NINPO SECRETS

NINPO PHILOSOPHY, HISTORY, AND TECHNIQUES

I dedicate this book to my beloved teacher,
Takamatsu Sensei.

TABLE
OF
CONTENTS

PART III
NINPO HISTORY

PART IV
NINPO TECHNIQUES

PREFACE

Already thirty-six years have passed since I first walked through the gates of the martial arts. Throughout this time, I have tried to study and train in both the martial arts and spiritual world. As a result I have found a purpose and mission in life as a human being and martial artist. This purpose and mission is to teach, with the martial art of *Ninpo*, the meaning of true self-defense of the body and heart to the people of the world.

The three forms of defense I hope you can master are the defense of the body, the defense of the heart, and last the defense of God. Lead a harmonious life with the body and heart using these three forms of defense, and happiness will not elude you.

I have tried to explain in this book exactly what the secrets of *Ninpo* are, including the philosophy, history and techniques, because at present *Ninpo* is not correctly understood. I have compiled this book to serve as a guide to those who wish to learn *'Ninpo Bugei* 忍法武芸'. Please note that all the Japanese names are written in the Japanese way (i.e. family name first, then given name).

Mrs. *Tane Takamatsu*, wife of the late *Ninpo* grandmaster *Toshitsugu Takamatsu Sensei*, for whom I have deep respect, has sent me the following letter of encouragement:

> "I have just found out you are in the process of writing a book on the martial art of *Ninpo* despite being very busy. I await the completion of this book from the depths of my heart. I truly believe my husband would also be very glad. Please follow my late husband forever and develop the "Martial Wind". I pray that you look to the eastern skies. *Tane Takamatsu*."

It is to the late *Takamatsu Sensei* and all other *Ninpo* ancestors who kept the spirit of *Ninpo* throughout their lives, that I dedicate this book.

4th October 1992
Shoto Tanemura

Mrs. *Tane Takamatsu* and I
(She died on 4th February 1991.)

NINPO SECRETS
NINPO PHILOSOPHY, HISTORY and TECHNIQUES

PART I
WHAT IS NINPO?

01.
NINPO (忍法)
AND
NINJUTSU (忍術)

Though the term *Ninpo* has been in use since World War II most people only recognize the art of the *Ninja* (忍者) through the term *Ninjutsu*. For these people there is only a slight or insignificant difference. The two terms, *Ninpo* and *Ninjutsu*, are vastly different and the distinction should be made clear for interested persons.

The names of many martial arts include the character or ideogram *Do* (道) which means way; however, when referring to *Ninpo*, *Do* is not used. Instead *Ho* (法) (read as *'Po'* in some combinations) is used. *Ho* is frequently found in the names of religions, as in *Buppo* (仏法), translated as 'Law of Buddha', with the literal meaning 'eternal truth'. *Ninpo* uses *Ho* because this martial art has deep religious significance. *Ninpo* succeeded in combining two parts: martial arts (*Bumon*) and religion (*Shumon*). As an analogy considers *Bumon* as a right hand and *Shumon* as a left hand; possessing both of them provides a balanced body. This is comparable to the blending of the masculine force *Yo* (Yang) and the feminine force *In* (Yin) in Chinese philosophy for a balanced universe.

The terms *Jutsu*, *Do* and *Ho* have different meanings, best understood by imagining a mountain. In this content an explanation of a technique for climbing the mountain is *Jutsu*. The range of available routes, from pleasurable to difficult, leading to the mountain's summit is *'Do'*. *Do* is not exclusive for martial arts, but also applies to such activities as dancing, music and painting. The martial arts that use the term *'Do'* teach ways to reach the summit of the mountain. It is rare to find those who have succeeded in reaching that goal, and once they have arrived, where else can they go? *Ho* is the cloud floating in the sky above the same mountain. *Ninpo* practitioners ride on this cloud, enjoy pleasurable times with nature and live on forever. The Chinese character for *Ho* (法) is made up of two radicals. The first *Sanzui* (氵), means water and the second *Saru* (去) means going forth. Putting them together literally results in 'water going forth', but at a deeper level implies the water cycle. From the clouds above, rain falls on the mountain and travels down into the valley becoming a stream. This stream combines with other streams becoming a river, eventually flowing to the sea. There, the water rises towards heaven and becomes a cloud once more.

This is the eternal law of the water cycle that is meant by *Ho*. In the ancient Sanskrit language of India, *Ho* meant 'Daruma'. It is in India that the famous personification of the eternal truth, Daruma, exists.

The enlightened warrior (*Shinobi*) will not be content with just a way (*Do*). His goal is to understand the eternal truth, to live within natural laws, and to fully develop martial techniques. By maintaining the spirit of enlightenment, a practitioner can build up as perfect a society as possible. In conclusion, this martial art should not be called *'Nindo'* or *'Ninjutsu'*, but instead its spiritually significant name, *'Ninpo'* should be used. This ancient martial art, like the rain of the water cycle remains fresh and in motion.

> "If the heart's eye comprehends, and one catches the mystic sword,
> one can control it like heaven."

02.
THE NAME NINJA

A *Ninja* is a master of stealth and disguise: *Shinobi* in Japanese. During the *Asuka* period (592-710) *Shotoku Taishi*, a great historical figure for the propagation of Buddhism in Japan, came up with this term. When translated, *Shinobi* (志能便) means an expert in the field of information gathering: *Shi* (志) meaning a doer, *No* (能) meaning an expert, *Bi* (便) meaning information. From this source the term '*Ninja*' evolved, but the historical antecedents go back centuries to an origin in China. In the following account, the Japanese reading of ideograms will be first, followed by the Chinese reading in parentheses.

From 2,300 B.C., through the reigning periods of Emperors *Fukki* (*Fushi*), *Shinno* (*Shen Nong*), and *Kotei* (*Huang Di*) continuing through the reign of Emperor *Ken-en-Tei* (*Shen Wuen Tei*) around 1,900 B.C. to China's Spring and Autumn War from 722 to 481 B.C., *Ninja* were known as *Kan* (Chen 間). The Chinese book of strategy, *Sonshi*, refers to the use of *Kan*, calling these agents the most important part of an army. The literal meaning of *Kan* is 'gap', as in a gap between two sliding screens through which ventilation takes place. Consider a command given to an agent to observe, through a gap between two screens, the enemy preparing his plans. If the agent actually enters and steals the plans then the agent has applied this definition.

Kan also has the nuance of 'between', as in the space between two objects. An application of this involves the separation or division of people. Examples include creating a rift between a commander and his officers so a division takes place. In action against two allied provinces, one of the allies would be attacked while the other would be sent false information testifying that everything was peaceful. No support would arrive for the besieged province rendering the alliance useless. For protection against this kind of misinformation most monarchs and government officials ignored officers who spoke out, for fear they were *Kan*. Skepticism developed as a form of security.

In the last chapter of *Sonshi* a reference to *Kan* states: "If one is not an intelligent leader, one cannot use an agent intelligently. If one is inhumane and a mere leader, one cannot use a *Kan*. If one is not a subtle leader, one cannot judge the truthfulness of a *Kan*." In the same chapter *Kan* are compared to the sun shining through an entrance. This is a literal interpretation of the Chinese ideograms or characters. The character for gate (門) is combined with that of sun (日) to read as *Kan* (間). Just as sunshine filters through a crack in the wall, so must the agent gathering intelligence. This same principle is expressed in a *Ninpo* poem:

> "If there is a village on which the moon shines,
> for a person who wishes to see it, it is there."

This verse implies that if you have true intentions, you will find a way, even if it is deep into enemy fortifications. However, if you do not have true intent, no matter how hard you try, you will not succeed. This verse teaches one of the greatest lessons a *Ninja* can learn.

Kan were also called *Cho* (*Teie* 諜), which meant 'to spy and discover'. These agents actually penetrated enemy camps and gathered information.

In China from 480 to 221 B.C. espionage agents were known as *Saisaku* (*Shintuo* 細作), *Yutei* (*Whowan* 遊偵), or *Kansai* (*Chenshi* 姦細). *Saisaku*, the makers of elaborate plans, would infiltrate an enemy camp, search personal effects for information, and return. The commander would then use cunning means to attack. *Yutei*, a combination of detective and actor, entered enemy camps in the guise of a musician or dancer to gather information. *Kansai* were skilful in the art of deception.

In the ancient Chinese book *Rikuto* (*Rhu Tao* 六韜), actor/warriors were called *Yushi* (遊士) and in the book *Inkyo* (*Yng Cho* 陰経) these agents were known as *Gyojin* (行人), literally translated as 'going person'. Disguised and in search of information, the *Yushi* and *Gyojin* entered enemy camps.

The Chinese book *Gozasso* (*Wu Tso Tsu* 五雑俎), called experts at disappearing, *Tongyo* (*Toen Shin* 遁形). From this origin, *Ninpo*'s most advanced techniques received the name *Tongyo-no-Jutsu* (遁形の術).

In Japan, *Ninja* have operated under a variety of titles. Many of the roles performed by Japanese parallel their historical counterparts, the Chinese. In Japan from the *Kamakura* (1192-1334) and *Muromachi* (1368-1603) periods until the beginning of the warring era, the *Sengoku* period, the following names were used:

Shinobi : an agent of stealth.
Kusa : grass; implying someone is hidden in the grass or trained from a young age to be in place when needed.
Kamari : crouching in concealment for a surprised attack.
Suppa : hunting for information and exposing the discovery.
Rappa : spreading disinformation.
Toppa or *Tsuppa* : to direct to information or a place.
Denuki : to advance beyond another through advantage.
Ukamibito : an agent who appears friendly, but is gathering information.
Homen : a traitor released from prison to spy.

Prominent feudal lord *Takeda Shingen* during the *Sengoku* period used the term *Mitsu-mono* that translates as 'three persons'. *Mitsumono* were divided into three parts: *Kaiken* - those peering in, *Kenbun* - those watching and listening, and *Metsuke* - those checking on other operatives. *Uesugi Kenshin* another feudal lord of the *Sengoku* and *Azuchi-Momoyama* periods used the term *Nokizaru* meaning an 'eave's monkey', implying eavesdropping. *Oda Nobunaga* (1534-1582) an expert at warfare and one of the greatest figures in Japanese history used the word *Kyodan* when referring to agents who could use 'sound waves' to gather information. Prior to the beginning of the *Edo* (*Tokugawa*) period the mysterious sources of information were called *Kanja*, *Choja* or *Kancho*. These terms are formed with various combinations of the same ideograms. *Kan* has been previously explained, *Cho* meaning eavesdropper, and *Ja* implying a practitioner of these activities. During the *Tokugawa* period many different terms were applied, including:

Shinobi : a master of stealth and disguises.
Shinobi no Mono : emphasized a person involved in stealth and disguises.
Onmitsu : literally translated as 'silent and secretive', in reference to persons who spied.
Koga Mono : *Koga* area *Ninja*.
Iga Mono : *Iga* area *Ninja*.
Negoro-Shu : *Negoro* (*Wakayama*) mountain warriors skilled with firearms.
Saika-To : *Saika* (*Wakayama*) area *Ninja*.
Haya-Ashi Gumi : a group named because of their fast running couriers.
Kohayato Gumi : a group ranked lower than the *Haya-Ashi*.
Karasu Gumi : a group named for the black clothes they wore.

Specialization also led to an acquired title. When in the unusual circumstances that a *Ninja* had authority over *Samurai* he was called *Shinobi Metsuke* or with partial authority, *Yoko Metsuke*. A scout was called *Monomi*, eavesdroppers were called Monokiki and castle guards were *Oniwaban*.

In Japan since the *Meiji* period, various terms have been used when referring to agents who used all possible means, including disguises to gather required information: *Mittei* indicated a secret searcher, *Tantei* indicated a deep searcher, while *Kansai* implied being tricky or sly. The term *Kansai* relied on the same meaning of *Sai* which was used long before in the previously mentioned Chinese term *Saisaku* (*Shi Tsuo*).

Other terms implied organizational division like within the police force of *Edo* (*Tokyo*), where agents with controlling power were known as *Yoriki*. The *Yoriki* controlled subordinates known as *Doshin*.

Many terms referring to the clandestine agents have survived. Words like *Kanja*, *Choja*, *Kancho*, *Sekko*, *Ninja*, *Mittei*, and even 'spy' that has been borrowed from English, can be heard in present day Japan.

Within the class hierarchy of Japanese society the *Ninja* were low, preventing them from revealing themselves for fear of jeopardizing their true identities and occupations. Yet for centuries, *Ninja* have perceived themselves as the most vital part of an army. Within their own secret circles the *Ninja* referred to themselves as the 'jewel of the country'. The various historical names that have been used to label *Ninja* operatives do not reveal much of the secretive and specialized techniques that developed *Ninpo* into a 'near science'. In contrast *Ninpo* practitioners have the privilege of openly admitting admiration for their martial art.

This privilege does not apply to everyone wanting to adopt the title 'Ninja'. Spies, survivalists, and military personnel not representing the 'tradition' are excluded.

From the end of the *Edo* period until the *Meiji* period (1868-1912), *Toda Shinryuken Sensei*, kept this martial art alive. His knowledge was passed to *Takamatsu Sensei*, who as the only true *Ninja* of the time maintained the tradition from the *Meiji* era, through the *Taisho* era and into the *Showa* era.

Ninpo represents a significant part of Japan's traditional martial art culture. Even the word *Togakure* from *Togakure-Ryu Ninpo* means a situation where the enemy believes that you are far away, when in fact you are near. This definition is strikingly similar to the definition of *Kan* a word used so long ago. *Ninpo* is more than the evolution of terminology, as a Grandmaster, I maintain that *Ninpo* is the most highly evolved martial art. For the betterment of individuals and societies, *Ninpo* the enduring martial art, once shrouded in secrecy is available for everyone to learn.

"Later he shall see me with a heart of fantasy."
Ancient *Ninja* Grandmaster.

Takamatsu Sensei performs the *Kenbu* (traditional sword dance) and *Koppo-jutsu Kamae*

03.
TRAITS OF THE NINJA

Three traits make up a *Ninja*. The most important one, honesty, is not only required in *Ninpo* but also applies to everything. A person with strength, skill, and intelligence, will loose everything if he is dishonest. Honesty, purity, and righteousness are the path to enlightenment. When one walks an honest road, things learned penetrate the body and heart like water entering sand. Then a person can judge what is right and wrong with the heart as a mirror.

Ninja, sometimes use a dishonest road, but only as an instrument. Diversionary tactics (*Kyojitsu-Tenkan* 虚実転換) are a temporary means and as such are not important, the dark way is not the true way. The true *Ninja* has the ability to use both honesty and deception to arrive at an honest goal. Deception is not the 'end' only a 'means".

The second trait involves taking an interest in everything. This produces common sense, general knowledge, and finally enables critical judgment. The *Ninja*'s essential techniques (*Sanjurokkei*) require this special insight or refined spirit (*Seishinteki Kyoyo*), because without this, in addition to having bad manners, an agent can easily fall into enemy traps. Martial art (*Bumon*), religion/spirit (*Shumon*), meteorology (*Tenmon*) and knowledge of the earth (*Chimon*) must be deeply understood. Knowledge of culture equates intelligence, but it is not enough to be only an intellectual. It is important to be able to use cultural knowledge in practical ways. Develop intellect with an honest heart, and unlimited wisdom (*Chie*) results; leading to spiritual refinement.

The third trait involves effort. To be a *Ninja*, a person must have a level of endurance that cannot be broken even in the most impossible of circumstances. To achieve this trait a practitioner must train both the body and the mind to the point of regurgitation. It is impossible to explain the way I trained to obtain my patience, because it has resulted from an entire way of life with *Ninpo*. However, with this trait the most difficult or impossible barriers can be overcome. Talent is not required for there is no relationship between talent and effort. Effort alone can defeat even a genius. Lack of talent should not bring despair, instead there should be a commitment to try harder.

To be a true *Ninja*, develop these three traits to the best of your ability. *Dojo* principles should always stress the development of these traits. Consider what these times honored *Dojo* principles, which go back to before the time of *Takamatsu Sensei*, emphasized.

i   One must learn patience within the time it takes a cigarette to burn.

ii One must learn that the way of man is righteousness.

iii Forget desire; forget easiness; forget stubbornness.

iv Think of sadness and grudges as destiny. One must comprehend the immovable heart (*Fudoshin*).

v   Do not distance one's loyalty from one's parents and rulers. Try deeply to master culture and martial arts.

"What are the martial arts?
If you understand the answer, that is the correct way.
This is the most mysterious point one gains without learning."

The 'Dharmas' seven fall down but the eighth gets up
(Painting by *Takamatsu Sensei*)

04.
NINJA SPIRIT

The character for *'Nin'* (忍) used in the words *'Ninja'*, *'Ninjutsu'* and *'Ninpo'*, consists of two radicals or parts. The upper radical is called *'Yaiba'* (刃).

Yaiba means the 'cutting edge of a blade'. The lower radical is read as *'Kokoro'* or *'Shin'* (心) meaning heart. In the *Ninpo* book Bansenshukai that means "All Rivers Flowing To The Sea" it says:

> "When entering an enemy camp on a dangerous mission, your heart must be as hard, cold, and sharp as the blade of a sword. If the heart is soft and weak, whenever an enemy confronts you, panic results and the mission fails. If the heart is unstable, the enemy will be able to see this hesitancy easily. This situation will not only cost your life, but will also endanger your leader, or for that matter, your country. A practitioner of *Ninpo* needs to have the type of heart that when touched can cut, and as with the blade of a sword, it should always be kept free from impurities, sharp, and cold to keep enemies on constant alert."

Most *Ninpo* scholars follow this interpretation, but I believe this is only half of the real meaning. With this simplistic understanding trouble may result. Several examples can be mentioned: for instance, there was a man who misunderstood the true meaning of *Nin*. Daily he would practice evasive techniques using a real sword with his twelve-year-old son. The father and son would take turns thrusting at each other. The father held the opinion that if he were to kill his son during this training, it would not be murder. During these training sessions he totally ignored his wife's tearful pleas to stop. Finally the son was admitted to a hospital with a strange illness; a nervous breakdown accompanied with many physical ailments. Another person, before going to sleep every night, suspended a sword from the ceiling with the tip of the blade only 10 centimeters from his forehead. He did this because he believed it was the best way to develop his spirit. Knowing if the thread snapped the sword would kill him, he would say to himself that death was of no importance. These two examples show how some people are ridiculous and misinterpret what *Nin* means.

The character for *Nin* is also used to write *'Nintai'* (忍耐) which means perseverance or patience, implying the important thing for a *Ninja* (*Shinobi no Mono*) is to be patient under impossible circumstances and persevere when he cannot find a way to succeed on a mission. This form of thinking, the spirit of perseverance, is called *'Ninja Seishin'* (忍者精神). If one receives an insult from another person, one must be able to endure it without holding a grudge and then discard such feelings as anger and jealousy. This combination of endurance and humility is known as *'Ninniku Seishin'* (忍辱精神). The Bansenshukai says:

> "The essential element for a *Ninja* is a pure heart. If a *Ninja* pursues the wrong course using trickery or plots, his heart cannot be pure and his judgment will always be misguided, never permitting an honest course of action. If such a person uses *Ninjutsu* for only his benefit or that of an evil superior, their actions will betray them showing they were responsible. There may be initial success providing money and fame, but they will tumble from their high pedestals before long. The heart of a *Ninja* is pure and honest."

Many people have forgot sincerity and humility. Some practitioners claim special status and make themselves out to be more than they are. Plenty of money can be earned by turning *Ninjutsu* into a business. A student once said, "I am a grandmaster of my school and because of this I can do anything I wish. I will be rich and famous..." Making this statement, he has shown no regard for the true meaning of *Ninpo*. These people have already lost the true *Ninja* heart. There are now international networks where this type of spirit is taught. These individuals, whenever they can, try to prevent others from reaching the true teaching sources in Japan.

In the United States and some other countries, *Ninja* suits and weapons such as throwing stars and swords are being sold by postal order. Newspapers report the occasions when people purchase these weapons and kill or injure others. This kind of trouble will undoubtedly continue; there is now an international problem. *Ninpo* will gain a dark reputation and be totally misunderstood by the international community. I worry about this situation and even if alone and isolated, I shall continue to keep the *Ninpo* martial art alive. I am glad, however, to find an increasing number of good pupils. Dangerous egoists never last long.

There is a *Ninja* verse that means that if one does not have a pure heart, heaven will never permit any pleasurable times.

> '*Chihayafuru Kami-no Oshiewa Tokoshieni*
> *Tadashiki Kokoro Mio Mamoruran*'.

The prayer *Ninja Seishin* is a traditional verse for guiding a *Ninja*'s heart. Recited at the beginning of each class by all *Genbukan* members, this verse acts as a link to connect one's heart with that of God's.

> '*Ninja Seishin-towa, Shin-shin-shiki-o Shinobu, Ninniku-seishin-o Konpon-to suru. Chijoku-o Shinon-de Urami-o Hoji-saru Nintai Seishin-o Yashinau Kotoni Hajimaru Mono-dearu. Nin-towa, Kokoro-no Ueni Yaiba-o Oite, Yaiba-de Hito-o Kizutsuke-tari Suruyouna Monodewa-naku, Kajo-Waraku, Hana-no Gotoki Joai-o Motte, Heiwa-o Tanoshimu Monode-aru. Yueni, Tai-o Motte Shizen-ni Aite-no Ken-o Sake, Sugata-o Kesu, Kyojitsu Tenkan-no Myo-o-e, Iccho Kuni-no Tame-toka, Gi-no-tameni, Chi, Sui Ka, Fu, Ku-no Daishizen-o Riyo-shite, Aite-o Seisuru (Taosu) Kotoga, Ninja-no Konpon Gensoku De-aru.*'

Translated:

"The essence of '*Ninniku Seishin*' is the spirit of the *Ninja* who has the power to use patience together with the body, mind and subconscious. It is this power that one must develop by training hard. The result will lead to the ability to pocket any insult and later throw it away together with all traces of resentment (*Nintai Seishin*). The true meaning of *Nin* is having a heart as peaceful, joyful, and lovely as that of a flower '*Kajo Waraku*' (花情和楽). One should never place the blade before the heart. It is also very important to acquire a good knowledge of diversionary tactics using both the heart and body, so that in emergencies one will be able to disappear. This is known as *Kyojitsu Tenkan*, and is for defeating evil with the powers of Earth, Water, Fire, Wind and Air in the defense of oneself or country."

In *Ninpo* there are many very dangerous techniques. It is bad for society if evil people use *Ninpo* to attain selfish interests. This is why in *Ninpo* the spiritual element is of primary importance. For many years the words *Ninja* and *Ninjutsu* when mentioned, brought to mind techniques rather than the spiritual aspects. Even some practitioners think that techniques are more important than spiritual development. It is the spirit that makes the *Ninja* and *Ninpo* seem very mysterious, clever, and superhuman, but in the eyes of some people, the spiritual element remains very low.

Until now, books introducing *Ninjutsu* have focused only on techniques. The spiritual part, if included at all, is vague, referring to either *Zen* or Esoteric Buddhism (*Mikkyo* 密教). This presents a very limited understanding and creates concern, so this book includes much on the spiritual aspects. Yet, you must understand that a great deal cannot be put onto paper because it is taught by word of mouth; from heart to heart. Study well the *Ninpo* techniques and *Ninja Seishin* to obtain proficiency in the true martial art and to enjoy a pleasurable life.

> "Without noise
> Without scent
> Without a famous name
> But the effect is cosmic."

05.
THE 36 NINPO ESSENTIALS

To begin, a *Ninja* must learn 18 categories of *Samurai* martial arts called '*Bugei Juhappan* 武芸十八般' (mainly *Samurai* martial arts) to become a true specialist, mastery of another 18 categories of secret techniques called '*Ninja Juhakkei* 忍者十八形' is necessary. Combined they are referred to as the 36 *Ninpo* essentials, '*Ninpo Sanjurokkei* 忍法三十六型'. The number 36 is special because it can be separated into 3 and 6. Adding 3 and 6 gives 9. Multiplying 3 and 6 gives 18. Then adding the 1 and 8 also gives 9. All these combinations produce the number 9 or numbers divisible by 9. In the martial arts, especially in China, the number 9 has special significance, with two important meanings. First, if one uses the techniques, one will never fail, and second, the number 9 indicates that the school incorporating it is very old and complete.

Ninja studies were never restricted to learning only the '*Sanjurokkei*'; success required an understanding of all fighting arts. The '*Ninja Juhakkei*' are presented in the following list:

① *Seishinteki Kyoyo* (精神的教養); Spiritual refinement
② *Taijutsu* (体術); Unarmed defense techniques
③ *Kenpo/Biken-Jutsu* (剣法・秘剣術); Sword techniques
④ *So-Jutsu* (槍術); Spear techniques
⑤ *Naginata-Jutsu* (薙刀術); Halberd techniques
⑥ *Bisento-Jutsu* (眉尖刀術); Battlefield halberd techniques
⑦ *Kusarigama-Jutsu* (鎖鎌術); Sickle and chain techniques
⑧ *Rokushaku Bo-Jutsu* (六尺棒術); Full staff techniques
⑨ *Sanjaku Bo-Jutsu/Han Bo-Jutsu/Jo-Jutsu* (三尺棒術・半棒術・杖術);
                                  Half and three quarterstaff techniques
⑩ *Shuriken-Jutsu/Senban Nage Jutsu* (手裏剣術・銛盤投術); Blade throwing techniques
⑪ *Kisha-Jutsu* (騎射術); Archery techniques from horseback
⑫ *Inton-Jutsu* (隠通術); Special disappearing techniques
⑬ *Hoko-Jutsu* (歩行術); Walking techniques
⑭ *Henso-Jutsu* (変装術); Disguise techniques
⑮ *Kakushi-Buki Jutsu* (隠武器術); Secret weapons techniques
⑯ *Nin-Yaku Jutsu* (忍薬術); Special medicine techniques
⑰ *Gunryaku Heiho* (軍略兵法); Strategies
⑱ *Tenmon Chimon* (天門地門); Strategies of Heaven and Earth

The '*Suikoden*', first introduced the '*Bugei Juhappan*', according to *Watatani Kiyoshi*, to Japan Chinese nobles of the *Ken-En-Tei* (*Sheng Weng Tei*) period, who listed them in the following categories:

① *Bo* (矛); Thronged spear
② *Tsui* (鎚); Battle hammer
③ *Kyu* (弓); Bow
④ *Do* (弩); Cross-bow
⑤ *Ju* (銃); Gun
⑥ *Ben* (鞭); Whip
⑦ *Kan* (簡); Ceremonial fan
⑧ *Ken* (剣); Sword
⑨ *Ren* (鏈); Chain
⑩ *Ka* (_); Iron rod for horses
⑪ *Fu* (斧); Battle axe
⑫ *Etsu* (鉞); Giant battle axe
⑬ *Geki* (戟); Spear
⑭ *Geki* (戈); Two-thronged spear
⑮ *Hai* (牌); Barriers
⑯ *Bo* (棒); Staff
⑰ *So* (槍); Spear
⑱ *Hatsu* (_); Battle plough

After this introduction to Japan, the *Bugei Juhappan* were reorganized in a book entitled '*Sansai-Zue*', written during the Ming Dynasty. The categories were:

① *Bo* (矛); Thronged spear
② *To* (刀); Singled edged sword
③ *Kyu* (弓); Bow
④ *Do* (弩); Cross-bow
⑤ *Hato* (把頭); Sleeve Cat
⑥ *Ben* (鞭); Whip
⑦ *Geki* (戟); Spear
⑧ *Ken* (剣); Double edged sword
⑨ *Sa* (叉); Restraining tools
⑩ *Ko* (稿); Iron rod for horses
⑪ *Fu* (斧); Battle axe
⑫ *Etsu* (鉞); Giant battle axe
⑬ *Eki* (殳); Wooden spear
⑭ *Kan* (簡); Ceremonial fan

⑮ *Jun* (盾); Barriers

⑯ *So* (槍); Single spear

⑰ *Hakuda* (搏打); Unarmed defence

⑱ *Kinjo Tobotsu* (錦縄套字); Tying with ropes

Later only the pronunciation of '*Ko*' was changed to '*Ka*'. Early in the *Edo* period, *Kaibara Ekken* published his books '*Wakan Meisu Zokuhen*' and '*Bukun*' which identified the following martial art techniques:

① *Katana* (刀); Sword

② Ishibiya (発_); Small cannon

③ *Teppo* (鳥銃); Gun

④ *Umanori* (騎); Horsemanship

⑤ *Yumi* (射); Bow

⑥ *Hiya* (火箭); Flaming arrow

⑦ *Bo* (棒); Staff

⑧ *Torite* (捕縛); Restraining

⑨ *Kama* (鎌); Sickle

⑩ *Suiren* (水練); Swimming

⑪ *Yari* (槍) : Spear

⑫ *Iai* (抜刀); Sword drawing techniques

⑬ *Ken-Jutsu* (撃剣); Sword techniques

⑭ *Yawara* (拳); Unarmed techniques

⑮ *Bisento* (眉尖刀); Battlefield halberd

In the *Bunsei* stage of the *Edo* period, *Hirayama Gyozo* wrote '*Bugei Juhappan Ryakusetsu*' in which he listed the following categories:

① *Ki Yumi* (木弓); Wooden bow

② *Oh Yumi* (大弓); Giant bow

③ *Kujira Hankyu* (鯨半弓); Half-bow made from baleen

④ *Kisha* (騎射); Horseback archery

⑤ *Ken-Jutsu* (剣術); Sword techniques

⑥ *Oh Naginata* (大長刀); Large halberd

⑦ *Yari* (槍); Spear

⑧ *Koranjo* (虎乱杖); Staff and Chain

⑨ *Ko Naginata* (小長刀); Small halberd

⑩ *Nodachi* and *Nagamaki* (野太刀・長巻); Long swords

⑪ *Ju-Jutsu* (柔術); Unarmed defence

⑫ *Iai-Jutsu* (居合術); Sword techniques

⑬ *Jumonji Kamayari* (十文字槍); Cross-shaped spear

⑭ *Saburi Yari* (佐分利槍); Saburi-ryu spear

⑮ *Nage Yari* (投げ槍); Spear throwing

⑯ *Bo-Jutsu* (棒術); Staff techniques

⑰ *Tessen* or *Jutte* (鉄扇・十手); Iron fan/rod

⑱ *Teppo* or *Taiho* (鉄砲・大砲); Gun/cannon

In the *Edo* period *Katsushika Hokusai*'s pupil, *Gekkotei Bokusen*, illustrated these 18 techniques in his book '*Shashin Gakuhitsu*':

① *Yumi* (弓); Bow

② *Uchimari* (打鞠); A Chinese ball game

③ *Uma* (馬); Horse

④ *Suiei* (水泳); Swimming

⑤ *Yari* (槍); Spear

⑥ *Naginata* (薙刀); Halberd

⑦ *Ken* (剣); Sword

⑧ *Ju* (柔); Unarmed defence

⑨ *Teppo* (鉄砲); Gun

⑩ *Hojo* (捕縄); Tying with ropes

⑪ *Iai* (居合); Sword techniques

⑫ *Suiba* (水馬); Swimming with a horse

⑬ *Yoroi-Gumi* (鎧組); Fighting with armour

⑭ *Hananeji* (鼻捻); Iron rod for horses

⑮ *Kisha* (騎射); Horseback archery

⑯ *Shuriken* (手裏剣); Throwing blades

⑰ *Ishibiya* (石火矢); Small Cannon

⑱ *Kusarigama* (鎖鎌); Sickle-and-chain

There has always been confusion regarding the content of the '*Bugei Juhappan*'. Time witnessed many additions and deletions, but from considering the enduring categories of a more realistic *Bugei Juhappan* are:

① *Ju-Jutsu* or *Kenpo* (柔術・拳法); Unarmed defence

② *Ken-Jutsu* or *Gekken-Jutsu* (剣術・撃剣術); Sword techniques

③ *Iai-Jutsu* or *Batto-Jutsu* (居合術・拔刀術); Sword drawing techniques

④ *Kusarifundo-Jutsu* (鎖分銅術); Weighted chain techniques

⑤ *Kusarigama-Jutsu* (鎖鎌術); Sickle-and-chain techniques

⑥ *Bo-Jutsu* (棒術); Full staff techniques

⑦ *So-Jutsu* (槍術); Spear techniques

⑧ *Naginata-Jutsu* (薙刀術); halberd techniques

⑨ *Suiren* (水練); Swimming
⑩ *Ba-Jutsu* (馬術); Horsemanship
⑪ *Kisha-Jutsu* (騎射術); Horseback archery
⑫ *Jo-Jutsu* (杖術); Three-quarter staff techniques
⑬ *Kyu-Jutsu* (弓術); Archery
⑭ *Yoroi-Kumiuchi* (鎧組打); Fighting with armour
⑮ *Hojo-Jutsu* (捕縄術); Tying with ropes
⑯ *Jutte-Jutsu* (十手術); Iron rod techniques
⑰ *Ho-Jutsu* (砲術); Cannon techniques
⑱ *Nageken-Jutsu* or *Shuriken-Jutsu* (投剣術・手裏剣術); Blade throwing techniques

Of all the categories for a *Ninja* to master, two remained the most important: spiritual refinement *Seishinteki Kyoyo* involving the mind, and spirit; and unarmed defence *Tai-Jutsu* involving physical movements and techniques. When combined, miraculous powers are reaped for the mind, body and spirit are unified *'Shin-Gi-Tai Icchi* 心技体一致'.

With spiritual refinement, an understanding of strategies, and mastery of body movement, any martial art can be mastered. The fundamentals of movement *Ninpo Tai-Jutsu* presented in this manual, when blended with hard training will lead to this unified attainment *Shi-Gi-Tai Icchi*.

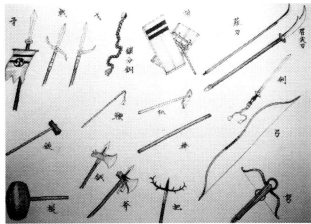

Weapons

Ninpo Essentials.

PART II
NINPO
PHILOSOPHY

01.
SPIRITUAL REFINEMENT

The most important thing when training in *Ninpo* is spiritual refinement (*Seishinteki Kyoyo*). Every martial art has its own form of spiritual guidance but in *Ninpo*, if the spirit is not correctly developed with utmost care, a practitioner might accidentally kill someone or use the techniques of self-defense for a crime. Compared to other martial arts, the practitioner of *Ninpo* needs a more refined spirit, a purer heart and harder physical training. *Ninja* philosophy and spiritual refinement are covered in more detail in the sections that follow.

"Maintain the Ninpo jewel."

The poem's meaning;

"The cherry trees invite good fortune
with smiling blooms
through out the entire
cold and hot seasons."

Painting by *Takamatsu Sensei*

A.
GOD'S HEART, GOD'S EYES

Martial art techniques are only for self-defense. Within *Ninpo* the highest quality self-defense techniques are found. *Ninpo* is a system to defend the body, mind, and spirit. If a martial artist's spirit is improperly developed, it will serve to defeat him. This applies to all other pursuits. For example, the goal of people should be to help others to live as good a life as possible. Yet, some people only want to exploit others to become wealthy. Some sell drugs illegally or negligently do things that result in death. There are cases when people acquire newborn infants because their mothers are not prepared to look after them. Couples unable to have children will purchase these infants. This type of unethical behavior goes against the true spirit of humanity. There must be safeguards to prevent such activities from taking place.

There are cases where people have lost their dedication. Eating and drinking are processes for maintaining a healthy life and any over-indulgence is bad for the body. Recent publications regarding natural food or health food explain what to eat and what not to eat, but an un-natural diet will break the balance, opening the body to a variety of illnesses. Many people spend lots of money on health-food products. A foreign student of *Ninpo* and natural-food consumer was told by a Japanese naturalist, for whom he had great respect, that if he ate twenty raw eggs a day he need not eat anything else. After two months on this diet, his energy level dropped dramatically. While training, he would frequently sit on the floor with a very pale face. Telling him that he was not a sick man, that all he needed was to return to a balanced diet, had no influence on him. Laughing, he replied that he was fine and he had vitamin pills. Shortly after, he left my *Dojo*. He misunderstood the meaning of preserving good health. *Takamatsu Sensei* used to eat any thing, including the famous *Kobe* beef. Throughout his life he was very healthy, living to be 85 years old.

Consider a country's government that has ministries to handle different functions. One ministry controls the land; another is responsible for the defense of the nation. If a minister is greedy, seeking power, money and life without hardship, the country soon becomes unbalanced and the nation as a whole begins to deteriorate.

Even religions are affected by this problem. A religion that is sincere naturally radiates, through its followers, honesty, kindness, and generosity. These attributes enable a follower to defend the body and spirit. Life for families becomes enjoyable, eventually creating peace and happiness for society. A bad religion ruins people, resulting in the slow deterioration of a whole country.

The way of heaven '*Tendo*', keeping heaven-like sincerity and a pure heart, is of the utmost importance. Living creatures cannot live without the earth, sun, water, or air. Imagine if the sun were not pure and charged us for light. What if the earth turned faster for no apparent reason? The universe displays a pure, merciful heart in total harmony with its elements. Through *Ninpo*, skilled practitioner can attain insight into the meaning of life '*Kanjin Kaname*'. Written in different characters it means "God's heart, God's eyes", *Shinshin Shingan*. In martial art philosophy these concepts have great significance. A human with a pure heart fits well within the heart of nature and heaven.

Whenever I am about to teach *Ninpo* to someone, from the very beginning I always try to see whether the person's spirit is good or bad. It is after this that I decide whether this person will be my student or not. This is a '*Genbukan Dojo*' rule. People's hearts are constantly changing and it is difficult for them to keep the same type of heart over time. For this reason, after people have entered my school, their hearts sometimes change for the worse. For me it is easy to see such changes, but a strange phenomenon happens during such times. A student whose heart has changed, leaves of his own accord without a single word from me. For this person, the feeling of an honest *Dojo* makes him leave because the *Genbukan Dojo* is a *Shinshin Shingan Dojo*. If an enemy attacks with a weapon, the people of this type of *Dojo* can defend themselves without resorting to weapons. They need only spiritual power. Only a person whose heart reflects *Shinshin Shingan* is able to do this. For this reason the *Ninja* desire to train in all martial art categories, master martial strategies and understand all religions. By doing so, a true *Ninja* can develop spiritually, never losing dedication by wandering. He can also exemplify the law of both God and the martial artist; never kill anything except as a last resort '*Shin Bujin Fusatsu no Ho*':

"The water is a mirror,
I cannot see the bottom,
Yet I feel ashamed,
For the bottom sees me clearly."

The seven gods of good fortune

B.
CODE OF CONDUCT

"The martial artist who practices good etiquette as well as humanism from the moment that he wakes till the moment he goes to sleep exemplifies a code of conduct *'Bufu'*. The acts of a true *Ninja* are governed by such precepts."

The code of conduct leaves no room for the components of thoughtlessness; carelessness, indelicacy and impoliteness. Instead a sincere, calm and well-composed attitude consisting of an air of dignity, balanced with modesty, discretion, and carefulness must be nurtured. With this commitment true affection can be shown while the qualities of a flower and the spirit of bamboo are kept. With honor, courage, and energy resist rude and violent acts that contradict the code of conduct.

A homo sapiens, unlike other animals, are able to smile. If you receive an insult or are disgraced in any way, do not allow your heart to wander from its path, just smile. The ability to do this, is the sign of a man with true courage. This is perseverance, *'Nin'* of the mind. Restraint in using martial art techniques is perseverance, *'Nin'* of the body and true martial power.

A martial artist once said:

"Keep your heart and spirit like the scene on an autumn morning when the sun shines brightly on the frost-covered fields. Your spirit must have dauntless courage. Never forget the heart of affection and benevolence blowing like a spring breeze, making the plants gently sway. If you can do this, you can possess a mind with graceful elegance."

A person who has truly adopted this code of conduct respects both martial arts and culture in balanced proportions. Gaining an elegant and graceful heart. Maintaining this conduct throughout life *'Bufu Ikkan'* is a tremendous achievement.

We are often instructed to aid the weak and dispirit the strong, but one must always be careful since a seemingly weak man can sometimes turn against you. If you wish to help a weak man, it is not good to fight to fulfill that purpose. As a last resort a martial artist may use the means necessary to help a weaker man.

The essence of *'Kajo Waraku'*
(Painting by *Takamatsu Sensei*)

Closely related to the notions of "God's heart, God's eyes" and the code of conduct is 'Banpenfugyo' the importance of self-composure. When any great incident occurs, from a massive typhoon to the longest of earthquakes, never be surprised or afraid. Control yourself and act according to your judgment. Following the code of conduct with "God's heart, God's eyes" leads naturally to the acquisition of self-composure.

In the past, *Ninja* were taught the way to avoid mental weakness to self-composure, through three important principles, *'Sanbyo no Imashime'*.

① Do not keep fear within one's heart. To overcome fear develops an immovable heart.

② Do not look at an adversary as an inferior. Be cautious with anyone who seems to be weak. Remember that there have been many cases where a weak man has suddenly become fierce. Use courage to do what is necessary.

③ Do not over think. When confronted by a situation, do not analyze it too much; by then it may be too late. The ideal is to do boldly what is necessary with the greatest possible care.

> "To calm waters or rough waters,
> If I give my body,
> I may have the chance to float."

C.
MARTIAL ARTS VIRTUE

'Butoku' is martial art virtue. According to the Japanese dictionary Butoku means to make oneself better by behaving with upright conduct or to have high morality. In my opinion one should have 10 to 14 qualities including:

① *Jin* (仁); benevolence or compassion
② *Gi* (義); courageousness
③ *Rei* (礼); etiquette or manners
④ *Chi* (智); wisdom
⑤ *Chu* (忠); loyalty
⑥ *Ko* (孝); obedience
⑦ *Shin* (真); truthfulness
⑧ *Bi* (美); gracefulness
⑨ *Zen* (善); goodness and kindness

It is fundamental to develop these qualities, but it is using them that are of utmost importance. All my pupils should have justice, righteousness and goodness within them. There will, of course, be times when it will be difficult to judge what is good and what is bad. However there is a saying that goes, "If one sees an injustice and does not intervene, this is a worse injustice".

A few years ago, an incident occurred as I was returning home after teaching a class in *Yokohama* I was accompanied by one of my foreign students, and as we were changing trains at *Akihabara* Station in *Tokyo*, we saw on our platform a salary-man being beaten up by three Japanese gangsters (*Yakuza*). His face was covered in blood and he was on the verge of collapsing. It looked as if his life was truly in danger. On the opposite platform many people looked on as if they were the audience at the local cinema. On our platform, the commuters just walked by, looking over their shoulders to see what the commotion was about. There were no police or station guards around.

I looked around trying to judge their strength, how high their adrenaline levels, and whether they were carrying concealed weapons. I removed my overcoat and placed it on a bench with my bag. "Stop please!" I requested, only to see them ignore me altogether when suddenly they attacked us with punches and kicks. We avoided them as if training in a *Dojo* with friends. During this time the salary-man tried to run away, but was caught by two of the gangsters.

My student was preoccupied with one of them so I took off after the other two, catching them by the shoulders at a pressure point creating pain. Then I kicked them and they fell to the ground, and I knelt on the weak points of their arms to prevent them moving. They both looked helplessly at me as if questioning why they were unable to move. (Not injuring *Yakuza* is very important to avoid revenge from other *Yakuza*. So it is best not to injure them). I wanted the salary-man to run away, but he had been caught by the one who was with my student.

Throughout this time I had been using *Yo-Jutsu* (as in *In/Yo* or *Ying/Yang*), changing to *In-Jutsu*, I whispered in the ear of their leader, persuading him to go. He then replied, "Oh, that's a good idea. Let's go!", and his men followed. The salary-man fled and everything ended happily. This is what is meant by martial art virtue.

A few days later a tragic incident occurred in *Yokohama* that was in all the newspapers. Some university students helped a man who was being attacked. Two of them managed to catch one of the attackers and when they were in front of a police box, the man overpowered them and stabbed them, one fatally. It is indeed very saddening to hear such things and it makes me think that if they had been studying a martial art like *Ninpo*, no one would have died. If martial art virtue leads one to do something positive as in the incident above but finds that the evil is too powerful, experience in a martial art is necessary to win. I hope my students will successfully defeat evil, but constant training and studying are required.

> "If one enjoys teaching with a child's heart,
> Then the martial wind shall dance with the
> spring flowers"

Children class *'Tsubute Sabaki'*

D.
SPIRITUAL CONCENTRATION

All martial arts have, as a goal, the development of spiritual concentration 'Seishin-Toitsu'. In *Ninpo* this is the most fundamental teaching. For most, the meaning of *Seishin-Toitsu* is the ability to reach a state of nothingness, through meditation, but for a *Ninja* it is very difficult to reach this state because in living he places himself on the border between life and death and must take action.

For centuries, the *Ninja* have used secret chants '*Jumon*' and energy channeling to control both mind and spirit '*In*'. Powers from heaven are solicited for different purposes through the chanting of different verses. Special knots with the fingers (*Ketsu-In*) are used to tie the heart to heaven. When used for good deeds, help is received from a good spirit resulting in happiness. When the purpose is evil, the contact is made with bad spirits preventing success. For this reason discretion must be used with these techniques.

Today most people find this totally unbelievable or just dismiss it as self-hypnotic control, but for the *Ninja* who does it with conviction power is generated. This power allows him to place his adversary under his control. Psychologists constantly remind us how the human mind is under-utilized. Ten percent is used for conscious functioning including all senses and thought processes. Ninety percent remains unused or as the "subconscious". A person who attempts to control the subconscious portion, may realize another twenty percent. Physical training has clearly imposed limits but mental training seems limitless. Someone with evil intentions may study mind development and obtain a few "miracle-like" powers but limits will be reached without peace of mind. A sincere person trying even harder than the evil counterpart will need a tremendous amount of patience and courage but after expanding his power, he will retain it and live with a peaceful heart.

It is important to understand that the mind and the body are two separate entities that co-exist. The seat of consciousness is located not in the brain but in the trunk of the body. Spherical in shape, it is in absolute harmony with the body. By means of God and the soul lifeline *Reishi-Sen*. The proof lies in one's sleep. During sleep, the mind and body are as apart as the distance from Heaven to Earth but contact is kept through the life line (*Reishi-Sen*). If someone insults you while you are asleep, although your hearing is functioning perfectly, the mind is far away, unable to perceive it. If while sleeping, a noxious smell enters the room, although the nose is working, the mind does not sense it. It is as if the body were a car and the mind its driver. The car will only start if and when the driver is in it. If the car has broken down, the driver cannot operate it. When the lifeline has been severed and the mind cannot return, this is death. The activity of the brain during sleep can be seen clearly on an oscilloscope, but if the activity ceases, the person is dead and the lifeline has been cut. In hospitals, if a body is working perfectly but the brain has stopped, the person is dead. With appropriate chants (*Jumon*) and finger knots (*Ketsuin*) the level of spiritual concentration increases and eventually the sincere practitioner can summon this power at will. With control of the mind, come the ability to correctly channel energy into a yell (*Kiai-Jutsu*), the ability to judge another person's heart, and the ability to predict future outcomes.

Within the *Genbukan Dojo* there are various tests to analyze a student's character, wisdom, and above all mind control. The tests are not merely focused on the student's mastery of techniques. For instance, in the test for teacher '*Kyoshi*' given only to 5th *Dan* students, the student sits in the center of the *Dojo* in front of the other pupils, and I as Grandmaster/*Soshi* stand behind the student with a bamboo sword *Shinai* above my head. Striking down towards the student's head with all my power but as silently as possible, I emit my killing intent *Sakki*. If my student is able to perceive this intent and consequently evades the *Shinai*, he has passed the test and awarded the title *Kyoshi*. He can then be considered a true martial artist.

The test for the title assistant master '*Jun Shihan*' given only to 7th *Dan* students or above is done in the same manner. The student is invited to my home where he (or she) kneels in the center of my main room meditating to control the mind. This time I enter the room silently carrying a newly made sword that has never shed blood and prepare myself behind the student. A moment before cutting I emit the (cutting spirit) *Zanki*, and then silently cut towards the student's head, ending the stroke about a foot off the ground. If my student escapes, he (or she) is given the title *Jun Shihan*. Until now there are but eight pupils who have passed this test, *Okayasu Yoshikazu*, *Nagamoto Jin*, *Ohno Keimi*, James Wright, Roy Ron and others.

The test for master *'Shihan'* given to 8th or 9th *Dan* students, is done under the same conditions as for *Jun Shihan*. This time I will not emit any spirit, so the student must be able to feel the spirit of the sword itself with the seat of consciousness. I will cut twice at full speed, first vertically, then immediately after horizontally. If the student can evade both cuts, he (or she) will be given the title *Shihan*. To this day (28th April 1989), no one has been selected for this test.

There is also a test for the 10th *Dan*. Near midnight my pupil and I will walk to either a mountain or forest where no one else is present. Neither of us shall be thinking of life or death; we shall have natural hearts. After searching each other's heart, and when I get a pleasant feeling as that of God, I shall start cutting in all directions without thinking. My pupil must then evade and catch the blade with his bare hands with the gracefulness of a butterfly. This is called Shinken Shiraha Dori: literally translated as "the catching of the tempered line of a real sword". If the student succeeds, he (or she) will already be a first-class martial artist. The title of chief master *'Shihan-Cho'* will then be awarded.

> "In a mountain river, the deep troughs have
> calm waters, and the shallows are rough"

E.
PRESERVATION OF SPIRITUAL HEALTH

There are two main creeds to preserve spiritual health: *Yojo Shiketsu* and *Hasshodo*. *Yojo Shiketsu* as taught by *Takamatsu Sensei* teaches four main points to preserve health:

① Avoid anger to preserve personality. Being patient requires more effort than becoming angry. With humility, develop your personality.
② Avoid excessive worrying to preserve the nerves. Don't spend too much time thinking about trivial matters, otherwise you will become irresolute. Worry less and develop strong nerves.
③ Avoid excessive speaking to preserve the spirit. Refrain from jabbering too much so as to store up the power of your spirit.
④ Avoid desire to preserve the heart. The problems of the mind are usually expressed as desire: 'I want this', 'I want that' or 'I want to be rich and belong to the upper class', etc. Try hard to avoid such desire and, instead, cultivate a good mind and heart.

I trust that you will make every effort to live up to these four points in your daily lives, so that, in time, a true martial artist will surely be cultivated. These points are very difficult to put into practice, but you can be sure to get positive results by trying. So please make the effort.

'Hasshodo' expresses the eight ways for the correct mental state Buddhism. Consider how the conscience works when a man lies to another but never to himself. With a pure conscience, it is possible to walk on the very narrow path between good and evil, leading to peace of heart and mind. *Hasshodo* is the needle of the compass that guides the way down the path.

Hasshodo (八正道)

Shoken (正見) ·········· seeing correctly

Shogo (正語) ·········· speaking correctly

Shoshi (正思) ·········· thinking correctly

Shogyo (正業) ·········· working correctly

Shomyo (正命) ········ living correctly

Shoshin (正進) ········ going correctly

Shonen (正念) ········ praying correctly

Shojo (正定) ·········· meditating correctly

Shoken means looking with a proper perspective and not by hesitating or looking out of the corners of the eyes. It is not enough to look at just the surrounding scene. It is important to perceive the truth within the scene. Don't change the appearance of the scene to fit a judgment.

Shogo means having a correct way of speaking. Words reflect the used soul. The most beautiful of words without a love-filled heart, will never enter another's heart. With love and truth in the heart, the roughest of words can be used, but if the heart trembles when speaking, so too will the words.

Shoshi means the correct way of thinking. Thinking is a direct result of what is seen and heard, and it is after this that we act. If we don't think about the narrow path on which we are walking, we will only fall. A schemer will be brought down when discovered; honesty is the best policy. In Japan there is a saying, 'if one wishes something bad for another, one has set two traps: one for the other person and one for yourself'. Do not forget that thinking is the same thing as doing. It is important to cut away ill feelings from the heart without leaving traces of jealousy, grudges, or slander behind.

Shogyo means the correct way of working. We can spend our entire lives working and keeping our families peaceful. We must have gratitude in our minds for our work. A humanitarian can develop either by studying or working; a student must study and in society, a person must work. These two roles must provide a purpose in life and lead to a balanced society.

Shomyo means living a correct life. Gratitude must be in the heart for everything and at all times. The source of misfortune lies within oneself. If misfortune occurs, discover it and remove the source to establish a new life. Always keep gratitude in the heart and evaluate yourself from the point of view of another.

Shoshin means putting effort into leading a correct life. Always keep an honest mind and go down the path correctly. The correct way for martial artists has been outlined in *Shoken*, *Shogo* and *Shoshi*.

Shonen means praying correctly. Wishes sometimes move like waves and work like animals. There are times when they appear very strong. If a person wishes for something positive, a beam of light will shine; if a person wishes for something negative, there is only waiting. A *Ninja* wishes only when he finds himself in a dark society. By wishing, he turns on that single beam of light, the shining martial art virtue *'Butoku-Iko'*. In this way, when a resident of that dark society, whether animal or person, appears, the light will be blinding. Positive wishes come forth with wisdom and encouragement, rising like water vapor from the surface of a pond. A bad wish does not rise; it results in misfortune.

If one thinks and does improper things, it is best to reflect upon those actions and correct them. The power to reflect upon oneself is a gift from God. It is his love and mercy. Don't be ashamed to correct your ways.

Shojo means meditating correctly. The true meaning of meditation is self-reflection which cleanses the heart like a rinsed mirror, leading to the state where "seeing without looking and hearing without listening" is possible. This attainment is a natural heart like that of God's. With this power of comprehension *'Satori'* you will know your own mind. Understand exactly your own mind to maintain harmony with the body. Undertake all action through the harmony of mind and body. Trying to build a peaceful society is most important.

> "If there is a village on which the moon shines,
> For a person who wishes to see it,
> It is there."

F.
THE POWERFUL LIGHT OF WISDOM

The universe moves according to laws. As humans, it is important to understand and follow the universal laws of nature to bridge the conscious and subconscious mind that will lead to enlightenment. There are ways to do this.

In Buddhism, there is a very famous petition, *'Namu Ami Da Butsu'*. It's true meaning is a pledge to follow the teachings of the Buddha Amida. The mere repetition of phrases without understanding or sincerity does not result in enlightenment. Everything has depth, so we must expose the roots to understand the deep meaning.

In *Genbukan Ninpo* the benediction, *'Shikin Haramitsu Dai Komyo'* is repeated at the beginning and end of each training session. 'Shikin Haramitsu Dai Komyo' when translated into English means "the powerful light of wisdom". The word Shikin has four dimensions:

> The first dimension is a merciful heart expressing love for everything.
> Second is a sincere heart to follow what is right.
> Third is a heart in tune with natural order.
> Last is a heart dedicated to a chosen pursuit.

Combined, these four elements produce great wisdom, *Haramitsu*, yielding a powerful aura, *Dai Komyo*. The energy emitted is like a nuclear reaction continuing forever. A *Ninja* must penetrate the depths of knowledge for complete enlightenment.

If you understand the deep meanings and pray throughout your life, the effect will be enormous.

> "The light of mercy travels vertically,
> The light of the heart travels horizontally,
> With them, it can spin,
> That is the heart of nature's cycle."

02.
HEART AND SPIRIT

A.
INDOMITABLE SPIRIT

Takamatsu Sensei once said, "The heart supports us in the ups and downs of life". To have an indomitable spirit means getting up after every fall. No one can reach his or her goal without this spirit. A *Ninja* needs an exceptionally strong spirit, like the grass that is stepped on many times but never gives up living. It is from this notion that the *Ninja* were once called *Kusa* (grass).

My spirit has always been strong. At the age of nine, I began to learn martial arts, and from that beginning I have suffered many injuries. Once a *'Kenpo'* teacher, with all his might, struck the back of my head with a *'Shinai'* leaving me with a concussion. Arrested breathing and a spinal injury resulted from a throw. *'Jujutsu'* Sakaotoshi cracked my neck, *Oni Kudaki* training dislocated an elbow, and *Oyagoroshi* broke a thumb. *Zutsuki* fractured my nose that I quickly set; fighting back tears I continued to practice. On many occasions, the small bones of my hands and feet were damaged, the pain was endured and training continued. In *Bo-jutsu*, an explosive blow to my shin, left it grotesquely swollen. The intense pain made walking difficult but on the way home I pretended to be fine. The entire night I held my shin and by controlling my thoughts I convinced myself it was not serious, overcoming the pain. With a *'Yari'*, I sliced open my hand. Through summer typhoons and winter blizzards, if I was able to walk, I attended class. Despite these injuries I was never worried; my life was safe.

An unskillful student when compared to the others, I practiced harder than they did. The greater the injury the more I exerted myself. I used to think to myself, "This is training!". Through my trials, I have developed and I continue to do my best with this same spirit. Of course, there have been times when I wanted to stop martial arts altogether, because of mental hardships that I was going through. My experience has convinced me that *Ninpo* is the only martial art for me. My purpose in life is to find the truth in martial arts with *Ninpo*. My mission is to teach and show people the blossom of virtue. With strong conviction, I will strive for both my students and for myself.

A martial art is different from a sport. In a real fight, your opponent will not show any mercy toward you for your disabilities. It is a mistake to be discouraged by a few broken bones. Remember this during regular training, otherwise the strong spirit required for physical and mental self-defence will not be there when you need it most.

> "From a high peak to a low plain,
> This is the water's habit.
> But this is but the beginning."

B.
EXISTING AND NOT EXISTING

Understanding the concept *'Yu'* is not a problem in that all objects and living things are expressions of it. The problem is nonexistence or naught *'Mu'*.

Philosophers and followers of *Zen* say, "*Mu* is like not being, but it is, and if you think that there is, then there is; if you think that there is not, then there is not". This is a very strange explanation and nobody really understands it.

For me, *Mu* definitely exists. For example, we cannot see air, but it exists and nobody doubts it. What about the concepts of heart, mind and spirit? You cannot perceive them with the senses, but they exist and are discussed academically. A simple explanation is the following: with your eyes open, what you see is the *Yu* world; with your eyes closed, what you see is the *Mu* world. You do not see what is around you, but it is there.

What exists is said to result from that which does not exist i.e. *Yu* arising from *Mu*. Consider the universe with the sun, planets, and stars. Even though these heavenly bodies are sometimes shielded from our vision they exist *Yu* in space *Mu*. Their very existence is said to have resulted from particles reacting with energy. Does not what exist *Yu* arise from that which does not exist *Mu*?

The term zero should not be expressed as nothing; it is something in itself. In addition and subtraction, when a zero is involved, it seems as if it is not there, but it actually is; it is invisibly present. In division and multiplication, zero changes the result into nothing. This is the *Yu* and *Mu* pattern. Zero conceals an extremely strong power and it is the greatest natural power in existence. It is not confined to the mathematics world alone; it applies to all natural phenomena.

You must understand the essence of *Mu* and understand the truth concerning an object or an event. This way you will be able to move miraculously, just like *Yu* arising from *Mu*, with unarmed self-defence techniques *Taijutsu* and life alike. Go your way guided by the notion of zero.

"The mystery of the martial arts is to
use the opponent's power.
That is the heart of the willow
against the wind."

C.
TRUTH AND DECEPTION

Truth and deception are not easy to judge. If a liar is clearly aware of the reasons that motivate his actions, it is all right for him. But if he loses control over the unrealistic world that he creates with his lies, danger then arises. Though he may be able to deceive others, he cannot deceive his own conscience. Even the imposter has a conscience.

"Deceive rather than be deceived" is a saying that should not be followed by the martial artist. It is not even advisable to use this as a form of strategy. It is best to deal with everyone and everything with your true heart. If you try setting traps and deceiving while facing someone with superior skills, you will easily be defeated. Honesty, truth, and sincerity are usually taken as weaknesses, but they are the best self-protection. They turn your heart into a mirror in which the opponent sees himself free of all of his artificialities. He will then collapse as do those who are to skillful and end up getting trapped in their own schemes. Heaven and the *Ninpo Bugei* will assist those who walk the path with proper intentions and sincere hearts. They will then possess the perfect life (*Kajo Waraku*).

If motivation comes from personal desire concerning money and fame through this art, the path will never lead to perfection (*Kajo Waraku*). Observe and remember that if one's heart is not correct, one's art will also be incorrect.

> "The body's posture and encouragement is
> explained in the martial arts,
> But, in reality, the highest point is
> the posture of the mind and spirit."

D.
FORTUNE AND DESTINY

At different points in life, two expressions are used: 'I was lucky' and 'I was unlucky'. Life consists of destiny and fortune. Destiny is determined before birth and lasts until death; and therefore, one cannot do anything about it - only heaven can. So no one can choose when one will be born but one can, to a certain extent, choose when to die. Everybody who goes to Heaven does so at a predetermined time.

Fortune, however, enhances our lives and comes in the form of continuous large and small waves. The crest of the wave carries fortune and the deepest trough carries misfortune. The best time to be active is while the wave is rising and the best time to store energy is while it is receding. Usually people are too happy to be cautious when the wave peaks, but here they should preserve energy. At this point it is advisable to stop business transactions. When the wave recedes, one should be defensive. The lowest point of the wave is the time to remain motionless, taking only a defensive attitude and never becoming impatient. People may become confused at this point and begin resistance, making their trough go deeper instead of replenishing energy. Those people who lead fortunate lives understand these waves without having to think about them. By learning how to use these waves, you can achieve a very happy and fortunate life.

There are other types of waves: the spiritual wave 'Ki' and the physical wave the 'Tai'. But the most common type of wave is considered to wave of consciousness. These waves can move in any direction throughout life. I hope that you will put effort into learning about this subject.

> "In the large river,
> comes the seed of the horse chestnut.
> If the seed is not there,
> The husk floats."

E.
RELIGION AND MARTIAL ARTS

In the martial arts, if one teaches with the wrong heart, the result is the same as giving a sword to a crazy man. This applies to the teaching of religion, with the result being the same as giving heroin. It is vital to find the true reason for entering either a martial art or religion.

I think of religion and martial art as being the same. Once a middle-aged pupil became very interested in a new religion that had sprouted up here in Japan. This pupil became so involved that he was no longer as earnest with his work as he used to be. And as a result, his family began to have difficulties and he was unable to train in this martial art.

A mother who came to one of our branch *Dojo* with her three children wanted them to begin training with us but because her family were followers of this religion, she laid down one condition - if her children were to begin training, they were not to bow before the *Shinto* altar or recite our ritual prayer (*Shinzen Rei* and *Shikin Haramitsu Daikomyo*). This made teaching these children very difficult because they were not allowed to show respect for tradition and the martial way.

A grandmaster of another martial art has seven or eight small shrines side by side in one room, and every morning he chants a prayer to each one individually, later repeating the same process in the evening. He does this because he wants to possess the super senses of God and he is now convinced that he has attained this goal. From time to time he writes religious types of charms found in most shrines and temples or even declares, "I am now God. I can do anything I desire. If during the rainy season, I wish the following day to be clear and sunny, it will be so." In reality, the weather only takes notice of him about 50 % of the time. Oddly enough, he has always claimed belief in absolute destiny, but whenever he travels, he buys expensive shrine or temple charms. He is also very indecisive about many things. If he makes a rule for his *Dojo* in the morning, by nightfall he has changed his mind. Due to this, his pupils are unable to commit themselves.

The meaning of true religion is the everlasting rule of the cosmos. The martial arts have to teach the rules and laws necessary for an honest life so they can become true martial artists. The martial arts do not only involve winning or losing, cutting or being cut. Both religion and the martial arts stand for one thing - Happiness. If by doing them, one is not happy, then it is best not to do them at all. What is happiness? It means having your heart, life and income united.

At my *Genbukan Dojo* the teaching of *Ninpo* is the teaching of martial arts as well as religion one step at a time.

> "A person usually says,
> 'the techniques are mine',
> but without knowing,
> it was with God's guidance."

F.
DISTANCING AND THE IMMOVABLE HEART

The concept of distancing *'Ma-ai'* has two applications. The first, which is most common, is the calculation of the physical distance between yourself and your opponent. This distance is determined, to enable an attack or retreat. The second application of distancing *Ma-ai* is that between two minds, the *Ma-ai* of *'Ki'*. If an enemy attacks in any way, it should not be a surprize; the heart should not flutter, and the mind should not wander. This state of consciousness is called the immovable heart - *'Fudochi'*. When your heart and spirit remain motionless like those of God; you can maintain a distance between your heart and that of an opponent.

With unrestricted freedom and insight almost like Gods, the attainment is the immovable heart - *'Fudoshin'*. In Buddhism, this level of consciousness is of the highest spiritual attainment *'Kanjizai'*, easily enabling understanding of an opponents course of attack beforehand.

Teaching the physical *Ma-ai* is very simple and is done in the *Dojo*, but the second *Ma-ai* is not so easy. Each pupil is different, with a different degree of spiritual and physical power and talent. The only way to obtain immovable heart easily is by training continuously. This also applies to those who are injured; they can train with their eyes. During training one should never give up because of pain or weariness or, even worse, because of thinking, "I have no talent for this; I can't study it. I can't make it work". Effort is the most important thing. A person who is unable to make an effort will never be able to understand the immovable heart, or of course, the distance of mind. If the person manages to obtain a wise immovable heart, and is never caught unaware of any change in circumstances, then this person will have a wise immovable heart, to be used like radar to hold his or her power of freedom, direct from God. I call this God's direct heart *'Shinden'*.

If you can't find the effort necessary for training or even for a real fight, you will surely be injured or even killed. This too can be called *Ma-ai*, but in this sense the characters used are different, meaning a meeting of devils.

In Japanese, the word *'Ma-ai'* can be expressed with other characters to mean either good or bad timing which in fortune telling implies good or bad luck.

As students of *Ninpo*, your goals must be set beyond the attainment of physical skills, reach an immovable heart.

> 'One must note that *Taijutsu's* highest point
> is the fundamental of peace.
> If one studies, one gets *Fudoshin*.'

G.
PURPOSE AND GOALS IN LIFE

If you ask yourself questions about your purpose or goals in life, you will find it impossible to see down the road of life. Are you after money, status, authority or pleasure? If you were to die now, you could not take these things with you. They will all disappear. Everyone should hope for a life with happiness and peace - true ideals. True happiness and peace can never be bought with money. This also applies to honor and status. Our true mission in life is to build a world of peace, health, and happiness.

Of course, this ideal is very difficult to establish because we must make a tremendous effort with an unyielding mind and spirit. Effort is the best way. Our lives are unpredictable. No one can predict the future. So it is fundamental that we cherish and enjoy every second of our lives. The "second" as a unit of time is most important, in contrast to the notion that "tomorrow" is important. A household is made up of a husband, wife, and children; each person has a personal mission to fulfill. Society is made up of people of different social levels with different forms of employment, yet each individual has a mission to carry out. The person who has a sense of this but still asks what they have to do will become separated from those whose goals are different, as in the relationship between clouds and the earth. It is only natural.

My purpose and mission in life is bound to the 'Ninpo' martial art. I have cleansed both my mind and body. I have begun to teach my pupils how to experience pleasure as well as self-defence. With this martial art, we can build a utopia together as international friends. This is the best way. We must endeavor throughout our short lives, so that when they eventually cease, our souls will be eternally peaceful and satisfied. Do your best! *Ganbatte!*

> If one holds a sword,
> One's spirit must be like a sword,
> If one holds a staff,
> One's spirit must be like a staff,
> If one holds nothing but air then,
> One's spirit must be as air.

*Takamatsu Sensei
Kenbu*

NINPO SECRETS
NINPO PHILOSOPHY, HISTORY and TECHNIQUES

PART III
NINPO
HISTORY

01.
THE LEGENDARY HISTORY
OF NINPO

A.
HEAVEN'S CAVE AND NINPO

Due to her brother's violent attitude, the Sun Goddess and most respected Goddess of the heavens, *Amaterasu Ohmikami* decided to become a recluse. Deeply offended, she entered a cave and had a gigantic rock placed in front of its entrance to seal herself inside. Her action left heaven and earth in complete darkness and disorder. Since this continued every day, the people began to suffer crop failures and thieves plundered the countryside.

The other Gods in heaven, who observed the suffering and darkness in the world, held a meeting to try to find a solution. Their leader, *Omoikane no Kami*'s first proposal was to try to get *Amaterasu* out of the cave by placing as many roosters as possible in front of the cave. The roosters would begin crowing at dawn, their usual ritual to summon the arrival of a new day, and hopefully, *Amaterasu* would emerge from the cave. The plan failed and the world remained dark. *Omoikane no Kami*'s next idea was slightly more complex, so to ensure success he solicited the assistance of a prophet. In ancient times, prediction involved the removal of a shoulder blade of a female deer from Mount *Ama no Kaguyama*. Once the bone was removed a circular cross section was cut from it. The bark from red cherry trees was then stripped and burned to bake the bone.

According to the marks on the bone, the future could be determined. When the bone was examined, the prophecy indicated a certain measure of success. As a result, *Omoikane no Kami* hastily continued with his plan, including the removal of some holy trees from *Ama no Kaguyama* to permit the divinities to hold a mock festival. To ensure realism, he even had decorative shrine ornaments made by suspending colorful stones (*Magatama*), mirrors (*Yata no Kagami*), and strips of cotton cloth from a blue hemp rope (*Tamakazari*). The large ornament (*Magatama no Tamakazari*) was to serve an additional function. He also ordered some ironwork to be undertaken, including the production of an iron mirror. Four other gods were chosen for important roles. *Futotama no Mikoto* would hold the mirror and decorate the entrance of the cave with the *Tamakazari*. *Ame no Koyane no Mikoto* was to pray out loud to *Amaterasu* in front of the cave's entrance. *Ame no Tajikarao no Mikoto*, the strongest, was to stand next to the rock. Last was *Ame no Uzume no Mikoto*, the Goddess of dance, who would entertain. Dressed in a *Kimono* with vines around her shoulders to keep her sleeves out of the way and around her forehead to keep her hair out of her eyes, she presented a striking countenance.

For the celebration, a table was placed in front of the cave, on which *Ame no Uzume* began an amusing dance in front of all the other Gods. With music they clapped and sang merrily. The faster they clapped, the faster she danced. Then her *Kimono* began to open and to the joy of all those present, her breasts were completely revealed. Totally aware of what was happening, she continued to dance until her navel was exposed. The merry making of the divinities aroused *Amaterasu*'s inquisitiveness. She started to wonder about the celebration. Yielding to temptation she opened the entrance a fraction, to see what was happening.

After silently observing the festivities, *Amaterasu* inquired about the nature of the celebration. *Ame no Uzume* stopped dancing, faced *Amaterasu* and replied that the celebration was in honor of a god who commanded more respect than her, *Amaterasu*. At this point, *Ame no Koyane* and *Futotama* positioned the mirror in front of the opening. Catching her own reflection, a brilliant beam, *Amaterasu* the sun Goddess was convinced that they had truly found someone superior to her.

When she opened the entrance to get a clear view of this new God, *Ame no Tajikarao* used his strength to force the entrance open, he took her by the hand and brought her out into the open. *Futotama* seized the opportunity to decorate the front of the cave with the ornaments in a way that would prevent her re-entry. He petitioned her never to enter the cave again. From that day on, the world was blessed with her divine light.

In order to understand the significance of this legend considers an analogy. If the god who did the planning and his accomplices were *Ninja*, one can conclude that during the dark period, it is the *Ninja* who comes out to seek a way to bring back the light in people's hearts.

At Mount *Togakushi* in northern *Nagano* Prefecture, central *Honshu*, a noted training ground for mountain ascetics, is a shrine that enacts a version of the same story in a dance. This form of dance is called *Kagura* that means 'Sacred music and dance'. Some of the *Kagura* dancers at this shrine were students of the *Genbukan Dojo*.

There are other legends and historic stories in the hidden old scrolls that bear relationships with this, I will briefly summarize them.

In 600 or 700 B.C., during the age of the gods, a ship from India was blown off-course and landed in Japan. Aboard was King *Mima-Oh*, a Brahmin priestly scholar, and his three servants. He helped *Amaterasu Ohmi Kami*, the Goddess Queen, to help set up an efficient central government. He shared his knowledge on religion, philosophy, astronomy and astrology, governing systems, Indian history, and on martial arts....

In 550 B.C., another group of Vedic peoples arrived and tried to take over some territory in *Yamato* (*Nara* Prefecture). The Imperial Army defeated them, while having a base camp at the foot of Mount *Miwa Yama*. One condition of the surrender agreement was that this group could settle at *Iso-jo*. Because of the extreme differences in styles of warfare many new ways of effectively using weapons, strategies, and types of warfare were developed.

In 10 B.C., the Imperial Army gathered at *Ise* and *Toba* (in *Mie*) for the start of a ten-year campaign to unify the country and defeat opposing parties. It was at this time that the first historically recorded emperor took power. In the territory of Mount *Miya*, *Isuzu Hime no Mikoto* (a royal princess) was received by him at a royal reception honoring their betrothal and marriage. At *Yamato Kashihara*, the coronation ceremony for the emperor *Jinmu* was held.

These stories help to shed some light on the sources of the history and traditions of Japanese *Budo* and *Ninpo*.

B.
EMPEROR JINMU AND NINPO

a. EMPEROR *JINMU* AND *YATA NO KARASU*

Before *Kamu Yamato Iwarehiko no Mikoto*'s legendary accession as the first Emperor (*Tenno*) and years before he received the posthumous title, *Jinmu*, given him in the late 8th century, he resolved to conquer the *Yamato* region to the east in the *Nara* basin. He left his family behind in *Hyuga* (what is now *Miyazaki* Prefecture in *Kyushu*) and together with *Itsuse no Mikoto*, his brother, set off on an expedition that lasted several years. They made their way along the inland sea and conquered various regions until they arrived at *Naniwa* (now modern *Osaka*). From *Naniwa*, it was *Kamu Yamato*'s intention to proceed to *Yamato* but local chieftains resisted fiercely.

Tribal chieftain *Nagasunehiko* had a particularly resistant command. During an engagement *Itsuse no Mikoto* was fatally wounded by an enemy arrow. This defeat caused *Kamu Yamato* to withdraw from the region. By ship, *Kamu Yamato* sailed to *Kumano* (in present day *Wakayama* Prefecture) where he observed a three-legged raven (*Yata no Karasu*) which legend claims were sent to him by *Amaterasu Ohmikami*, the Sun Goddess. The raven was to serve him as a guide through the treacherous jungle-like terrain from *Kumano* to *Yoshino* (near *Yamato*).

During the march *Kamu Yamato*'s procession encountered light resistance from a local chieftain but they easily defeated his forces. Their march continued until they arrived at their destination, there savage fighting occurred between the forces of *Kamu Yamato* and his nemesis.

During this engagement the sky turned unnaturally dark and a howling wind arose assisting the flight of a large golden kite that descended on the tip of *Kamu Yamato*'s bow. From there it produced a powerful, blinding light that shone directly into the eyes of the enemy. The outcome was a decisive victory for *Kamu Yamato*.

Yamato province turned into a peaceful province and at the *Kashiwara* Shrine, the young leader sat on a throne and became Emperor.

Are you wondering about the significance of this legend? At first, one may assume that there is little relationship between this legend and the historical development of the *Ninja*. Let me assure you that this is not the case. Even to this day, the three-legged raven (*Yata no Karasu*) is a symbol of the *Ninja*, while the Golden Kite is the symbol for reflection techniques with mirrors (*Kinton no Jutsu*) and also fire techniques (*Katon no Jutsu*). It may well be because of this legend that my teacher, the late Grandmaster *Takamatsu Toshitsugu*, chose to live in a house situated in front of the *Kashiwara Jingu* Shrine with Mount *Ama no Kagu Yama* in the background.

Emperor *Jinmu* an expert strategist, deserved the title of *Ninpo* master. It is interesting to note that *Ninpo* martial artists have always maintained a close relationship with the Emperor's family, providing assistance throughout the centuries. A recent example of this aid took place at the end of the *Edo* period when the people of Japan were divided on the issue of concessions to foreigners. *Tokugawa* and his supporters believed that Japan should be closed to outside influence. The Emperor held the opposing point of view with the desire to permit foreign influence. The *Tokugawa Shogun*s were successful in imposing their will and excluding disruptive foreign influence. During this dissension the Emperor's chief bodyguard and aid was *Ohkuni Izumo* of the *Togakure-Ryu Ninja*. During different stages of the 268 years of the *Edo* period (1600-1868) other *Ninja* families lent assistance to the imperial cause. Notably among these were both the *Kusunoki* and *Hattori* families. These are not the only accounts where *Ninja* families have lent assistance to the imperial household, as early as the *Nara* period (710-784 A.D.) the *Ohtomo* family performed the same function. My own family lineage can be traced back to the Emperor *Uda*.

Yata no Karasu.

b. EMPEROR JINMU AND NINJA

According to mythology, six years after the first Emperor of Japan and the founder of the present reigning dynasty took the throne, he was involved in a battle that had little prospect of victory. It was August 2nd and the Emperor *Jinmu* was in the small village of Iware in *Yamato* province (now known as *Nara* Prefecture). The opposing forces were an army from *Shiki* province. The battle was going so badly that at night before retiring, he prayed for divine help.

During his sleep, he dreamt that a god had spoken to him. Emperor *Jinmu* had been instructed to retrieve some clay from the base of Mount *Ama no Kagu Yama* and produce 80 *Sake* vessels from the clay. When the *Sake* vessels were complete they were to be offered to the god. This offering would ensure victory.

The following morning, immediately upon awakening, the Emperor summoned to his quarters two of his retainers, *Shinetsuhiko* and *Ototokashi*. With the knowledge that he had to send these two men through the enemy lines to get to the mountain, Emperor *Jinmu* ordered *Shinetsuhiko* to disguise himself as an old peasant by wearing a weathered straw hat. *Ototokashi* was ordered to disguise himself as the peasant's wife concealing himself in a tattered straw raincoat. After they had prepared their disguises, the Emperor told them secretly that they must penetrate the enemy lines, reach the base of *Ama no Kagu Yama* mountain, and return with clay from the mountain. He confided that the outcome of the battle depended entirely on their action.

The two retainers avoided confrontation with the enemy. In their clever disguises they reached the mountain and returned with the clay. The vessels were made and on the first of October, Emperor *Jinmu* performed a ceremony at the *Niyu* River to present them to the god. Immediately after that he returned to the battlefield and went on to defeat his enemy.

The survivors of the defeated side joined the Emperor's forces by pledging their allegiance to him, as was the custom in those days. However, *Jinmu* was uncertain whether his new recruits were dedicated or if they still maintained loyalty to their dead leader. *Jinmu* decided to test his conscripts. Secretly he contacted his highest-ranking officer whose name was *Michino Omi no Mikoto* (also known as *Hi no Omi no Mikoto* who later established the *Ohtomo* Family). *Michino* was ordered to take the army from *Kume* province to the village of *Osaka* (not the present day city of *Osaka*) where a massive excavation was to be undertaken. The regional forces of that area would be invited to attend a festivity inside the excavated chamber. At an opportune moment *Michino*'s followers were to annihilate their guests. Any of *Michino*'s men who refused to enter the chamber were to be taken aside and executed.

Michino strictly obeyed *Jinmu*'s command for the rapid excavation. When the chamber was finished and the day of the festivity came, *Michino* had his men mingle with the guests. Many of *Michino*'s men were secretly seated amongst the unsuspecting guests, the others were strategically seated in an outer ring. Before undertaking this mission, *Michino* held his own secret meeting in *Kume* Province. He told his men that if he stood up at the peak of the festivities and began to sing a song, they were to stand up and kill anyone who remained seated. This precaution was done so that any spies that may have infiltrated *Michino*'s army after leaving *Kume* would be unaware of the plan and when the time came, they too would be seated and killed. *Michino*'s plan was an unparalleled success. This technique became known as '*Fuka Togo no Jutsu*'.

Emperor *Jinmu*
(By *Yamato Sakura*)

C.
YAMATO TAKERU NO MIKOTO AND NINPO

Ousu no Mikoto, son of the 12th Emperor, *Keiko*, was dispatched to eliminate the dissident *Kumaso* tribesmen, led by *Kawakami Takeru*. *Ousu* at only 16 years of age faced a powerful opponent. The *Kumaso* tribesmen were veteran warriors so victory seemed unlikely. After contemplating the problem, the young man thought of a possible solution.

At some point during the warfare, *Kawakami Takeru* decided to hold a feast. Learning of this event, *Ousu* dressed himself as a young woman of exceptional beauty, enhanced by his fine features and fair complexion. Without arousing any suspicion, he entered the party and was soon spotted by *Kawakami*. His appearance was so startling, that he was asked to sit next to *Kawakami Takeru* and serve him drinks. Throughout the festivities, *Ousu* conversed in a submissive, feminine voice and poured *Kawakami* so much alcohol that he was soon drunk. *Kawakami* was unable to resist when *Ousu* drew a short sword from his *Kimono* and stabbed the chieftain through the heart. As *Kawakami* lay dying, he asked the girl who she was. He was astounded to hear the reply. In his dying breath he issued a proclamation that henceforth *Ousu no Mikoto* shall be called *Yamato Takeru no Mikoto*, literally, the master of Japanese martial arts.

An early instance of the art of impersonation and disguise (*Henso-Jutsu*) is recounted in this legend. The tactics employed by *Ousu no Mikoto* were those frequently used by the female *Ninja* (*Kunoichi*). Feminine charm has accomplished many deeds.

Yamato Takeru no Mikoto stabbed *Kawakami Takeru*
(By *Yamato Sakura*)

D.
RYUJU BOSATSU AND NINPO

The term *Bosatsu* is a reverent title used for Buddhist saints who are on their last pass in a human existence before attaining the state of perfect blessedness, nirvana, when the soul is absorbed into the Great Spirit. *Ryuju Bosatsu* or *Ryumo* as he is otherwise known, was born into a high Brahman caste family in the Kosara Province of India 500 to 600 years after the death of Buddha (*Shaka*).

Ryumo was a genius, for every one sentence that he heard, he understood at least 10 different interpretations. His intelligence enabled him to become a very respected figure.

During his youth, he had many other brilliant friends of the same age. At one point, he and three of those friends began to talk about invisibility (*Onshi no Ho*). The subject then turned to what they would do if they had this capability. One particular idea appealed to their sense of adventure. They desired to enter the king's palace and secretly have sexual relations with his highest-class courtesans. Obsessed with this, the four friends went to a master of invisibility and persistently begged him to teach them the secret. The master thought that if he gave them a sample, they would leave and he would not be troubled by them. He produced a sample that *Ryumo* examined carefully for a short time, and then bewildered the master by reciting all the ingredients. The master taught *Ryumo* the proportions of the ingredients and the brewing techniques. They left the master and excitedly prepared the potion. Drinking it, they became invisible. They then entered the palace grounds and accomplished their lustful objective.

Within a short while a tense situation arose at the palace when none of the king's courtesans could account for their pregnancies. They cried constantly in shame.

The furious king called to his presence many aged advisers. Some said that it was probably an evil spirit sent by devils, while others thought it was the work of fairies. If it was an evil spirit, special prayers would stop its activities. If it was the work of fairies, then the solution would be to scatter sand on the floor to observe the footprints. When the footprints appeared the guards would then surround the fairy and cut freely with their swords. The king chose the latter solution as it sounded more realistic. He had his guards scatter sand all over the palace and seal the exits. After their initial preparation, the guards maintained strict vigilance for the telltale signs.

It was not long when the sand began to shift and the recognizable pattern of footprints began to appear. The guards rushed forward to surround the area. As they hacked away at the empty space in front of them, all three of *Ryumo*'s friends were killed. *Ryumo* managed to stay alive by standing behind the king so that the guards could not kill him without risking the king's life. After his narrow escape, *Ryumo* began his study of Buddhism that lasted throughout his life. Eventually he became a monk of the highest order.

This legend traces back the origin of *Ninpo*. Throughout the centuries, Indian mystics have invented many potions and medicines with extraordinary capabilities. Even present day martial artists in Indian gain flexibility by using such ointments. They can make their muscles rock hard and yet maintain flexibility. Special products also are used to make their wooden staffs either harder or more flexible. Many of these discoveries found their way to China and eventually to Japan.

Ryuju Bosatsu

E.
JOFUKU AND NINPO

In the year 219 AD the Emperor of China, *Shiko-Tei* (*Suh Fong Tih*) was obsessed with finding the secret of eternal youth and life. *Jofuku* (*Shih Fuh*), one of the Emperor's retainers was ordered to find the potion and return with it from what are now known as the islands of Japan. So, with 500 aides, *Jofuku* made it to Japan and began searching at *Shingu* (*Wakayama* Prefecture). From there they searched all of the islands but were unable to learn anything of the potion.

Unable to return to China without the potion, they decided to stay in Japan. *Jofuku*, who during this time became known as *Oirotayuya*, taught the Japanese people how to catch whales, as well as make paper and fireworks. He and his followers also taught what would later be considered the origin of *Ninjutsu*. It was *Jofuku* who brought to Japan *Senjutsu*, techniques for attaining supernatural powers, and introduced it around the *Yamato* and *Katsuragi* provinces (now *Nara*). *Senjutsu* was originally practiced by the Brahman class of old India together with the Yogi Sutra (the origins of Yoga) and other mystical practices. During the sixth century B.C. *Senjutsu* found its way to China where it was further influenced by *Dokyo*, Chinese teachings on preserving youthful appearance. *Senjutsu* training utilized meditation, sojourns and potions to acquire the following supernatural skills:

① *Shingen Tsu* - An awareness of all events happening at the present time.
② *Shinju Tsu* - The ability to hear over vast distances.
③ *Shinsoku Tsu* - The ability to transport one's body instantaneously.
④ *Tashin Tsu* - The ability to read people's minds.
⑤ *Kio Tsu* - An awareness of all previous events.
⑥ *Mirai Tsu* - The ability to predict the future.

In Japan, the practice of *Senjutsu* was soon adopted by the *Shugendo* and the *Mikkyo* religions. Through these channels it influenced *Ninjutsu*. The most famous practitioners of *Senjutsu* (*Sennin*) in Japan were *Kume Sennin*, *Ohtomo Sennin*, and *Azumi Sennin*. Many legends herald their deeds.

The *Sennin*

The religion of *Shugendo* tried to obtain the spiritual unity of man and god through concentrated prayer and physical training. This is distinguished from *Ninpo* by three elements, physical training (*Taijutsu*), the academic study of tools and weapons (*Buki*) and finally mind control (*Seishin Toitsu*) was combined to obtain the final goal of a spiritual paradise. In *Ninpo*, the ultimate objective is to establish peace between people and not just attain self-elevated God-like status. It was this difference that distinguished *Ninpo* from *Shugendo* and other religions. However, *Ninpo* remained a paradox because it was deeply academic and rational yet mysterious. The components of *Ninpo* can never be learned from books or meditation only. The only way to learn is by practice and experience so that the study of *Ninpo* is complete.

Regarding the legend of *Jofuku*, there is another version of this tale that claims *Jofuku* returned to China, leaving behind two women. It is said that they settled in *Iga* (*Mie* Prefecture) and they taught the people to make cloth and the foundations of *Ninjutsu*. This version claims *Oirotayuya* was the name of one of the two women but it remains unclear as to which one.

It is more probable that *Jofuku*, a high-class warrior and personal envoy of the Chinese Emperor, would have had too much pride to return to China without the potion for eternal life. An intelligent man, he would not have been gullible enough to believe in the existence of such a potion in the first place. So it seems likely that Jofuku was also *Oirotayuya*.

02.
NINPO IN THE NARA PIRIOD

A.
SHOTOKU TAISHI AND NINJA

According to current scholarship, in 538 A.D., the Buddhist religion (*Bukkyo*) entered Japan. *Bukkyo* together with *Sonshi* (*Sueng Tsu*) the book of strategy arrived from the *Kudara* (*Paichi*) Province of Korea that was then ruled by King *Seimei-Oh* (*Sun Ming Wong*).

It was not until later on, in the same century, during the reign of Japan's first ruling Empress that Buddhism became prominent. For the Empress *Suiko* to rule the country alone would have been impossible, so she appointed *Shotoku Taishi*, the twenty-year-old son of Japan's 31st Emperor *Yomei*, as her regent.

Shotoku Taishi passed a law *Kan-i Junikai* that changed the social structure of Japan into twelve classes of people. The same year he drew up a constitution made up of seventeen fundamental articles. His plan was to centralize the government and strengthen the authority of the imperial institution. With this came the building of *Horyuji* and *Chuguji* temples and also a book on *Bukkyo* made up of selected topics, thus the Buddhist religion began to flourish. He also ordered *Ono no Imoko* to go to China (*Zui*) to absorb culture so that he could bring it back to Japan. The discoveries of the returned scholar strengthened Japan's cultural and political structure.

Shotoku Taishi employed another highly skilled individual, his name was *Ohtomo no Saijin*. *Ohtomo no Saijin* was employed as a spy. His particular field of work was acquiring information that *Shotoku Taishi* called *Shinobi*. In the year 587, a high-ranking *Samurai* of the *Mononobe no Moriya* clan began to disturb government officials by burning and defacing statutes of Buddha. *Ohtomo no Saijin* acquired information about these subversive activities; thus convincing *Shotoku Taishi* to finally confront and defeat the rebel forces. Eventually *Saijin* left the service of *Shotoku Taishi* and went to live in the *Koga* region, from there he finally moved to *Iga*. The relationship between *Ohtomo no Saijin* and *Shotoku Taishi* was very deep, so when *Saijin* moved to *Iga*, their shared values were implanted in *Iga*. From this beginning, *Ohtomo-Ryu Ninpo* became the backbone of both the *Iga* and *Koga-Ryu* traditions. Other than this, there is little known information of *Ohtomo no Saijin*'s activities.

Years later, *Shotoku Taishi*'s descendants were defeated by the *Soga* clan but within 60 years, the Emperor's family, once again with the assistance of the *Ohtomo* family defeated the *Soga* clan.

Shotoku Taishi was a remarkable man. It is said that he had the ability to hear the problems of ten different people simultaneously and yet give judgment to each one individually. His influence on the development of *Ninpo* was significant. The law of the twelve classes stated that the highest class title in the system would be that of '*Toku* 徳'. These select few were to have a deep understanding of the virtues of the martial arts. In the *Ohtomo* family there was an expression '*Butoku Iko* 武徳威光' which means "the virtue of the martial arts is the giving of a great light". A secret teaching passed exclusively to successive *Ninpo* Headmasters and understood by some *Toku* was *Shinbujin Fusatsu no Ritsu* which when translated means "the law of both God and the martial artist is that one must never kill anything." From this expression *Ninpo* has derived the principal "to win without drawing one's sword; to win without a fight is to attain the highest level."

Within the Seventeen-Article Constitution, *Shotoku Taishi* wrote in the first article,

> "The highest and most important virtue is that of peace and harmony. Carrying peace and harmony in your heart is the same as possessing the spirit of Japan (*Yamato Kokoro*). This is the backbone of the original Japanese people, the *Yamato* race."

This principle is also written in one of the *Iga Ninpo* records where it says,

> '*Bujin Wa o Motte Totoshi to Nasu*',

"The martial artist's most important achievement is that of peace and harmony."
This is the most important principle in all of the *Ninpo* scrolls.

In the second article it said that the people must have a deep respect for the three treasures of the country, which are prayers (*Butsu-i / Bu*), Buddha sutra (*Ho / Po*) and priests (*So*). Similarly, *Ninpo* scrolls also referred to three jewels (*Sanpo Hiden*); however, these refer to the three secret *Taijutsu* points:

    ① Eyes (*Metsubushi*)   ② Ears (*Happa*)   ③ Groin (*Suzu*)

The combination of three essentials, however, has far greater significance because in order to become a true *Ninja* one must train in three fundamental areas:

    ① *Bumon* (武門) : The martial art component consisting of the 36 *Ninpo* essentials (*Ninpo Sanjurokkei*; *Bugei Juhappan* and *Ninja Juhakkei*). From *Bumon* one derives power.

    ② *Shumon* (宗門) : The religious and spiritual aspect, where one must learn and understand different religions of the world without being tied down to only one. From *Shumon* one attains spiritual enlightenment.

    ③ *Bunmon* (文門) : This involves the learning and understanding of culture, history, philosophy and traditions. From *Bunmon* one gains knowledge.

A human can be considered as having three main parts: the body that gives power, the heart that gives spirit, and the mind that provides wisdom. Through the learning of *Bumon*, *Shumon*, and *Bunmon*, a *Ninja* develops these three parts and has them working together in complete harmony. When this integration is complete the practitioner is a *Ninja*.

In the tenth article of *Shotoku Taishi*'s Seventeen Article Constitution it states "one must stop anger from entering one's heart, and then be able to disregard that anger." These words are also found in a verse called 'The Spirit of the *Ninja*'(*Ninniku Seishin*), in which it says that if one is ridiculed by someone, one must not become angry or jealous. Instead throw any resentment into the river. Keep your heart like a flower. Keep your spirit like bamboo.

B.
EMPEROR TENMU AND THE NINJA

On December 3rd 671 AD, Emperor *Tenchi*, the 38th Emperor of Japan, died and the following year the *'Jinshin no Ran'*(the rebellion of the *Jinshin* period) occurred. The conflict was between the heir of the throne, Prince *Ohtomo*, and his uncle Prince *Oh-Ama* and lasted about a month (from June 22nd to July 23rd) in the year of *Jinshin*.

Oh-Ama's army left *Yoshino* (near *Nara*) on June 23rd and marched day and night for two days until they arrived at *Ise*. Their march took them through the *Iga* and *Koga* regions. The army had two battalions, the first led by three generals called *Kino no Omino Ahemaro*, *Ohtomo no Muraji no Makuta* and the *Fukei* brothers. The second battalion was commanded by only one man, *Murakuni no Muraji no Oyori*. The entire army consisted of thirty thousand men, all dressed in red and carrying red flags so they could easily tell the difference between allies and enemies on the battlefield. They attacked and defeated Prince *Ohtomo* at the *Seta* River near Lake *Biwako*, and it was at *Yamazaki* that Prince *Ohtomo* committed suicide. Prince *Oh-Ama* then changed his name to *Tenmu* and became the fortieth Emperor of Japan.

A warrior of Prince *Oh-Ama* from the *Yamato* Province earned recognition during this battle. He was the *Ninja Takoya*.

After *Tenmu* was installed as Emperor, Prince Seiko began a rebellion within the walls of his castle at *Atago* in *Yamashiro* Province. *Takoya* was ordered to enter the castle secretly and create a diversion. He succeeded and began to burn the castle while *Tenmu* attacked with an army. *Seiko* was killed during the siege. It is interesting to note that Prince *Ohtomo*'s mother was originally from the *Iga* region. Japan's history has always had a close relationship with the *Iga* and *Koga* regions.

Tenmu's wife, Empress *Uno no Kogo*, used a *Ninja* by the name of *Tsumori no Muraji no Toru* to help her rule Japan after the Emperor died (She was the 42nd ruler of Japan).

Tsumori, who concealed his true profession by working as a fortune-teller, had one of the most efficient information gathering networks of that time.

A revolution scene at the Emperor's palace.
(By Yamato Sakura)

C.
SONSHI AND NINPO

There is a collection of seven books on strategy which originally came from China called '*Sonshi* 孫子', *Goshi*, *Shibaho*, *Iryoshi*, *Rienko Montai*, *Osekiko Sanryaku* and *Taikobo Rikuto*. In Japan, these books are referred to collectively as *Shichisho* (seven books). There are many different accounts explaining how and when these books entered Japan. The most popular version says they were brought in by *Kibi no Makibi* when he returned from China after having lived there for twenty years as an emissary of the Emperor. His specific mission was to bring Chinese culture to Japan. This version claims he arrived in Japan on April 26th 735 AD. However, another tale claims that the books came along with the Buddhist Sutra from the *Kudara* Province of Korea in the year 538 AD. Another report says that it was around 600 AD, when Japan was invading Korea's *Shiragi* Province. It may have been a present from *Zui* (China) or perhaps it was a student of culture by the name of *Ono no Imoko* who brought it to Japan when he returned from *Zui* in 608 AD.

Nonetheless, in the year 593 AD, *Shotoku Taishi* was regent of the empire '*Sessho*' during the reign of Empress *Suiko*. He must have had access to these books because he made up the Seventeen-Article Constitution the '*Junanajo no Kenpo*' with the assistance of the seven books.

The book of *Sonshi* (*Suen Tsu*) was written by *Sonbu* (*Sun Tsu*). He was born in the Chinese Province of *Go* (*Wu*) in 541 BC and died in 482 BC. A thorough study of the fighting era of the Chinese armies (which began from about 772 BC onwards) as well as the strategies used about 2000 years before that enabled *Sonbu* to compile the necessary material. The book was made up of his personal opinions, and in the thirteenth and last chapter he wrote about the importance of '*Kan*' (the Chinese name for *Shinobi*).

In later years, the famous general *Takeda Shingen* developed his own system of strategies from *Sonshi*, and called it *Takeda-Ryu Gunryaku*, also known as *Koshu-Ryu Gunryaku*. From the seventh book of *Sonshi* he combined some characters (*Kanji*) from a certain paragraph to make '*Fu-Rin-Ka-Zan* 風林火山'(*Fu* meaning wind, *Rin* meaning forest, *Ka* meaning fire and *Zan* meaning mountain). He put this phrase on his flag as his motto. In *Sonshi*, the original meaning is, "To attack faster than the wind". However, its secret meaning is, "An army moves like the wind; silent as the forest; if it must attack it does so like fire; if it cannot move it remains as steadfast as a mountain". Later the famous *Shogun Kusunoki Masashige* also used it. His *Ryu* was *Kusunoki-Ryu Hyoho*. I am very fond of this phrase since *Takeda Shingen* is one of my ancestors.

It is the opinion of many that *Ninpo* developed from the book of *Sonshi*, but even before this book was imported and before the Buddha Sutra was brought to Japan, the Japanese religion was mainly *Shinto*ism (the natural way of God) and inside their shrines secret books on strategies were kept. These secret books, the backbone of *Shinto*ism, were traditionally the teachings of three families, *Ohtomo Bunsho*, *Mononobe Bunsho* and *Nakatomi Bunsho*. It is thus my opinion that the development of *Ninpo* came by combining the Japanese and Chinese.

D.
SHUGENDO AND NINPO

Shugendo, the religious order that encourages ascetic practices in certain mountainous regions, resulted from the mixture of esoteric Buddhism (*Shingon Mikkyo* and *Tendai Mikkyo*), *Shinto* teachings, secret Chinese strategies, Chinese *Dokyo* (Chinese *Senjutsu*, and Indian *Senjutsu*. Followers of *Shugendo* were known as students of *Shugendo* (*Shugenja*) or mountain warriors (*Yamabushi*). *Shugendo* was favored by the mountain warriors since it was a mixture of the *Shinto* Religion, practiced by the lower classes, and the imported Buddha Sutra, practiced by higher classes.

The unique combination of these ideas led to the development of many special practices enabling the followers to provide astonishing services to their people. Secret medicines used within religious ceremonies would cure those even near death. Hypnosis, mind control techniques, the development of the spirit through yelling, the writing of lucky charms, and the concocting of special medicines gave *Shugendo* great credibility. With this support and the *Yamabushi*'s knowledge of strategy, *Shugendo* became extremely powerful.

Although *Shugendo* has no documented historical founder, members ascribe its origin to *En no Ozunu* (*En no Gyoja*), a semi-legendary magician. His ancestors were probably from China or Korea. He was born in the year 634 in the *Yamato* Province at the *Kichishoji* Temple. At the age of 32 he went to *Katsuragi* Mountain where he began hard physical training and ascetic discipline to heighten spirituality and develop super powers. After successful attainment, he began to practice *Shugendo*. Other holy mountains where his exercises were performed included the mountains of *Ohmine*, *Kinbu*, *Imichi*, *Mikami*, *Koga*, and *Fuji*.

However, there are contradictory accounts explaining the way in which he managed to obtain his special power. One version maintains he received his power by praying in a special manner with the aid of the secret book of the Buddha Sutra called '*Kujaku-Oh-Jukyo*'. A second version states he got his special ability by training at *Akame no Ishi* in the *Iga* region. Another account purports he dreamt that it was a gift from *Fudo-Myo-Oh* a guardian of the heavens, who stands in front of a wall of fire with a sword in one hand to cut down evil spirits and a rope in the other to bind them should they try to harm the angels. Although his face displays his anger, his heart is pure. One-eye gazes upward representing the sun and his ability to see during the day while the other eye is cast downward representing his ability to see at night.

Akame no Taki

En no Ozunu derived satisfaction by helping pure-hearted commoners, but when it came to the local governors who caused misery, he would irritate them with his magical powers (*Genjutsu*) and super human skills (*Senjutsu*). Orders for the capture of *Ozunu* were given in 699 A.D., prompting the use of his best students in a guerilla campaign. The constant use of unconvential strategies as well as magic made life extremely miserable for the opposing forces. The governor was forced to enlist the aid of the national army. A plan was devised to take *Ozunu*'s mother hostage and force *Ozunu* to surrender. Love for his mother brought the predicted outcome and *Ozunu* was exiled to the penal island, *Izu no Oshima*.

Two stories exist about the way he managed to get out of prison. The first story claims that after three years, the governor gave consent to his release and allowed him to return to his home region. The other version claims that one night he managed to escape by flying to Mount *Fuji*. Other than the day marking the anniversary of his death, July 7th, nothing further is known of him.

Long after *Ozunu*'s death, Buddhists and *Shinto*ists continued to oppose each other. This ended at the end of the *Nara* period when *Gyoki*, a celebrated monk, appeared and in order to triumph over the ardent *Shinto*ists proposed a compromise that acknowledged *Shinto* Gods and Buddha as one and the same. The governing powers accepted his interpretation and the previously outlawed religion of *Shugendo*, a mixture of Buddhism and *Shinto*ism, was finally made legal.

The height of popularity for *Shugendo* came with the return of two monks from abroad and the establishment of their *Mikkyo* temples. *Saicho*, who studied in China for a short period, established on Mt. *Hiei*, the new *Mikkyo* religion *Tendai Shu* in 805. This religion is now known as the *Tendai* Sect of Buddhism. *Kukai*, after a two-year period of study in China, returned in 806 with *Shingon Shu Mikkyo* to open a temple in the *Koya* Mountains. This religion is now known as the *Shingon* Sect of Buddhism. *Shugendo* shared a close relationship with these two forms of *Mikkyo*. This relationship exerted a considerable influence on *Ninpo*. The *Ninpo* techniques for self-composure including spiritual self-defense (*Goshin*) energy channeling (*In*), and techniques to immobilize the enemy (*Fudo Shichibaku In*) came directly from *Mikkyo* through *Shugendo*. *Shugendo* taught future prediction (*Hachimon Tonko no Ekisen*), death wishes (*Jujutsu*), prayers and incantations (*Kaji* and *Kito*), and special techniques on 'flying' and endurance running (*Senjutsu*). This type of training alone was severe but the mountain warriors who practiced these techniques

En no Ozunu

also practiced staff fighting (*Bo-Jutsu*, *Jo-Jutsu*), defensive body movements (*Taijutsu*) and various teachings on strategy. the strategy of the mountain warriors (*Yamabushi Hyoho*) became the most influential subject in the development of *Ninpo*.

Ninpo, with its many inherited aspects, has not been clearly understood. Misunderstanding may have arisen on account of similarities between *Ninpo* and the deceptive *Genjutsu*. *Takamatsu Sensei* taught the way in which one can separate *Ninpo* from *Genjutsu*. This can be done through a comparison of the components of both *Ninpo* and *Genjutsu*. Shared components of both *Ninpo* and *Genjutsu* were:

TAI-JUTSU : Unarmed self-defense
SOSOKU-JUTSU : Rapid walking and running
SHURIKEN-JUTSU : Throwing sharpened projectiles
KODACHI-JUTSU : Short sword techniques
SEKKO-JUTSU : Army Command and enemy surveillance

Ninpo alone contained:

MUTODORI-JUTSU : Weaponless defense against an armed opponent
SHINTO HIHO : Mysteries of *Shinto*
HACHIMON TONKO JUTSU : Prediction of future events

Genjutsu alone contained:

GENJUTSU : Deceptive magic
SENJUTSU : Religious practices for super-human capabilities
DOKYO : Yoga and special ointments
MIKKYO : Esoteric Buddhism

Several religions including *Sendo*, *Dokyo*, and *Shugendo* used the title '*Doshi*' (Master) to refer to disciples of their highest orders until the *Kamakura* era about 700 years ago. In *Ninpo*, the title was also used until the same period for grandmasters, for example, the titles of some of *Togakure Ryu Ninja* Grandmasters were *Gamon Doshi*, *Garyu Doshi*, *Kain Doshi*, and *Hakuun Doshi*. The misconception that *Ninpo* is only trickery and evasion persists to this day; however, what must be understood is that *Ninpo* is a true martial art based on martial strategy, techniques, and practices that can be traced through *Shugendo* to *Mikkyo*.

03.
NINPO IN THE HEIAN AND KAMAKURA PERIOD

A.

MINAMOTO NO YOSHITSUNE AND NINPO

Minamoto Kuro Hogan Yoshitsune, born in 1159, was the 9th son of *Minamoto Samano-kami Yoshitomo*, the leader of the *Seiwa Genji* Clan, and *Tokiwa Gozen*, his mother.

Between 1159 and 1160, *Yoshitsune*'s father warred with *Taira no Kiyomori*, the leader of the *Kanmu Heishi* Clan the *Heiji* rebellion (*Heiji no Ran*), but was defeated. *Yoshitomo* fled towards the *Kanto* area (now *Tokyo* and *Saitama* Prefecture) but during his escape was killed by *Nagata Tadamune*, one of his own officers. *Nagata* had invited *Yoshitomo* to dinner and after *Yoshitomo* had drunk a lot, they entered the bath. *Yoshitomo* was at ease and during a relaxed moment, *Nagata Tadamune* killed him. *Tokiwa* headed for safety to the small village of *Ryumon* in *Yamato* Province carrying the baby *Ushiwaka-Maru* (*Yoshitsune*'s name as a child) and holding the hands of *Yoshitsune*'s elder brothers, *Otowaka-Maru* and *Imawaka-Maru*. Together they crossed the snow-covered area and finally reached *Ryumon*. Shortly after, *Taira no Kiyomori* kidnapped *Tokiwa Gozen*'s mother and used her as bait to lure *Tokiwa* and her children to his castle. *Tokiwa* had no choice but to go, although she may have gone for another reason. When *Kiyomori* saw her, he was stunned by her beauty and wanted to marry her. Using this for leverage she begged for the release of her mother and children from the castle grounds. The request was granted in 1166, when *Ushiwaka-Maru* was only seven years old. However, he was confined to *Kurama-Dera* Temple on Mount *Kurama* near *Kyoto*. The temple was established for children to perform religious duties. *Kiyomori*'s spies kept an eye on the young boy from time to time to make sure that he had not run away and to ensure he was not being trained in martial arts.

The *Kurama-Dera* Temple was built in 770 by a Chinese man, *Ganjo Wajo*, a high level student of *Ganjin Wajo* (*Chieng Tsuang Hashian*). *Ganjin Wajo* had been asked to come to Japan to teach the Buddhist Sutra (*Hosso-Shu*). *Hosso-Shu* was later adopted by the *Tendai-Shu* (*Mikkyo*). The temple's main statue was *Bishamonten* that stood with a *Yari* (spear) in one hand and a sword in the other to guard Buddha.

When *Ushiwaka-Maru* arrived at the temple, the head was *Zenrinbo Ajari Kakunichi* (*Zen* means *Zen*; *Rin* means *forest*; *Bo* means *part*; *Ajari* is the title given to the highest priest; and *Kakunichi* was his personal name). *Ushiwaka-Maru* stayed at the temple until he was 16, however, he hardly ever studied the Buddhist Sutra and instead studied the martial arts.

Once when *Ushiwaka-Maru* was training sword techniques against the trees in the *Sojogadani* valley by himself, he was spotted by *Tohkobo Ajari Rennin*, the *Kurama-Dera* Temple head before *Kakunichi*. This man was an expert swordsman. To keep his identity secret, he would wear a *Tengu* (demon) mask while teaching specialized sword techniques called *Hiko Kenpo* (flying sword techniques). *Ushiwaka-Maru* was thus taught martial arts and strategy. Eventually the boy was able to study the martial arts with the support and encouragement of his late father's retainers.

Ushiwaka-Maru had, as a girlfriend, a famous young dancer who had the freedom to enter the grounds of the home of *Kiichi Hogan*. *Ushiwaka-Maru* used her to get an introduction to this man. *Kiichi Hogan* had a secret scroll containing the highest strategic theories (*Rikuto Sanryaku Tora no Makimono*) that was given to the young man. (A different version says he stole it. This version seems more credible because he was too young to have it given to him.) Nonetheless, *Ushiwaka-Maru* grew up with the spirit of the *Genji* family that was, at that time, the correct attitude for becoming a *Samurai*. His martial training and knowledge of strategy were further developed by the *Yamabushi* and other warriors he encountered.

From this period, a legend arose *Gojo no Hashi* that made *Ushiwaka* famous. The story says that a *Hiei* mountain priest, *Musashibo Benkei*, attacked *Ushiwaka* while they were on a bridge. *Ushiwaka* jumped onto the railings of the bridge and continuously evaded *Benkei's* attacks. Suddenly *Ushiwaka* counter-attacked his rival with a fan, defeating the priest. After surrendering, *Benkei* asked *Ushiwaka* if he could become the young man's retainer.

In 1174, *Ushiwaka-Maru* became of age and wanted to escape the confines of *Kurama-Dera* Temple to go to *Ohshu Hiraizumi* where he could stay as a guest of the leader of that area, *Fujiwara no Hidehira*. To escape, the young man needed assistance. His accomplice was *Kaneuri no Kichiji*, a spy employed by *Hidehira* and well known to *Ushiwaka*. To conceal his identity, *Kichiji* worked as a gold merchant, transporting gold from *Ohshu* to sell in *Kyoto*. Because of this profession, he was able to give young *Ushiwaka* money and assist in his training while he was still at the temple. By this time, *Ushiwaka* was very skillful in escaping from the temple and going to *Kyoto* at the foot of the mountain. On the day he left for *Ohshu* he met the merchant in *Kyoto* to receive assistance.

On the way to *Ohshu*, he stopped at *Ohmi Kagami no Shuku*, where he changed his boyish haircut to a man's style and changed his name to *Minamoto no Kuro Yoshitsune*.

While *Yoshitsune* was traveling towards his destination, another man asked to be a retainer. He was *Ise no Saburo Yoshimori*, one of the highest-ranking *Ninja* of the time. There are two versions as to how they met. The first claims that on the way to *Ohshu*, *Yoshitsune* stopped at a farmhouse in a village in the *Joshu* area (*Gunma* Prefecture). The house had been that of a former *Samurai* so the owner's first son was given permission by *Yoshitsune* to use the name *Yoshi.*, eventually known as *Yoshimori*. The second account says that when *Yoshitsune* was making his way back to *Kyoto* from *Ohshu* to fight the *Heishi*, he was confronted by *Koroku*, the leader of the Suzuka mountain clan. Defeated, *Koroku* begged *Yoshitsune* to allow him to be a retainer. *Koroku* is said to have changed his name to *Yoshimori*.

Yoshimori, an expert in *Ninpo* strategy, was very active in the clashes against the *Heishi*, providing *Yoshitsune* with a personal *Ninja* group. *Yoshimori* is renowned for his 100 *Ninja* poems that had secret teachings.

For example:

"When moving towards the sun or moon one has no shadow;
But with a light behind, one grows a shadow."

This poem explains that when moving towards a source of light you are not preceded by a shadow that would give you away to the enemy. However, if you move away from a light, the shadow falls in front of you, announcing your arrival and broadcasting one's movements.

A second example is:

"When entering someone's property it is very importantthat one knows the opportunity."

The opportunity refers to the moment of vulnerability when the enemy is very tired or relaxed.

A third example:

"The techniques of the enemy are well known to me, But they never know mine."

To know everything about the enemy is of utmost importance. If the enemy knows absolutely nothing about you, then you are an expert *Ninja*.

At *Ohshu Hiraizumi*, *Yoshitsune* stayed under the protection of *Hidehira* until the age of 22. During this time he had the opportunity to study more about strategy from experienced *Samurai*.

In 1180, *Yoshitsune* received word that his eldest brother *Yoritomo* had assembled a massive army in Izu province to fight the *Heishi*. *Yoshitsune* wanted to fight with his brother, so against the advice of *Hidehira* he left. After meeting his brother for the first time, near the Kise river in the *Kanto* region, *Yoshitsune* was made second-in-command and began to war against his enemies.

In 1183, *Yoshitsune* started from *Kamakura* with his other brother, *Minamoto no Noriyori*, who was standing in for *Yoritomo*, to fight against his cousin *Kiso Yoshinaka*. The account of this campaign claims *Yoshitsune* had 25,000 soldiers under his command although the exact number could have been as low as five thousand, since history often distorts figures. On January 20th, 1184, *Yoshitsune*'s army arrived at the banks of *Kyoto*'s *Uji* River where they halted.

Yoshitune was facing *Yoshinaka* and his already assembled army on the *Kyoto* side of the river. Prior to *Yoshitsune*'s arrival, *Yoshinaka* had fortified the river with wooden spikes and nets. The boards of the bridge had been removed to make it almost impossible for *Yoshitsune*'s army to cross the river. After several unsuccessful attempts to cross the river, *Yoshitsune* dispatched *Noriyori* to go down river, cross over, and attack from the east. *Noriyori* was successful but not without great difficulty due to his incompetence and lack of experience. Yet, *Yoshitsune* and his men managed to get across the river and oust *Yoshinaka* and his army from *Kyoto* in only one day.

In the battle between the armies of *Yoshitsune* and *Yoshinaka* at the *Uji* River, *Yoshinaka*'s defense plan included placing pointed poles in the ground at an angle so the points faced the enemy. Under the water, he had many more pointed poles planted firmly in the riverbed to stop both swimmers and mounted warriors from getting across. Nets were also scattered around to trip any horses.

Yoshitsune ordered his men to enter the water and remove as many poles and nets as possible. Many men lost their lives to the rain of enemy arrows until a small area about 200 to 300 meters had been cleared. It was then that the famous *Ujigawa no Senjin* occurred. This was a race between *Sasaki Shiro Takatsuna* and *Kajiwara no Kagesue* to see who could get to the other side of the river first. As *Yoshitsune*'s men were preparing for the assault across the river, the two mounted warriors charged across the river. The race began with *Kajiwara*'s horse, *Surusumi* (meaning smooth black ink) taking the lead. In *Kamakura*, *Kajiwara* had asked *Yoritomo* to give him the best horse he had to ensure *Kajiwara*'s success on the battlefield. *Yoritomo*'s finest mount was called *Ikezuki* (meaning pond moon) but *Yoritomo* refused to hand over this horse because of his love for it. Instead he gave his second best mount, *Surusumi*.

Sasaki on the other hand, was riding *Ikezuki*. He had managed to get hold of the prized steed after having begged *Yoritomo* for it. In secrecy, *Sasaki* was given the horse because he threatened to commit *Seppuku* if he could not have it. *Yoritomo* gave in to the demand. *Surusumi*, the first into the water, left *Ikezuki* far behind. *Sasaki*, worried that he was going to lose and be forced to disembowel himself, shouted to his opponent, "It looks as if your saddle is not strapped on to the horse properly. You better take a look at it!" When *Kajiwara* slowed to check it, *Sasaki* took the opportunity to reach the other side of the river and win the race.

The *Asahi Shogun*, as *Yoshinaka* had been nicknamed, was a famous man in *Kyoto*. He had attacked *Kyoto* to drive away the *Heishi* several years earlier. With a pair of bull's horns on his head, he stampeded a herd of cows at the *Heishi* army. Then with his army he drove away the *Heishi* contingent of 100,000 men. This time it was his turn to flee. With only seven of his men, *Yoshinaka* arrived at *Awazu* near *Biwako* Lake.

Yoshitsune's men were in close pursuit and caught up with them. *Yoshinaka* and his men prepared for their final battle. Among them was *Tomoe-Gozen*, a powerfully built mistress of *Yoshinaka*. She took part in the battle but at one point, *Yoshinaka* ordered her to escape. Finally there were only two people left, *Yoshinaka* and *Imai Shiro Kanehira*. The two died together after committing *Seppuku*. *Yoshinaka* was only 31 at the time. His remains are kept at the temple of *Gichuji* (the same Chinese character can be read as *Yoshinaka*) in *Ohtsu*.

According to the history of the *Togakure-Ryu Ninja*, *Yoshinaka* had a retainer called *Shima Kosanta Minamoto no Kanesada* who came from a rich and powerful family in *Ise* Province. *Yoshitsune* was accompanied by about 3,000 saddled *Samurai* by order of *Hidehira*. The 16-year-old *Kanesada* attacked the 3,000 mounted warriors with a small army. In the ensuing battle *Kanesada* was severely injured. Yet he was able to crawl to a nearby mountain where he fainted. He was discovered by *Kain Doshi* (whose first pupil became *Togakure Daisuke* I) who saved the young man by taking him to the *Iga* area. Eventually, *Kanesada* became a pupil of *Togakure Daisuke* I and it was then that he began to learn *Ninpo*. He became the next authority of the *Togakure-Ryu*, changing his name to *Togakure Daisuke* II. It was he who established the school of *Togakure-Ryu Ninpo*. Many of *Yoshinaka*'s other soldiers also escaped to *Iga* and it was from these men that other different *Ryu* developed.

After this, *Yoshitsune* went on a campaign against the *Heike* (*Heishi*) army. Finding the *Heike* camped in *Ichi no Tani* Valley, *Noriyori* was to attack from the west side (called *Ikuta*) and *Dohi Sanehira* who had been given charge of the bulk of the army by *Yoshitsune* was to attack from the east. *Yoshitsune*, with only 100 to 200 troops moved in behind *Ichi no Tani* by going around Mount *Mikusa*. The mountain had no paths, so *Yoshitsune* recruited a young man with first-hand experience of that particular area to act as a guide. The only approach to *Ichi no Tani* from the mountain was down the vertical cliff and when *Yoshitsune* arrived at the top of the cliff (called *Hiyodorigoe*) he ordered everyone to try to climb down the cliff, but they refused saying it was impossible. To prove that it was possible, he had two horses attempt it but they slid all the way down to their deaths. This made *Yoshitsune*'s men even more afraid. *Yoshitsune* turned to the young mountain guide and asked him if there was any animal that could descend the slope. The boy said a wild mountain goat could. *Yoshitsune* gave the order for all his men to follow him as he began the descent, claiming that a goat would sit down and use its fore legs for stability. Their horses could be commanded to do the same. Once *Yoshitsune* began, they all followed.

The *Heike* army, naturally thinking that they could not be attacked from behind, was taken by complete surprise as *Yoshitsune* began his attack coordinated with the well-timed east and west attacks. In absolute panic, the *Heike* army took the only escape route available to them, which was by sea to their base on *Yashima* Island. In February 1185, *Yoshitsune* attacked the island and at last, on March 24th he accomplished the near annihilation of the *Heike* army on the ocean side of the island. During this final conflict, *Yoshitsune*'s style of fighting was very unconventional. He had moved his entire army by boat to *Yashima* in the middle of the night during a typhoon. They landed behind the enemy on the other side of the island. This, too, was very unorthodox because a *Samurai* always attacked from the front, never from the rear. *Yoshitsune* thought it was of no importance how one went about attacking the enemy, only winning was important. The survivors took to the sea again with *Yoshitsune* in close pursuit. During the crossing, one of the *Heike*'s top *Samurai* managed to board *Yoshitsune*'s boat and tried to kill him, but according to legend, *Yoshitsune* leaped from boat to boat until he was eight boats away from his attacker. This was done in full armour.

Since *Yoshitsune* had been very successful in his military campaigns, his brother *Yoritomo* was very jealous and began doubting his younger brother's loyalty. He gave instructions to have *Yoshitsune* hunted down and executed. In reality, *Yoshitsune* had always been loyal to *Yoritomo*.

Yoshitsune managed to evade his new enemies and on April 30th, 1189 he once again headed for *Hidehira*'s home to seek refuge. Unfortunately, *Hidehira* died from an illness and his son, *Yasuhira*, against his father's dying will yielded to *Yoritomo*'s pressure. *Yoshitsune*, together with his wife and children committed suicide. *Yoshitsune*'s second wife, pregnant at the time, was captured by *Yoritomo* and when the child was born, he threw the boy into the sea to perish.

Yoshitsune jumping from boat to boat.
(By *Yamato Sakura*)

History shows that *Yoshitsune*'s enemy, *Yasuhira* was later attacked by *Yoritomo*'s 28,000 men but was killed by one of his own officers. Thus it is true to say that an attacker eventually will be attacked. Another example illustrating this point concerns the Imperial family that originally ruled Japan with tight control over the military. It was *Yoritomo* who pioneered the Shogunate system (*Bakufu*) that made the military so powerful that it took control of the country away from the Emperor. Future generations of *Yoritomo*'s family ended when his grandson was killed by an officer of his wife's family, the *Heike* family. Vicious acts usually start circles of events. In Christianity it is said that if one lives by the sword, one shall die by the sword.

Interesting to note is that *Mizuhara Kuro Yoshinari*, a Grandmaster of *Togakure-Ryu*, was *Yoshitsune*'s illegitimate son born in *Mutsu*. He became very active between 1190 and 1199 when he governed a small castle in the *Mizuhara* area. Apart from being a Grandmaster of *Togakure-Ryu*, he was also an expert of sword drawing techniques (*Iai-Jutsu*) and held the grandmaster title for both *Kukishin-Ryu* and *Shinden Fudo-Ryu*.

Yoshitsune-Ryu Ninjutsu and *Yoshitsune-Ryu Gunpo* are the names for the schools that employed strategies developed by *Yoshitsune*; in addition, schools of swordsmanship (*Kenpo Ryu*), unarmed self-defence (*Ju-jutsu*), and signaling (*Jingai-jutsu*) also carry his name. A later era *Samurai*, *Kusunoki Masashige*, born in 1294, adopted strategy very similar to *Yoshitsune*'s to establish the *Kusunoki Masashige* system of warfare.

A pale short man, *Yoshitsune* was brave, decisive, and intelligent. His expertise included specialized swordsmanship (*Biken-jutsu Kenpo*) leaping and flying movement (*Taijutsu*), and his unparalleled strategy, especially for surprise attacks.

04.
NINPO DURING THE NORTH AND SOUTH DYNASTY PERIOD

03
NINPO
IN THE HEIAN
AND
KAMAKURA
PIRIOD

04
NINPO
DURING
THE NORTH
AND SOUTH
DYNASTY
PIRIOD

A.
KUSUNOKI MASASHIGE AND NINPO

The *Kawachi* and *Izumi* areas were the original home territories of the then disreputable *Kusunoki* family. Initially, the family was small and easily controlled by the provincial government, however, growth with the accompanying increase in power eventually threatened the government seat.

The Imperial agent administering taxes in the region lacked authority because of his non-*Samurai* background and requested assistance from the *Kusunoki* family who collected tax for the government in exchange for handsome payment. With this role they soon took control of the entire province. This act did not court favor with the government.

In April of 1294 at the foot of Mount *Kongo* in the village of *Akasaka*, *Kusunoki Tamonhyoe Masashige* was born. This area, known as *Kawachi no Kuni* includes what is present day west *Osaka*. His childhood name was *Tamon-Maru* that was changed in his adulthood to *Tamonhyoe*. His court name was *Kawachi no Kami Saemon no Suke* which from its length reflected the high social class his family had attained.

Kusunoki Masashige was educated at the *Mikkyo* Temple, *Kanshinji* where apart from the usual studies, he mastered many disciplines including martial arts and strategy. Initially taught by the priests, visiting mountain warriors (*Yamabushi*), and followers of *Shugendo* (*Shugenja*), *Masashige* was later singled out as a personal student of the expert strategist *Ohe no Tokichika*. From *Tokichika*, *Masashige* learned *Sonshi* strategy and the *Ohe* family secret strategy known as *Tosenkyo*.

In 1331, when *Kusunoki Masashige* was 38 years old, he was summoned before the Emperor *Godaigo*. The Emperor had arrived at Mount *Kasagi* on August 27th with an army to war with the *Hojo* family who controlled the Shogunate government (*Bakufu*). On September 3rd, standing before the Emperor, *Kusunoki* learned he appeared in the Emperor's dream. *Kusunoki* was ordered to topple the *Hojo* family. With confidence, *Kusunoki* replied that the strength of the enemy was of no significance and that he had strategies to ensure victory for the Emperor. *Kusunoki* boasted that even with battlefield defeats he could not be killed. He extended an invitation for the Emperor to seek refuge in *Shimo Akasaka* Castle on Mount *Kongo* if it became necessary. Returning to his territory and within the walls of the small castle, *Kusunoki* began to assemble an army. Time, however, was not in his favor. By September 30th the Imperial forces had been defeated. The Emperor, overtaken while fleeing, was exiled to the tiny island of *Oki*.

The army of the Shogunate marched on *Shimo Akasaka* Castle. The terrain of Mount *Kongo* reputedly made attacks difficult, while the castle itself had never been fully completed. Through exceptionally unorthodox tactics, *Masashige* with a mere five hundred men held out for four months against a force of twenty thousand. As the Shogunate's army was marching to the castle, *Masashige's* well-positioned men arranged a shower of arrows killing nearly one thousand of the enemy. As the enemy retreated to a small road at the base of the mountain, three hundred previously placed defenders attacked the regrouping army from both sides, demonstrating how much more difficult it is to manage an army of twenty thousand compared to a force of three hundred.

During the siege of the castle, *Masashige* arranged many surprises. Inside the castle, a second wall was erected, permitting the weakening of the outer wall's foundations. Against this wall many logs and rocks were placed and as the enemy began to scale it, the wall was allowed to collapse, creating an avalanche of rocks and logs that killed an estimated seven hundred of the enemy.

In a most unprecedented manner, *Masashige's* men took a farmer's implement used mainly to spread human feces as fertilizer in the fields (*Naga-Hishaku*) and showered the enemy with a mixture of boiling water and human feces. This six foot pole with cup attachment was used to effectively thwart the attack and annoy the attackers, *Samurai* never used farming implements. This type of technique became known as *Kusunoki-Ryu Ninpo*.

Knowing he could not hold out forever, *Masashige* had his men dig a trench within the castle into which they placed the corpses of both the enemy and his own men. One of the corpses was dressed in *Masashige's* own armour. They set the castle on fire from inside and in the confusion the surviving defenders escaped. Only the *Ninja Sahyoe* was to stay behind.

When the Shogunate army searched the burned out ruins, they found a scorched corpse in *Kusunoki's* armor. As planned, *Sahyoe* allowed himself to be captured and was taken to confirm the identity of the corpse. Leaping forward, he embraced the corpse and cried loudly. Without a reply, his action was enough to convince the Shogunate army. The *Shogun Hojo* was informed that *Kusunoki Masashige* was dead and the victory, their's.

After escaping from the castle, *Kusunoki Masashige* met his close personal friend Prince *Morinaga* who also vowed destruction of the Shogunate. In control of Mt. *Hiei* and its temples, Prince *Morinaga* had an estimated two thousand mountain warriors and followers of *Shugendo* under his command. These men frequently traveled and were well informed of events. Their visits to Mt. Koya in the *Kumano* Province and Mount *Ohmine* in the *Yoshino* Province established good channels of communication.

Kusunoki acquired the service of 48 *Iga Ninja* who were divided into three groups and sent to *Kyoto*, *Osaka* and Hyogo on spying missions. *Kusunoki* named them *Suppa* implying the exposers of personal secrets. These agents were especially skillful at acquiring local dialects to become indistinguishable from the locals (*Dakko-Nin*: literally taking someone's mouth).

To recover his castle, *Kusunoki* began an attack in December of 1332 against *Yuasa Magoroku* who was in command. *Yuasa* had ordered rice to be brought from the *Ki-i* area, which is present day *Wakayama* Prefecture. As the 200 -300 laborers were on their way back to the castle, *Kusunoki* ambushed them. The rice was taken out of its packing and replaced with weapons and armor. His men dressed as the laborers and proceeded to the castle gates. A second group of *Kusunoki's* men staged a mock ambush that allowed the laborers to cry for help and gain quick entry to the castle. At the granary these men put on their armor and coordinated their attack with the assault from outside. In the ensuing panic, the castle was taken. Once again in charge of Mt. *Kongo*, *Kusunoki* decided to strengthen his position by building the castle, *Chihaya*, at the top. It was not long until the *Hojo* army readied another attack. This time *Kusunoki* left two thousand men in his fortification to wait on the banks of the *Yodo* River in *Osaka*. As the six thousand-man army from *Kyoto* was near to crossing the river, *Kusunoki's* men defeated them and quickly dispersed. The five hundred reinforcements sent by the *Shogun* arrived to late to be of any help, *Kusunoki* and his men were on their way to *Tennoji*, a partially forested hill.

Kusunoki Masashige and his son
(By Yamato Sakura)

Thinking that *Kusunoki*'s army would attack from the forest, the *Shogun*'s army waited below the trees. Instead of a major engagement, *Kusunoki*'s men created ghostly flames and eerie sounds, preventing the enemy from sleeping at night. Within a few days the enemy returned to *Kyoto*. Then the *Shogun* raised an army of fifty thousand men to assault *Chihaya* Castle. From February 22nd to May 8th, *Kusunoki*, using strategic ploys, managed a seventy-five day defense with only two thousand men. The people of Japan were astonished and lost faith in the *Shogun*.

This battle at *Chihaya* Castle earned its place in Japanese history because of *Kusunoki*'s guerilla-style warfare. Rocks were used as missiles, avalanches were triggered on the mountainside, and bamboo devices were made that squirted oil on the enemies who could then be ignited by torches. Ambushes successfully captured the enemy food supply that was then available for the defenders. Several thousand life-sized dolls complete with armor and weapons were even placed outside the castle one night. Battle cries were shouted by the defenders from inside the castle. The enemy, fearing a sudden attack, mounted a counter-attack but as they reached the dolls, *Kusunoki*'s men attacked them from all sides. While *Kusunoki* was engaged in the defence of his castle, the Emperor *Godaigo* escaped from *Oki* Island. With *Ashikaga Takauji* and *Nitta Yoshisada*, both high-order *Samurai*, the Emperor raised an army to successfully defeat the *Shogun*. The Emperor reinstated his authority and the threat against *Kusunoki* and *Chihaya* Castle ended.

Then on October 22nd 1334, while *Kusunoki* was in the *Ki-i* area confronting an enemy, *Ashikaga Takauji* took Prince *Morinaga* as a prisoner. The following year on July 26th, Prince *Morinaga* was executed by *Takauji*'s brother Tadayoshi.

Although *Ashikaga* and *Nitta* were high level *Samurai*, they were of questionable loyalty. Originally they represented the *Shogun* and fought in his ranks. A sudden change of loyalty allied them with *Kusunoki* under the Imperial banner against the *Shogun*. Although *Ashikaga* and *Nitta* were distant cousins, they disliked each other intensely. With the defeat of the *Shogun*, *Ashikaga Takauji* took unofficial control of the *Kamakura* area, thinking the Emperor would eventually present it to him. *Nitta* went to *Kyoto* where he badly slandered *Ashikaga*. *Kusunoki* who considered *Nitta* useless, advised the Emperor that it was wiser to court favor with *Ashikaga*. Prince *Morinaga* differed with *Kusunoki*'s evaluation of *Ashikaga*. The Prince reported to his father that *Ashikaga* was power-hungry for the *Kamakura* area and dishonest. An obstacle in *Ashikaga*'s control of *Kamakura*, the Prince was captured and later executed. In addition, *Akamatsu Enshin*, a respected high-order *Samurai*, defected from the Imperial ranks to *Ashikaga*. He had been, along with *Kusunoki*, the Emperors' finest leader. Not having been given the customary packet of land for his military service, *Akamatsu* deserted the Imperial cause.

By October of 1335, *Ashikaga Takauji* raised an army to fight the Emperor. In December at Mt. *Hakone*, *Ashikaga* defeated the Imperial forces led by *Nitta*. *Nitta* retreated to *Kyoto* where the Imperial army was preparing its defenses. *Kusunoki* preparing to defend the southern part of the city, realized the weakness of their position by considering the past failures of others to provide a successful defense. Through a court noble and acting intermediary, *Kusunoki* wished to advise the Emperor that their position was not a good position for defense, so the plan should be revised. The court noble disregarded the message. To the best of his ability *Kusunoki* defended his area, however, *Ashikaga* won entry through the eastern and western defenses. *Kusunoki* assisted the Emperor in his flight to Mt. *Hiei*. From the mountains surrounding *Kyoto*, *Kusunoki* used numerous guerilla strategies to harass *Ashikaga*, including the interruption of his food supply. After *Ashikaga* left *Kyoto* for *Kyushu*, *Kusunoki* tried to convey his opinion that the Emperor should make an ally of *Ashikaga*. The intermediary ignored his plea.

At this period in the history of Japan, there were two Emperors. The north and south had separate Emperors, who were to exchange their positions every ten years. Emperor *Godaigo* had remained in the south for twelve years and refused to leave for the north. When *Ashikaga* returned, he bore the banner of the northern Emperor and was to dislodge Emperor *Godaigo*. *Kusunoki* evaluated the situation and maintained it would be better to allow *Ashikaga* to enter *Kyoto* without resistance. His comments ignored, *Kusunoki* was ordered to fight on the flat land near to the *Minato* River. From a premonition, *Kusunoki* realized this would be his last battle, so he sent his son to *Kawachi* Castle with a message to attack their enemies when the boy came of age. At forty-three, *Kusunoki* died in the battle at the *Minato* River. Touched by his rival's death, *Ashikaga* had *Kusunoki*'s head sent to the bereaved wife, rather than placing it on public display. After the Emperor was captured and

04

NINPO
DURING
THE NORTH
AND SOUTH
DYNASTY
PIRIOD

exiled, *Ashikaga* set up his own Shogunate government, the *Muromachi Bakufu*, in *Kyoto's Muromachi* district.

Interesting to note, relations between the *Kusunoki* family and the *Iga Hattori* family were very close. In fact, *Hattori* Kan-Ami, the founder of *Kanze-Ryu* Noh dancing, has as a mother, *Kusunoki Masashige's* sister.

What the Emperor *Godaigo* failed to do, was listen to his best adviser. If a leader listens to flatterers and those who are incompetent, his framework can easily be torn apart. If a leader has honest competent men to counsel him, his framework will be very strong. In history when a man gave his opinion to his leader, his life was at stake; any oversight could result in an execution. *Takamatsu Sensei* detested people who used flattery to achieve their objectives.

It was pointed out by *Takamatsu Sensei* that *Kusunoki Masashige's* father, *Masato* was a true martial artist, *Masato* had the secret scroll *Amatsu Tatara*, belonging to the *Fujiwara* no *Kamatari* family and learned the following poem:

> If one can understand that martial arts
> are the way and this is correct, this is
> the highest point and needs no learning.

Emperor *Godaigo* and *Nawa Nagatoshi*
(By *Yamato Sakura*)

04
NINPO
DURING
THE NORTH
AND SOUTH
DYNASTY
PIRIOD

05
NINPO
DURING
THE WARRING
PIRIOD

05.
NINPO DURING THE WARRING PERIOD

A.
TAKEDA SHINGEN AND NINPO

At *Chozenji* Temple, *Takeda Shingen* (1521-1573) devoted his youth to the serious studies of calligraphy, painting, poetry, and strategy. His study from the book *Sonshi* greatly influenced his thinking. His personal strategy evolved into what became known as *Koshu Ryu Gunryaku* and *Koshu Ryu Ninpo*, and strongly resembled *Sonshi* strategy. The symbol on his banner representing wind, forest, fire, and mountain (*Fu-Rin-Ka-Zan*) characterized his style of warfare that ranged from unrelenting waves, through forest-like patience, to gust-like retreats.

In the field of intelligence gathering *Takeda Shingen* was a master. With seventy agents which he named *Suppa*. *Takeda* had a substantial intelligence network. The wives and children of his select *Suppa* were kept as hostage to insure the loyalty of the agents. With his home region surrounded by three provinces under the control of *Murakami Yoshikiyo*, *Suwa Yorishige* and *Ogasawara Nagatoshi*, *Takeda* had to be kept informed. His thirty best *Suppa* were divided into three groups and were placed under the command of his officers, *Amari Bizen*, *Iitomo Hyogo* and *Itagaki Nobutaka*. *Takeda* was kept well informed on activities in all three provinces.

The *Ninja* employed by *Takeda* came from a collection of mountains in the *Shinshu* Province (now *Nagano* Prefecture). These mountains including Mount *Togakushi*, Mount *Iitsuna*, Mount *Kurohime* and Mount *Ontake* were renown for being *Shugendo* training centers. From the *Shugendo* came the *Yamabushi* that influenced *Ninpo*. The other region noted for *Shugendo* was in *Koshu* Province and included Mount *Fuji*, Mount *Kinpo*, Mount *Jizogatake*, Mount *Komagatake*, and Mount *Ho-oh*. The *Ninja* in this area were known as scouts '*Kamari*' or grass '*Kusa*' and would have served only as regional guides.

In addition, *Takeda* had twenty shrine priests in his employment. The priests walked vast distances to all points in Japan to give away charms. These *Suppa Samurai*, as named by *Takeda*, were in an ideal position to gather information. *Shingen* Shrine at the foot of Mount *Fuji* served as their base where they were known as '*Fuji Oshi*' (priests of *Fuji*).

Close allies of *Takeda Shingen*, the *Sanada* family developed talent for the effective employment of their *Ninja*. Stories credit the *Sanada* family for many accomplishments during the battle of *Sekigahara* including information leaks that made their force seem larger than it was.

Takeda Shingen and Uesugi Kenshin (By Yamato Sakura)

In opposition to *Takeda Shingen* were *Ninja* groups employed by his enemies, the *Hojo* family. Supporting the *Hojo* were the *Odawara Ninja* called *Rappa* from the mountains of *Nagano*. *Rappa* implied guide but these specialists were actually capable of penetrating deep into enemy territory and stealing supplies. Allied with the *Odawara* were the *Fuma*. The tall, hawk-faced leader of the *Fuma* was an expert in special fighting strategies. *Fuma Kotaro*'s appearance, further marred by two protruding teeth, was probably as remarkable as his strategy. Luring rivals into his territory provided terrific advantage and enabled surprisingly swift annihilation of those who came. Prearranged signals and responses were used to reveal enemy spies who managed to infiltrate his group.

For effective communication, *Takeda*'s network could not rely on messages delivered by riders because of the mountainous terrain. Instead, fires were used as signals. This system contrasted that of *Takeda*'s life-long rival from *Echigo no Kuni* (*Niigata* Prefecture), *Uesugi Kenshin*. *Uesugi* transmitted messages with mirrors in the famous system known as *Uesugi-Ryu Gunpo* or *Kaji-Ryu Ninpo*.

An *Iga Shinobi* nicknamed *Tobi* (Leaping) *Kato* is alleged to have sought employment by both *Uesugi Kenshin* and *Takeda Shingen*. His actual name was *Kato Danzo*, an acrobat capable of amazing feats. Stunned by *Kato*'s seemingly magical skill, *Uesugi* proposed a special test. *Uesugi*'s highest ranking retainer, *Naoe Yamashiro no Kami*, possessed the sword '*Murasame*' which *Kato* was to steal.

At night, *Kato* entered *Naoe*'s house completely undetected. By poisoning the guard dog with a piece of wild boar, *Kato* was able to get through the floorboards, lift a *Tatami* mat, enter the right room, and escape with the sword. Knowing that *Naoe* would have to commit ritual suicide for losing the sword, *Uesugi* decided to end the matter with *Danzo*'s execution, thus sparing the high-ranking retainer. *Danzo* somehow managed to escape from *Uesugi* and the *Echigo* area.

Arriving in the *Koshu* area, *Kato* sought employment under *Takeda*. To decide if *Kato* were to be employed, *Shingen* asked him to leap over a six-foot fence. In mid-air *Kato* spotted the thorny rose bushes on the other side and performed a backward somersault to land back on the same side. *Shingen* was able to judge *Kato*'s personality through this act of disobedience. *Danzo* was too crafty and posed too great a threat should he ever defect. *Takeda* instructed an officer to dispose of *Kato*. Invited to dine at the officer's house, *Kato* was given fine food and alcohol. The officer flattered *Kato* by telling him how impressed *Takeda* had been. *Kato* happily ate and drank to the point where he became drunk and was easily killed.

Another version of this story maintains that *Kato* again managed to escape but this does not discredit the fact that *Takeda* was a very intelligent leader and an expert in judging people and deploying *Ninja*. Even *Tokugawa Ieyasu*, who ran the *Bakufu* in the *Edo* period, had been defeated in his youth by *Takeda Shingen*. With the humiliation, *Ieyasu* tried to commit ritual suicide but was stopped by a close officer. *Ieyasu* began to admire *Takeda* and eventually became an expert in *Takeda*'s style of strategy. Most of the *Samurai* of the period had great respect for *Takeda* who would have surely have become the ruler of all Japan had he not died of an untimely illness.

Takeda Shingen's personal creed indicates what he valued most in people.

> "A person is like a castle;
> A person is like a stonewall;
> A person is like a castle moat.
> A kind heart is an ally;
> A fighting heart or a heart filled
> with hate is an enemy."

Kawanaka Shima Area

05
NINPO
DURING
THE WARRING
PIRIOD

06
IGA, KOGA
AND
NINPO

06.
IGA, KOGA AND NINPO

A.
PROLOGUE

In 1049 AD, *Ikai (Iko)*, the warlord of *Shiko (Su Chang)* Province in China met in battle the warlord of *So (Sung)* Province. *Ikai* was defeated, but avoided capture by escaping to Japan. Landing at *Ise (Mie* Prefecture) he went to the *Iga* region, where he lived in a cave and taught two people the beginnings of *Ninpo. Ikai*'s students were *Fujiwara no Chikado* (later known as *Gamon Doshi*) and *Hogenbo Tesshin*. They were taught a variety of skills including leaping and concealment (*Ongyo no Jutsu*), unarmed defence (*Kosshi-Jutsu*), throwing *Senban Shuriken (Senban Nage Jutsu)*, Chinese *Karate (Toda Jutsu)* and the 18 fundamental Chinese martial arts (*Kankoku Juhakkei*). A combination of these martial arts with native Japanese martial arts led to the development of *Ninjutsu*.

The same region that sheltered *Ikai* became a sanctuary for others later on in history. Between 1161 and 1163, defeated warriors from the war between the *Genji* and *Heike* found refuge in the *Iga* region. Both the famous *Iga* and *Koga* regions provided a haven for defeated troops during the war between the Northern and Southern Emperors and many refugees from China found their way to these sanctuaries.

Within established mountainous havens, the *Iga* and *Koga* traditions (*Ryu*) began, giving birth to many other *Ninja* traditions that were often in competition with each other. Sources vary as to the number of traditions there really were; some quoted 108, others 75 and still others 73. Different traditions spread all over Japan but the *Iga-Ryu* and *Koga-Ryu* were the oldest and most established. The *Tokugawa Bakufu* used the *Iga-Ryu* as well as the *Koga-Ryu* in an effort to end the long period of civil war. The numerous other groups resulted from the *Iga* and *Koga* sources. The following breakdown outlines the areas where 69 different traditions were known to exist. From this information it seems likely that there were no more than 73 different traditions.

Iga province

NINPO RYUS

Iga Area (*Mie* Prefecture) :
Iga-Ryu, Hakuun-Ryu, Togakure-Ryu, Kumogakure-Ryu, Genjitsu-Ryu, Ryumon-Ryu, Tenton-Happo-Ryu, Goton-Juppo-Ryu, Kadono-Ryu, Kukishin-Ryu, Gyokko-Ryu, Rikyoku-Ryu, Tsuji-Ichimu-Ryu, Hattori-Ryu, Taki-Ryu, Yoshimori-Ryu, Uchikawa-Ryu, Gikan-Ryu, Takino-Ryu, Sawa-Ryu, Minamoto-Ryu, Momochi-Ryu.

Shiga Area (*Shiga* Prefecture) :
Koga-Ryu, Tarao-Ryu, Ohtomo-Ryu, Sasaki-Ryu, Shinpi-Ryu, Kuriya-Ryu.

Nagano Area (*Nagano* Prefecture) : *Akutagawa-Ryu, Aoki-ryu, Ito-Ryu.*

Yamanashi Area (*Yamanashi* Prefecture) :
Koshu-Ryu, Koyo-Ryu, Ninko-Ryu, Takeda-Ryu, Matsuda-Ryu, Inko-Ryu.

Wakayama Area (*Wakayama* Prefecture) :
Kishu-Ryu, Natori-Ryu, Shin-Kusunoki-Ryu, Saika-Ryu, Negoro-Ryu.

Fukui Area (*Fukui* Prefecture) : *Minamoto-Ryu, Yoshitsune-Ryu.*

Kanagawa Area (*Kanagawa* Prefecture) : *Fuma-Ryu, Hojo-Ryu.*

Nara Area (*Nara* Prefecture) :
Yagu-Ryu, Hicho-Ryo, Hidesato-Ryo, Kyushu-Ryu, Kusunoki-Ryu, Gamo-Ryu.

Yamagata Area (*Yamagata* Prefecture) : *Haguro-Ryu*

Niigata Area (*Niigata* Prefecture) : *Uesugi-Ryu, Kaji-Ryu.*

Aichi Area (*Aichi* Prefecture) : *Akiba-Ryu, Ichizen-Ryu.*

Aomori Area (*Aomori* Prefecture) : *Nakagawa-Ryu.*

Nagasaki Area (*Nagasaki* Prefecture) : *Nanban-Ryu.*

Okayama Area (*Okayama* Prefecture) : *Bizen-Ryu.*

Gifu Area (*Gifu* Prefecture) : *Mino-Ryu, Hatano-Ryu.*

Hiroshima Area (*Hiroshima* Prefecture) : *Fukushima-Ryu.*

Gunma Area (*Gunma* Prefecture) : *Negishi-Ryu.*

Tochigi Area (*Tochigi* Prefecture) : *Fukuchi-Ryu, Matsumoto-Ryu.*

Fukushima Area (*Fukushima* Prefecture) : *Shirai-Ryu.*

B.
HISTORY OF IGA-RYU NINPO

The most fundamental rule of the *Ninja* was to teach directly by word of mouth only and this tradition continued for one thousand years or more; even with changing times, the rule remained intact. Very few written records were kept, making research difficult in piecing together this history.

The Chinese military leader *Ikai*, in 1049 AD, sought refuge in *Iga*. Having taught to a select few what is now known as *Ninjutsu*, *Ikai* had as successors *Fujiwara no Chikado* (*Gamon Doshi*), *Garyu Doshi*, and *Iga Hattori Heinai Hyoe Yasukiyo*. The third successor, *Yasukiyo*, established *Iga-Ryu Ninpo*. Confusion exists as to when *Fujiwara no Chikado* was active as a warrior. Different accounts mention the periods 661 to 670, 781 to 805 and 946 to 966. *Takamatsu Sensei* claims it was from 1065 to 1069, which would have enabled successor *Iga Yasukiyo* to establish *Iga-Ryu Ninpo* between the years 1096 to 1099. The following accounts illustrate the roles of the significant personalities and families in establishing the *Iga-Ryu Ninpo*.

Fujiwara no Hidesato (*Tawara no Tota*) gave his family name a place in history with his victory in the *Taira no Masakado* rebellion, fought from 934 to 941. Later, his grandson *Fujiwara no Chikado*, as *Chinjufu Shogun*, held one of the highest ranks open to people outside the Imperial family. At some point between the years 1060 and 1069, out of dissatisfaction, *Chikado* demanded that the Emperor give him a ranking second only to the Emperor himself. The Emperor's refusal prompted *Chikado* to go to Mount *Takao* in *Iga* where in a large fortified cave in the village of *Taneo*, *Taga-Gun* district, he sought sanctuary. From this mountain fortress *Chikado* mounted attacks on the Emperor's forces, deploying four superior *Ninja* known by the nicknames *Fuki* (wind demon), *Suiki* (water demon), *Kinki* (gold demon) and *Ongyoki* (concealed demon). *Fuki*, skilled in using fire techniques (*Katon no Jutsu*), directed walls of flame at the enemy when wind prevailed. Specialized in water techniques, *Suiki* built massive dams at strategic points that he would destroy when the enemy reached a designated position. A gigantic wall of water capable of destroying an entire army was released. *Suiki* was also an expert in using weapons that propelled poison. *Kinki*'s specialty was reflection (*Kinton no Jutsu*); using polished iron plates he reflected sunlight to blind the enemy. The same plates were also used to make loud noises to startle the enemy. *Ongyoki* was very skillful in disappearing (*Onshin Tongyo no Jutsu*). These four demonic agents used their tactics to repeatedly defeat the Emperor's forces. They are mentioned in the ancient *Iga* area history, *Jungoki*, and in another local study of *Iga*, *Shinpen Iga*

Chishi. In reality they were mountain warriors (*Yamabushi*) named *Yama no Chuki*, *Mikawa-Bo*, *Hyogo Risshi* and *Tsukushi-Bo*.

After many defeats, the Emperor raised a mightier army. The commander *Ki no Tomo-o* decided *Chikado* must be separated from his four *Ninja*. To do this, he wrote a poem and had it delivered to the four *Ninja*. Translated it reads:

"All the grass, all the wood, is for the Emperor,
so where can demons live?"

Through this poem they realized the futility of opposing the Emperor and abandoned their leader. *Chikado* was subsequently crushed by the Emperor's forces.

Successor *Yasukiyo*, as a reward for helping *Minamoto no Yoritomo*, had been given a piece of land in *Iga* where he built a castle. From this location he founded *Iga-Ryu Ninpo*. *Iga Hattori Heinai Saemon Ienaga*, a descendant ten or twelve generations after *Yasukiyo*, gave the retired Emperor, *Rokujoin*, a demonstration of his skills in archery around 1165 or 1166. The retired Emperor continued to hold the real power and actually controlled the government while the reigning Emperor spent his time attending elaborate ceremonies. *Rokujoin* was so impressed by the demonstration that he honored *Ienaga* by presenting him with a family emblem, two arrows within a wheel, called 'Yahazu-Guruma'.

Later, *Ienaga* fought as an officer of *Taira no Tomomori*, son of the *Shogun Taira no Kiyomori*, but they lost a battle against the *Minamoto* (*Genji*) family in which *Tomomori* was killed. There are two versions of *Ienaga*'s fate; the first states he was killed at *Dan no Ura* (near *Shikoku*), the second says that he sought refuge in the *Yono* area of *Iga*, where he changed his name to *Yasunaga*.

Regarding *Yasunaga* there are slightly different accounts. It is not clear whether *Yasunaga*'s three sons or three grandsons established independent families. Nonetheless, the oldest of the three direct descendents, *Heitaro Koreyuki*, was given permission to establish an independent family under the name *Kami Hattori* (upper *Hattori*). Since the *Hattori* family originally came from China and occupied several provinces there, this family was also known as *Kan Kuni no Hattori* meaning the *Hattori* from *Kan* (*Hang*) Province. His family emblem 'Yahazu Nihon' consisted of two arrowheads. The second eldest, *Heijiro Yasuyori*, who was given the family name *Naka Hattori* meaning middle *Hattori* which implied ties with China's *Go* (*Wu*) Province. His emblem was an arc 'Ichitomoe'. The third son, *Heijiro Yasunori*, was given the name *Shimo Hattori* (lower *Hattori*), but was also known as *Aekuni no Hattori*, the *Hattori* from *Ae* (*Kang*) Province. His emblem, the 'Yatsu Yaguruma', consisted of eight arrowheads in a circle. The most famous *Ninja* leader of the *Tokugawa* period (1603-1868), *Hattori Hanzo* was said to have been a direct descendant of the Kami *Hattori* family through

Momochi Sandayu's Monument

either the *Heitaro* or *Chigachi* lines.

The *Momochi*, *Hattori* and *Fujibayashi* families were regarded as the leading families in *Iga*. These families were all well established descendants of *Ohtomo no Saijin*, a member of one of Japan's oldest families. The *Momochi* family and the *Hattori* family, because of a common origin, wore the same crest. The *Momochi* family achieved fame for their exploits during the *Tensho* Rebellion (1578 to 1581). A famous grandmaster at that time was *Momochi Sandayu* (*Momochi Tanba Yasumitsu*), who owned three small castles: *Ryuguchi*, *Hojiro* and *Yamato Ryuguchi*.

The *Fujibayashi* family maintained their castle in *Yubune's Ayama-Gun* district. Their best-known grandmaster was *Fujibayashi Nagato no Kami*. The activities of the *Momochi* and *Hattori* families are fairly well documented, where as very little is known of the *Fujibayashi* family. Some historians consider *Fujibayashi Nagato no Kami* and *Momochi Sandayu* to be the same man. At one point, reports of *Momochi's* activities ceased and those of *Fujibayashi* suddenly began to appear. Several new *Ninpo* groups appeared after the *Tensho* Rebellion in September 1581 making a definitive explanation impossible. This information is the only support for the view that *Fujibayashi* and *Momochi* were the same person.

In 1676, the *Ninpo* book 'Bansenshukai' was written by *Fujibayashi Yasutake*, a *Samurai* of *Iga-Ueno* castle, and in 1681 'Shoninki' (Correct *Ninjutsu* Memories) was written by *Fujibayashi Masatake* (*Natori Sanjuro*) a *Samurai* in *Kishu* (*Wakayama* Prefecture). The similarity of these authors' names suggests a connection.

In 1653, a book on *Ninpo* called 'Ninpiden' meaning "Secret Teachings of *Ninjutsu*" was written by *Hattori Hanzo Yasunaga* (or *Hattori Hanzo Yasukiyo*). Bansenshukai, Ninpiden and Shoninki remain the best books on the subject of *Ninpo*. There are 26 volumes of *Bansenshukai*, 3 volumes of *Shoninki*, and 4 volumes of *Ninpiden*. Bansenshukai was possessed by both the *Iga* and *Koga Ninja*; however, *Ninpiden* and *Shoninki* were kept exclusively by the *Iga Ninja*. Since the authors of all three books were *Iga Ninja*, the *Iga Ninja* appears to be the true *Ninpo* specialists.

Accounts differ regarding how many families were active as *Iga* area *Ninja*. Different versions claim there were 38, 45 or even as many as 66 families. Records have been located identifying the following family names.

Abe, Kadono, Momochi, Shima, Arima, Kanbe, Mori, Shindo, Fujiwara, Kaneko, Narita, Shinmon, Fukui, Kashiwara, Natori, Suzuki, Hata, Kataoka, Nomura, Taira, Hattori, Katayama, Odagiri, Tajima, Ibuki, Kazama, Ohkuni, Togakure, Iida, Kimura, Ohtsuka, Toda, Iga, Kuriyama, Sakagami, Toyota, Ise, Minamoto, Sasaki, Tozawa, Izumo, Mizuhara, Sawada, Ttsutsumi.

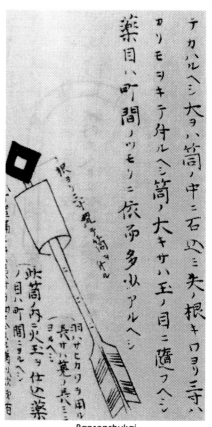

According to *Bansenshukai* and *Takamatsu Sensei*, *Oda Nobunaga* attacked *Iga* with a massive army in 1568. By this time the *Hattori* Family had escaped to *Mikawa* (*Aichi* Prefecture) that was the home of *Tokugawa Ieyasu*. When *Nobunaga* attacked, some eighty *Ninja* fled to many parts of Japan, some going to *Yamato* Province and the protection of the *Ochi* Family; others to *Yamashiro, Iwaki, Tanba*, and *Kawachi*. Later their descendants taught and spread *Ninjutsu* throughout Japan.

Although there are conflicting accounts and inconsistencies regarding dates, from historical sources and rare volumes we can reasonably conclude that *Ninpo* was established in Japan sometime between 1024 and 1077. The *Ninja* were most active for about 450 years from 1181 to 1644 reaching the height of their activities between 1467 and 1615.

Bansenshukai

C.
HISTORY OF KOGA RYU NINPO

The southeastern area of *Shiga* Prefecture is called *Koka-Gun Ryubosshi*; scholars outside *Koka* read the name as *Koga*. In 939, *Mochizuki Saburo Kaneie*, the third son of the governor of *Shinano* Province (near *Nagano*) served as a warrior on the side of the Emperor in the *Taira no Masakado* Rebellion. For his participation he was made the ruler of *Shiga*. Accepting the position he changed his name to *Koga Ohmi no Kami Kaneie*. His son, *Ohmi no Kami Ieshika*, a cultured man renowned for martial art ability, lived in an area of *Koga* called *Ohtaki no Sho Tatsumaki*. *Ieshika*, the pioneer of *Koga-Ryu Ninpo*, learned 'Genjutsu' and 'Ninjutsu' from a man named *Tatsumaki Hossi*.

In time, five families evolved and maintained the *Koga-Ryu Ninpo* tradition: the *Mochizuki, Ugai, Naiki, Akutagawa* and *Koga* families. Between 1487 and 1489, there was a rebellion against the *Ashikaga* family in the *Koga* region known as *Magari no Jin* Rebellion, in which these five families fought on the front line for the *Sasaki* Family. The heads of the five *Koga* families were *Mochizuki Yajiro, Ugai Senshu, Naiki Gohyoe, Akutagawa Tenpei* and *Koga Saburo* II.

During the *Nanboku-cho* period when the country was divided into north and south dynasties, an influx of defeated *Samurai* from both Imperial sides raised the number of families in the *Koga* region from 5 to 53; however, the original five families remained the most important. Each family retained between ten and thirty *Ninja*. Of the 53 families, eight were later known as *Koga Hachi Tengu*. *Tengu*, legendary creatures with wings and long noses, were thought to inhabit woods and mountainous areas. *Hachi* is the Japanese word for eight. The *Koga Hachi Tengu* consisted of the five original families plus the *Kadono, Tomo* and *Nagano* families. There were also other clans (*Gumi*), including the *Hiryu-Gumi, Byakuru-Gumi, Taira-Gumi, Tomo-Gumi, Fujiwara-Gumi, Tatara-Gumi, Sugawara-Gumi, Ishu-Gumi, Kawachi Yon Tengu Gumi* and *Tachibana Hachi Tengu Gumi*.

Unsurprisingly, *Koga-Ryu Ninpo*'s leading family was the *Koga* Family. *Koga Saburo* I, leader of the second generation, had three sons. In order of birth they were *Tenryu* (Heaven's Dragon) *Koga, Chiryu* (Earth's Dragon) *Koga* and *Aranami* (Rough Sea) *Koga*. These three brothers built up a very powerful family even before the *Magari no Jin* Rebellion, which introduced the *Koga Ninja* and placed their name in the history of Japan. During this rebellion on June 5th, 1570, *Sasaki Jotei* gathered an army of *Iga* and *Koga* warriors on the banks of the *Yashu* River for a final conflict to destroy the army of *Oda Nobunaga*. The warriors were from *Samurai* families in *Koga*, but had received extensive training as *Ninja*. They were proud to be *Samurai*, but were not inhibited by *Samurai* ethics and felt free to use *Ninjutsu* when necessary. *Sasaki*'s forces were divided into three groups, the front group consisted of four top *Ninja* groups; the *Mikumo, Mizuhara, Takanose* and *Inui* clans. Next were groups from the 53 *Koga* families, followed by a third column consisting of *Sasaki*'s own men. The *Tanemura, Niimura* and *Kawai* family

Koga Province

warriors totaling three thousand men were held in reserve.

In this battle, *Mikumo Iyonokami*, suddenly changed sides and attacked *Sasaki* forces from behind. The defeated *Sasaki* managed to evade capture.

In 1573, *Nobunaga* and *Shogun Yoshiaki* were warring with each other. The *Shogun* gathered warriors (*Daimyo*) and *Ninja* clans including: *Daimyo Asai, Daimyo Asakura, Daimyo Miyoshi, Daimyo Matsunaga,* warrior priests (*Sohei*) from the *Enryakuji* Temple at Mount *Hiei* and from *Honganji* Temple, and *Iga/Koga* area *Ninja* groups. He also maintained close contact with the powerful *Daimyo Takeda Shingen*. Despite such extensive support he was eventually defeated and imprisoned by *Nobunaga*, thus ending his reign (*Bakufu*).

The following year, *Nobunaga's* forces continued their campaign against *Sasaki's* army and killed *Sasaki* at *Ishibe* Castle in *Koga*. *Nobunaga* finally controlled the *Iga* and *Koga* areas.

During this war between the *Shogun* and *Nobunaga*, a *Koga Ninja*, *Tanimura Yozen*, settled in *Echigo Nagaoka* which is now part of *Niigata* Prefecture. A fifth generation descendant *Tanimura Ihachiro* headed the *Koga Ninja* for many years. He revealed many *Ninjutsu* techniques to the writer *Ito Gingetsu* who later wrote the classic '*Ninjutsu no Gokui*', meaning the highest techniques of *Ninjutsu*. These techniques are very similar to those of *Togakure-Ryu Ninpo*, indicating the fighting systems of the *Iga* and *Koga Ninja* were very similar.

The *Sasaki* family can be traced back to the 59th Emperor of Japan, *Uda Tenno*. The eighth son of *Uda Tenno*, Prince *Atsusane* was also known as *Ninnaji no Miya* after the temple where he lived. His grandson, *Naruyori*, ruled *Ohmi* Province, and later *Naruyori's* grandson, *Tsuneka* ruled the *Ohmi* and *Sasaki* Provinces. *Tsuneka* changed his family name to *Sasaki* when he became ruler of those provinces. *Tsuneka's* grandson *Hideyoshi* had five sons who became famous figures during the *Kamakura* Period. As leaders under *Shogun Yoritomo*, all five were victorious in their battles. In order of birth they were *Sadatsuna, Tsunetaka, Moritsune, Takatsuna* and *Yoshikiyo*. They were the pillars of *Yoritomo's* rule. The fourth brother, *Shiro Takatsuna*, earned honor when he charged his horse across the *Uji* River initiating a battle.

In 1185, the *Shogun* presented the provinces of *Ohmi, Nagato, Iwami* and *Oki* to *Sasaki Taro Sadatsuna*, eldest son of *Sasaki Hideyoshi*. His family was later sub-divided into the *Rokkaku* and the *Kyogoku* families. The second son, *Jiro Tsunetaka*, was given the provinces of *Awaji, Awa* and *Tosa*. The third son, *Saburo Moritsuna*, received the provinces of *Kozuke, Echigo, Sanuki* and *Iyo*, and fourth son, *Shiro Takatsuna*, was given the seven provinces of *Bizen, Aki, Suoh, Inba, Hoki, Izumo* and *Hyuga*. *Goro Yoshikiyo*, the fifth son, later received the provinces of *Oki, Izumo* and *Hoki*. As rulers of these areas the *Sasaki* family developed a deep and lasting relationship with the *Koga Ninja/Samurai* groups. I am proud to be able to say that I am a descendant of *Shiro Takatsuna*. One of *Takatsuna's* sons changed his name to *Tanemura* and took his family to the *Kanto* region. The family settled in the *Matsubushi* area and have remained there for the last few hundred years. A grandson of

Sasaki Shiro Takatsuna (By *Yamato Sakura*)

Takeda Shingen came to the *Matsubushi* area and was adopted into the *Tanemura* family, mixing my family's blood with that of the *Takeda* family.

The symbol of the *'Tanemura'* family is a combination of the *Sasaki* emblem and the emblem of *Takeda*; a secret not recorded in any Japanese books. The *Sasaki* emblem was called the *'Yotsume Yui'*; *Takeda*'s was called *'Waribishi'* or at times *'Takedabishi'*. Custom dictated that families from the higher levels of feudal society have separate emblems for men and women. The *Tanemura* emblem for males called *'Maruni Yotsuishi'* consists of four stones within a circle. For females in the *Tanemura* family, the emblem is called *'Gosan no Kiri'*; a similar emblem is used by the women of the Imperial family.

Interesting to note, the male emblem of the *Tanemura* family is also found in a scroll (*Makimono*) containing *Kukishin-Ryu Ninpo*'s highest teachings. One of the most advanced sections of the scroll (*Sanpo no Reiho*), where the emblem is found, contains instructions on the saying of prayers. A possible connection between this emblem and the *Kukishin-Ryu* scroll is an association of the emblem design with a belief in the importance of the cluster of stars next to the north star. This information is substantiated by artifacts including swords and armour still kept by my family.

Hundreds of years later, I am teaching both *Iga-Ryu* and *Koga-Ryu Ninpo*. It seems my destiny to continue on the same road as my ancestors.

07.
NINPO DURING THE AZUCHI MOMOYAMA AND EDO PERIOD

A.
TOKUGAWA IEYASU AND THE NINJA

Oda Nobunaga (1534-1582) cherished things modern and detested anything old. He was the first man to use the gun as a weapon of warfare and because he was unconventional, he finally managed to rule all of Japan. *Nobunaga* was responsible for ending Japan's civil war period and for this accomplishment, he had the massive *Azuchi* Castle built on open land instead of the usual hilltop location. Still there were rulers of some provinces who resisted him and it was during this peaceful time that he first began acts of genocide. His victims were the two groups of society he hated the most - the priests and the *Ninja*. He set fire to Mount *Hiei*, where many *Mikkyo* temples were situated, and on Mount *Koya* he had thousands of priests slaughtered. For 11 years his men continuously attacked the *Hongan* Temples, which housed many believers in the *Ise*, *Nagashima* and *Echizen* provinces. Tens of thousands died as a result of either being burned alive or cut down with swords.

In September in the 9th year of *Tensho* (1581), *Nobunaga* attacked the *Iga* area with an estimated 44,000 warriors and started the war known as '*Tensho Iga no Ran*'. Most of the *Ninja* families were wiped out with their homes burnt to the ground. On June 2nd of the following year, *Nobunaga* was assassinated by one of his lieutenants, *Akechi Mitsuhide*. At that time *Nobunaga* had been living in the *Honnoji* Temple which was set on fire by *Akechi*. Finding no way to escape, *Nobunaga* committed suicide, and then perished in the flames.

Nobunaga's revulsion of the *Ninja* was based on his parents having him marry the daughter of an enemy (*Saito Dosan*) to try and better their situation. The women known as Princess *Noh* had as a true name, *Kicho*. *Nobunaga* intensely disliked such 'political' marriages although an even stronger reason against the marriage could have been his homosexuality; nevertheless, he complied with his parents wishes. Princess *Noh* turned out to be a spy working for her father. *Nobunaga* eventually succeeded in recruiting her as his spy and used her to assist in the defeat of her father, *Saito Dosan*. *Nobunaga* loathed the *Ninja* and used a term of contempt when speaking of them. If *Nobunaga* had pursued martial art virtue, and respected others he would not have died as he did.

Nobunaga was succeeded by his best follower, *Toyotomi Hideyoshi* (1537-1598) who was born in the village of *Naka* in *Owari* Province. His father was a poor peasant but from this class of society *Hideyoshi* rose to the top *Samurai* ranks and eventually ruled Japan. He was a very talented man, but did not get to be ruler of Japan with only talent; destiny also aided him. Among his forces were *Kuroda Kanbei*, an authority on army strategy, and *Hachisuka Koroku*, an instructor of army strategy. It was in *Osaka* that *Hideyoshi* built Japan's largest castle.

During *Hideyoshi*'s time a very famous *Ninja*, *Ishikawa Goemon*, emerged. His fame grew as a result of his activities as a good thief (a Japanese Robin Hood, now the subject of *Kabuki* and *Joruri* plays). *Goemon*, as he is popularly known, learned *Ninpo* from his master, *Momochi Sandayu*. According to stories about him, *Goemon* fell in love with one of his master's wives, named *Okan* or *Shikibu* and they eventually eloped. Later he killed her by throwing her down a well and then went into hiding. For several years, *Goemon* tried to kill *Hideyoshi* without success. To support himself he began to steal from the rich. *Goemon* was finally captured by *Hideyoshi* and, together with all his living relatives was boiled alive. His famous dying words were, "Even if I, *Ishikawa*, die and all the sand on all the beaches were to disappear, the thief will still be here".

This version of the story about *Goemon* and his lover is incredulous. The most conceivable story is that he was given a secret order to go and kill *Hideyoshi*. To avoid panic and confusion in *Hideyoshi*'s area, an elaborate cover-up plan was made. The order to assassinate *Hideyoshi* was probably given because *Hideyoshi* had been a keen follower of the man who tried to exterminate the *Ninja* completely. A typical *Ninja* strategy is to send a pupil on a mission so that there are no repercussions for the master.

07
NINPO
DURING
THE AZUCHI
MOMOYAMA
AND
EDO PIRIOD

Grandmaster *Takamatsu Sensei* once said that people such as *Goemon* never die that simply. It is hard to believe that *Goemon* could have died that easily. It is extremely difficult to believe the *Kabuki* plays and dramatizations. A skilful *Ninja* such as *Goemon* would never have given his true identity or said he was a thief, even at death.

In popular stories *Momochi Sandayu* wanted *Goemon* dead. As a grandmaster of *Iga Ninpo*, he would have resorted to *Kuji-Kiri* or *Juji-Kiri*. Still, *Goemon* was *Momochi*'s top student and he would have known how to defend himself from the *Kuji-Kiri* and *Juji-Kiri*, enabling him to survive.

After *Hideyoshi* died, the next ruler of Japan was *Tokugawa Ieyasu* (1542-1617). His *Bakufu* utilized the talents of many 'Shinobi' enabling a reign of three hundred years. *Ieyasu*'s wisdom and honesty combined with his knowledge of strategy helped him succeed in life.

Ieyasu used the *Ninja*, *Hattori Hanzo Masanari*, whose father, *Iwami no Kami Hanzo Yasunaga*, was from Northern *Iga*. *Yasunaga* was said to have been adopted by the *Chigachi* Family in the *Yono* District of *Iga* and became a lieutenant of the *Shogun* Yoshiharu. Later he became a lieutenant of the *Matsudaira* Family in *Mikawa* Province (now *Aichi* Prefecture). *Yasunaga* had three sons, *Yasutoshi*, *Yasumasa* and *Masanari*. They worked for the *Matsudaira* Family, serving throughout the lifespan of three of its leaders; *Kiyoyasu*, *Hirotada* and *Motoyasu* (*Motoyasu* became *Ieyasu*).

Historically, the eldest son of the family carried the father's title but *Masanari* became *Hattori Hanzo Masanari* because his elder brothers had been killed in battle. While he was employed by *Ieyasu*, *Masanari* spent most of his time fighting wars and managed to do many great things as both a *Shinobi* and lieutenant.

In 1570, during the *Anegawa* War, *Masanari* was so effective that *Ieyasu* presented him with his best spear called the demon killer *(Onikirimaru)*. Its total length was three meters with the blade constituting 1.2 meters. He became popularly known by the nickname *Yari no Hanzo* (*Hanzo* of the spear). In 1572, after the *Mikatagahara* War, *Ieyasu* appointed *Masanari* leader of 150 *Ninja Samurai*. In 1574, during the battle of the *Takatenjin* Castle, 30 of his mounted *Monomi* (scouts) worked so effectively that the castle was taken. Later *Masanari* was given a total of *Hassen Goku*, a piece of land so large it could produce 8,000 *Goku* of rice every year, making him almost the same as a feudal baron (*Daimyo*). He was given the title *Iwami no Kami* (Lord of *Iwami*) and a massive house in the *Kojimachi* district, just outside *Edo* Castle's west gate. Later, he moved to *Yotsuya* district's *Iga-Machi* and *Kita-Iga-Machi*.

The west gate of *Edo* Castle (in present-day *Tokyo*) was the *Tokugawa*'s escape route in the event of an attack. The *Tokugawa* would escape, while *Masanari* and his men would hold back the enemy. For this reason the west gate was called *Hanzo-Mon* (*Hanzo*'s gate) and it still stands today.

Masanari was later given charge of 30 *Yoriki* and 200 *Doshin*. *Yoriki* were high ranking *Ninja* permitted to ride horses; a rare accord in those times. The *Doshin*, however, had low status and were mainly from the *Iga Ninja* Clans. These men were the *Edo* period's police force. The *Doshin* were truly active as police while the *Yoriki* kept up appearances.

Tokugawa's relationship with the *Ninja* was not only through the *Hattori* Family. His contact with the *Ninja* began during the years 1566 to 1581, when *Nobunaga* attacked the *Iga* Province. A great many *Ninja* sought refuge under *Ieyasu*, who accepted them and looked after them. More importantly, when *Nobunaga* invited *Ieyasu* to *Kyoto* to declare peace in 1582, but was assassinated at the temple, *Ieyasu* had to run for his life. *Akechi Mitsuhide*, the assassin, had also attacked *Ieyasu*. From *Kyoto*, *Ieyasu* had to return to his province as quickly as possible but all the routes had been closed off. So he decided to go through the rugged terrain of the *Iga* and *Koga* Mountains, the home of *Hattori Hanzo*. *Hanzo* asked the *Iga Ninja* to guide *Ieyasu*, and 200 *Ninja* protected him constantly. By June 5th, *Ieyasu* was at *Okazaki* Castle where he raised an army and returned to *Kyoto*. On June 14th he was at *Narumi*, *Owari* Province (now *Aichi* Prefecture) and it was there he declared the same 200 *Ninja* to be his lieutenants.

Just after the *Edo Bakufu* started, the *Iga* group worked as *Oniwaban* (garden sentries) that gave them total access to all areas of the castle. They were frequently summoned to go and spy in other provinces. Their work as *Oniwaban* was to conceal the real nature of their positions.

Ieyasu's son and successor, *Hidetada*, demoted the *Iga Ninja* from *Oniwaban* to lower positions such as house guards. Treated as inferiors to the *Koga Ninja*, the *Iga Ninja* became very angry, especially since their work as *Oniwaban* had always been very dangerous.

In 1596, the leader of the *Iga Ninja* was 18 years old *Hattori Hanzo Masanari*, son of the famous but deceased leader of the same name. The younger *Masanari* was very violent, without any martial virtues, and did not take care of his men. In 1605 nearly all the *Iga* group went on strike and at *Sasa* Temple in *Yotsuya* appealed to the *Tokugawa* for better treatment. This was the first official strike in Japan, lasting about a month. *Masanari* was replaced by *Hattori Naka Yasumasa*, a lieutenant of *Ieyasu*. He was given command of 70 *Doshin*. The original 200 *Doshin* employed by the *Bakufu* were divided into six separate divisions; *Yasumasa* was given command of only one of these six. The other five divisions were under the direct command of the *Tokugawa* himself. This separation disrupted the organization of the *Iga Ninja* and by the end of the *Edo* Period there were no true *Iga Ninja* leaders left.

The relationship between *Ieyasu* and the *Koga Ninja* group began about 20 years before his relationship with the *Iga* group. As early as 1562, *Ieyasu* had used the help of 280 *Koga Ninja* to attack *Udono* Castle and defeat the enemy.

In 1584, during the war in *Komaki* and *Nagakude* provinces, *Ieyasu* was controlling many *Ninja* groups, while his enemy had only a few individual *Ninja*. This fact may have prompted *Hideyoshi* the following year to attack *Negoro* Temple in *Saika* Province (*Wakayama* Prefecture). The temple, headquarters of the *Negoro Ninja*, was surrounded by their land that produced 80,000 *Goku* of rice per annum. The temple was burnt to the ground and most of the *Ninja* died. Those who survived were widely dispersed but eventually joined forces with *Ieyasu*. By 1626, the *Negoro Ninja* had developed skill with the matchlock and a special group of 100 marksmen was formed. This group, known as the *Negoro Hyakunin Gumi* served as the guards at the main gate of *Edo* Castle (*Ohte-Mon*) and served as the armed escort accompanying officials carried in palanquin outside the castle. *Ieyasu* also sent a number of the marksmen to guard the castles of his son and brother.

This period introducing the age of the firearm, brought a decline in the overall activities of the *Ninja*. Japan was becoming a peaceful, unified country and the need for *Ninja* had lessened considerably. The technical skills that had made the *Ninja* legendary, were no longer even guaranteed of being passed on to future generations. The books *Bansenshukai* and *Shoninki* were written because many believed their art would disappear completely.

Embarking on a major engagement in 1600, *Ieyasu* left approximately 1,800 warriors to protect his home, *Fushimi* Castle. From nearby *Osaka* Castle, *Ieyasu* and his *Samurai* marched on *Uesugi Kagekatsu* Castle in *Aizu* Province (now *Fukushima* Prefecture). In *Ieyasu*'s absence, enemy under *Ishida Mitsunari*'s command attacked *Fushimi* Castle. In the defence of the castle, *Yamaoka Kagetomo* (*Doami*) with 300 *Ninja Samurai* fought valiantly against the enemy numbering over 10,000 men. The defense lasted 75 days, until 40 of the *Ninja* turned against their leader and gave entry to the enemy one night. The loyal *Ninja* were nearly all slaughtered but *Ieyasu* had been given enough time to complete his mission and was on his way back. Upon his return, the historic *Sekigahara* battle was fought and won by *Ieyasu*. With his victory, the undisputed leader of Japan, *Ieyasu*, summoned the sons and grandsons of the *Ninja* who gave their lives in defence of *Fushimi* Castle, and made the descendants his lieutenants. This *Koga Ninja* group, composed of ten *Yoriki* and one hundred *Doshin*, was known as the *Koga Hyakunin Gumi* (the *Koga* 100 member clan). *Doami* was named the leader of the group which he referred to as the *Koga Gumi* (*Koga* clan). With its headquarters in *Aoyama*, the group guarded the three main gates of *Edo* Castle.

Japanese scholar *Nakanishi Yoshitake* once wrote:

> "The complete *Koga* clan was made up of three groups. One group was the *Aoyama Koga Gumi*. The second group consisted of bodyguards stationed at *Kishiwada* Castle, and were known as the *Gojunin-Shu* (the fifty man group). The last group was the *Koga Gojusan-Ke* (the *Koga* fifty-three families) who lived with their own values apart from society. It is my conclusion that the *Koga Hyakunin Gumi* were just spies

because they lacked important values."

07

NINPO
DURING
THE AZUCHI
MOMOYAMA
AND
EDO PIRIOD

Nakanishi Yoshitake mentioned an important premise; a true *Ninja* would never sell his techniques or services to anyone. The *Koga Hyakunin Gumi* sold themselves to *Ieyasu* who would have resorted to any means to ensure his triumph. When a *Ninja* uses his skill for the betterment of society, he will offer his services for free. If this sense of propriety is lost, that person is a mere spy.

In 1608, *Ieyasu* appointed *Todo Takatora* as the head of a 120,000 *Goku* area in *Iga*. However, instead of living at *Iga Ueno* Castle, he lived in his main castle *Ise Tsu* and placed a descendant of the *Iga Hattori* Family named *Yasuda Uneme Motonori* (later known as *Todo Uneme Motonori*) in *Iga*. *Todo Takatora* lacked confidence in controlling a province dominated by many *Ninja* groups. By choosing a descendant of the well-known *Hattori* Family, and later adopting him into the *Todo* Family, he was able to control *Iga* Province indirectly. Occasionally he would grant the *Ninja* families the title of *Samurai* to keep them in reserve for emergencies. Whenever these *Samurai* visited his main castle, they were always given fine treatment.

Motonori was also ordered to open a file on every family in *Iga*. This information was very detailed, consisting of the number and names of all members of the families (especially the sons), where they lived, and other pertinent facts to prevent them from joining other armies that might rebel against the *Tokugawa* government. This type of planning shows how intelligent *Ieyasu* was. The filing system was very thorough and disrupted the evolution of the *Ninja* groups. As when wild animals are kept in a zoo; after some time they cease to be wild. The *Ninja* families became tame.

In 1637, the *Shimabara no Ran* occurred with 40,000 Christians rebelling against the government. Sent by the *Tokugawa*, the forces included *Ninja* who were to gather information as spies. However, they were far from successful because as the *Tokugawa*'s employees, these *Ninja* were already out of touch with their training. True *Ninja* living in *Koga*, *Iga* and other provinces could still have been effective.

The first signs of the disappearance of the *Koga Ninja* became obvious in February 1789, when a *Koga Ninja*, *Ohara Kazuma*, went to *Edo* Castle with two other leaders and literally begged for help because their *Ninja* groups were experiencing hard times and could not continue much longer. They requested financial help from the *Bakufu*.

Edo Castle

Of the 21 *Koga Ninja* families that existed in the *Edo* period, only 11 were still practicing their art. Eight of the *Ninja Samurai* families, due to poverty, no longer practicing their art and other two had lost their ancestor's skill already.

The three leaders brought with them the *Bansenshukai* and another book on *Ninja* strategies, but their trip was in vain. The *Bakufu* only gave them a few silver coins and told them to return home.

In 1853 at the end of the *Edo* period, Commodore Perry's black ships arrived at *Uraga*. The *Bakufu* ordered *Sawamura Jinzaburo* of the now tamed *Iga Ninja* to go and spy on these ships. He boarded the ship with *Bakufu* lieutenants. Once on board, *Sawamura* wanted to bring back proof he had been successful but unable to do so, he went to the ship's crew and asked one member to write a letter. The crew wrote the following:

"Engelsch meid in de bed, Fransch meid in de keuken, Hollandsch meid in de huishouding. Stille water heeft diept grond"

Translated: English maid in the bed, French maid in the kitchen, and Hollandsch maid in the housekeeping. Still waters run deep.

Sawamura returned to his master with this as his prize, showing the extent the salaried *Ninja* had lost their skills by the end of the *Edo* period.

The times had changed and the *Bakufu* no longer had a need for the *Ninja* and their techniques. There are two explanations for this. The first is that the *Bakufu* felt that the period was peaceful, hence, there was no need to maintain any *Ninja* groups. The second explanation is that the *Koga Ninja*'s techniques and skills had already become useless. Either way, the most disheartening aspect was that the *Ninja* were already in a situation where they were begging for assistance. From this period, the techniques of the *Koga Ninja* quickly deteriorated.

08.
NINPO SINCE THE MEIJI ERA

07
NINPO
DURING
THE AZUCHI
MOMOYAMA
AND
EDO PIRIOD

08
NINPO
SINCE
THE MEIJI
ERA

A.
NINPO LINEAGE TO THE PRESENT DAY

From the end of the *Edo* period (1867) and throughout most of the *Meiji* period (1867-1912) only two people kept the art of *Ninpo* alive. They were *Toda Shinryuken Masamitsu* and *Ishitani Matsutaro Takakage*. *Shinryuken* was the Grandmaster of a martial art school established by the *Bakufu* in *Kyoto*, and *Ishitani* was the seventh generation of the chief advisor to the *Iga Hattori Ninja* Family on the subject of strategies. Both *Toda* and *Ishitani* passed on their knowledge of *Ninpo* and all matters relating to *Ninpo* as well as other martial arts to *Takamatsu Toshitsugu* (*Uoh/Chosui*), making him the next Grandmaster. *Takamatsu Sensei* was the only person throughout the *Meiji*, *Taisho* and *Showa* periods (until the 46th year of *Showa* or 1971) who was a true *Ninja*.

Takamatsu Sensei taught many people this martial art (look at the lineage section) and one in particular was *Akimoto Fumio*, who was the senior instructor and disciple after having trained under *Takamatsu Sensei* for the longest time. Fortunately his son, *Akimoto Koki*, and I are good friends and he has helped me in many important ways. As an example, he has showed me all of his father's secret scrolls that had been written by *Takamatsu Sensei*, and has told me many interesting stories of *Takamatsu Sensei* and his father. *Kimura Masaji Sensei* was given grandmasterships from *Takamatsu Sensei*. He gave me all of his titles and told me many secret true stories about *Takamatsu Sensei* as well as a lot of *Kuden*. He passed away when he was 100 years old. Kimura *Sensei* and *Akimoto Sensei* were the highest and the oldest private students of *Takamatsu Sensei*.

Nowadays some people are trying to sell *Ninpo*. The only thing they want to do is to turn *Ninpo* into a business to attain material wealth. Slowly the people who are still faithful to *Takamatsu Sensei*'s spirit are gradually disappearing. *Takamatsu Sensei* used to say all the time;

> "Use *Ninpo* and other martial arts to build a Utopia
> with the motto: Love, generosity and peace."

Takamatsu Sensei and I

However of the few who used to follow this while he was alive, many have neglected it after his death. Having been a pupil of *Takamatsu Sensei*, I believe if this attitude continues, this beautiful and unique martial art will turn stale and eventually disappear forever. My aim is to continue this style of martial art without having to resort to its spying and strategic aspects. I do not wish to have a martial art that only focuses on spying and killing techniques. My martial arts *Ryu* concentrates only on the self-protection of one's body and spirit this is how I wish to keep it. For this reason, on November 27th 1984, I established the *Genbukan Dojo* so I may teach all interested persons the true art of *Ninpo*. My final aspiration is to make up a true *Ninja* group with a view to making the international community a more peaceful place with this martial art. Hopefully it can become a true Utopia.

Again we will go back in time. Spying is among the many skills credited to the *Ninja*. The following are brief accounts of people who, although they were not *Ninja*, were true spies.

Katsura Kogoro (later known as *Kido Takayoshi*) was a high-ranking official of the *Meiji* Government. He also worked with a group of people preparing to overthrow the government. He carried out his duties in a style similar to a *Ninja* on an assignment. He was very skillful in gathering information by disguising himself as a beggar. Whenever times were too dangerous for him, he would quickly change and disappear without a trace. He was also very proficient in the *Samurai* martial arts. (In those times, the best martial artists were able to study some *Ninja* techniques from available documents.)

The famous number one *Samurai* of the *Meiji* period was *Saigo Takamori*. During his youth, he had been a mere *Oniwaban* at *Kyushu*'s *Satsuma* Castle. (He was most probably given this work because his family probably was *Oniwaban*.)

Around the end of the *Edo* period from 1854 to 1860, the *Ninja* authority *Ohkuni Izumo* (also Grandmaster of *Togakure-Ryu Ninpo*), was a personal bodyguard to the Emperor's top aids.

These three helped overthrow the *Edo* government and establish the *Meiji* goverment, and so became heroes. This was the beginning of a new Japanese culture based on European ideals. It was also the time when the *Samurai* system was dismantled, with all swords being confiscated. From this time on the need for martial arts declined rapidly because the new armies now had guns. This also affected *Ninpo* and sport-oriented martial arts began to appear instead. But still, *Ninja* spying techniques proved very useful throughout the China-Japanese War, Russia-Japanese war and both World Wars.

A certain *Fujita Seiko* declared himself as the '14th Grandmaster of the *Koga-Ryu Ninja*,' and according to him, had been teaching from the eleventh year of the *Taisho* Period (1922) at the *Toyama* Land Forces School, the Infantry Officers School, at a University for top-class officers, the Navy's University and also *Nakano* Ground Forces Spy School. At this last school he taught *Ninja* spying techniques and was later given a direct order from the Japanese Imperial Army to go to Mongolia and assassinate the president of China, *Shokaiseki* (*Chang Kai Shek*). This order however, was cancelled by the head of the Japanese forces in Mongolia, *Daihara*.

Fujita Seiko had studied the *Bansenshukai* in great depth, so in my opinion he was just a good scholar specializing in the subject of *Ninjutsu*; when it came to the true *Ninpo* techniques, he was just a *Gyoja* (a mountain priest). What he considered *Ninja* techniques were such acts as putting long needles through his limbs and lying on beds of nails. He never displayed any form of fighting techniques. The late *Takamatsu Sensei* was also in Mongolia during the war and, while there used true *Ninpo* techniques earning him the nickname *Moko no Tora* (Mongolian Tiger).

In the First World War, the famous European spy, Matahari (1876-1917) could also be considered a *Ku no Ichi* (female *Ninja*). Born as Guertrude Margaret Tsuer in Holland, she went to Paris where in 1905 she debuted at the Moulin Rouge as a dancer. From there, she became a sexually promiscuous star. She later began acting in many opera theaters in Paris as well as in Italy's Scalar Theater. Her private life was that of a playgirl, with her lovers being such noble people as high-ranking government officials and foreign ambassadors living in Paris. At one time the German army accused her of being a spy, but she was indifferent.

The German army then brought her to Germany, where they trained her in their spy schools. Her code number was H-21 and she became the most effective spy in the Great War (1914-1918). Of the estimated 11,000 other female spies working for the German army, she was the most prized. For example, she got information from a British Field Marshal that the Allies had built a tank, capable of killing some 10,000 soldiers. She also got information from a Russian officer about secret plans to attack the allied forces that later resulted in the death of about 20,000 allies. Her cover remained being a dancer and whenever she was able to get vital information, it would be placed in a special diplomatic bag and would go to Germany via a neutral country. In February 1917, Matahari was caught by the allies and on the October 15th of the same year she was put in front of a firing squad and executed. She was only 41.

Another spy that became famous in Japan during World War II was the German Reiheil Sorge who worked for the Russian forces. He came to Japan in September 1933 from Russia as a professor of geology, economics and politics. He became friends with ten people in Japan including *Ozaki Hidemi*, one of the highest aides to the Prime Minister of Japan, and formed a secret spying organization. On September 6th 1941, in a meeting in front of the Emperor, the Japanese Imperial Army made it's decision that Japan must fight America, England and Holland. Plans were to begin sometime near the end of October that year.

Sorge was able to get this information directly from *Ozaki* and passed it on to Russia in mores code. The Russian High Command realized Japan was not interested in attacking Russia and so were able to focus their attention towards the counter attack of Germany. This turned out to be fatal to Japan's chances of winning the war. Sorge was caught by the military police in October 1941 and on November 7th 1944 was executed.

During the same war, there was also a famous Japanese spy called *Amagasu Masahiko*, a captain in the Japanese Military Police. In September 1923, he was imprisoned for the multiple murder of the head of an anarchist movement, *Osugi Sakae*, and some of it's members. He was released after three years and went to France. In 1929, he went to Mongolia where he joined the Imperial Army based there. He moved around the underworld and at one point was able to invite the ex-Emperor of China to sit on Mongolia's throne. He committed suicide by drinking poison on August 20th 1945 (probably influenced by Japan's surrender on August 15th).

Even now, spy stories remain very popular here in Japan. Some examples are the 007 series and some *Ninja* films from the United States, but these are not new. Before 007 there were many popular Japanese films such as 'Shinobi no Mono (The *Ninja*)'. Novels and other films in which either spies from many countries are fighting each other or the 'hero' country has a specialized elite group the other side does not, are forever popular.

Kimura Masaji Sensei and I

Akimoto Fumio Sensei

I strongly support the using of *Ninja* techniques for anti-terrorist organizations and have advised the Japanese Police on dealing with hijackings. However, I am completely against the use of *Ninpo* for guerrilla wars, etc. The fundamental part of the *Genbukan Ninpo* is *Goshin* (defense of the body and spirit) and my purpose is to teach just that. This *Ninpo* is not only based on techniques, but also on martial strategy and humanity, with the primary goals being for a martial arts Utopia and an enjoyable art. From now on, the future of *Ninpo* depends on its practitioners having this type of spirit. If it does not, it can never continue to develop, let alone exist.

PART IV
NINPO
TECHNIQES

01.
NINPO TAIJUTSU 「体術」
(UNARMED DEFENSE TECHNIQUES)

A.
HOKO-JUTSU 「歩行術」,
SENKO JUTSU 「潜行術」,
HICHO JUTSU 「飛鳥術」
(WALKING, INFLTRATING AND LEAPING TECHNIQUES)

The *Ninja* practiced techniques involving ways of using the feet (*Sosoku Ho* techniques) called *Sokushin Sosoku Ho* (literally 'fast spirit, moving fast'). *Aruki Kata* is the methods of walking, *Hashiri Kata* is the methods of running and *Tobi Kata* actually part of the other two techniques, are the methods of jumping. *Aruki Kata* has many different forms such as sideways walking (*Yoko Aruki*), sometimes called crab walking (*Kani Aruki*). With the sideways walk, three steps cover the distance of five normal steps, enabling a person who normally travels about four kilometers in an hour to cover seven kilometers.

Traveling like this, a person can cover about 120 to 160 km in a day. He would not get too tired since by changing sides, the legs can be rested alternately. This type of walking is excellent for moving through very narrow areas, enabling one to see in any direction. A person waiting by the roadside could be avoided easily by a change in direction. It also allows *Shuriken* to be used while on the move.

To do the sideways walk, first stand with the left leg crossed over the front of the right leg and cross the forearms in front of the chest with the fists clenched. Then move the right leg to the right, opening the legs wide, and repeat the process. A variation involves crossing the arms in front of the stomach. At first this may be difficult but after some time it usually becomes very easy.

Another form of *Aruki Kata* is *Ukimi no Jutsu* involving walking on ice with wooden thonged sandals (*Geta*). A *Kendo* master used to scatter small beads over the floor of his *Dojo* for practice balance. However, ice is far more effective and can be used effectively in winter. This type of training is for mastering the use of one's center of gravity. Even the more sophisticated techniques can be done in this way.

Hoko-Jutsu

Yoko Aruki (Sideways walking) ①

Yoko Aruki (Sideways walking) ②

The ancient book *Shoninki* refers to ten ways of walking called *Ashinami Jukka-Jo*. They are: walking silently by peeling one foot off the ground heel first, then placing the sole on the ground (*Nuki Ashi*), walking silently similarly to Japanese *Noh* dancers (*Suri Ashi*), walking by lifting the heel first and putting it down first (*Shime Ashi*), doing a small jump using the toes (*Tobi Ashi*), hopping on one foot (*Kata Ashi*), walking with long strides (*Oh-Ashi*), walking with short strides (*Ko-Ashi*), walking with the stride covering only the length of one's foot (*Kizami Ashi*), walking with the feet pointing in opposite directions (*Wari Ashi*), and normal walking (*Tsune no Ashi*).

According to the *Bansenshukai*, there are four ways of walking: walking over marshland with boards tied to the feet; the *Uki Ashi* (flying walk), *Kitsune Ashi* (fox walk) or *Inu Dori* (dog walk) for infiltrating an enemy's house; the *Usagi Ashi* (rabbit walk) for walking on a wooden floor; and walking using the scabbard of the sword to feel one's way through a dark place (*Za-Sagashi*).

For the use of disguise (*Henso-Jutsu*) it is important to know how to walk like a drunkard or injured man, both with and without a walking stick. Knowing how to move through water, both above and below, is also important. One must study these things constantly.

These techniques are not only limited to how one should walk or not walk depending on the circumstances, but also involve learning how to judge another person's character, profession, mood, etc., by observing the way he walks.

Tobi Kata consists of six main forms called *Tobi-Roppo*. These are: jumping forwards (*Mae Tobi*), jumping backwards (*Ushiro Tobi*), jumping upwards (*Taka Tobi*), jumping a specific distance (*Haba Tobi*), jumping sideways (*Yoko Tobi*), and jumping diagonally (*Naname Tobi*). In my *Dojo*, I teach the *Tenchi Happo Tobi*, which consists of jumping in a total of ten directions: up, down, forwards, backwards, sideways and diagonally forwards and backwards. I also teach the somersaulting (*Tobi Kaiten*): somersaulting using the hands (*Happo Tenkai*) and somersaulting without using the hands (*Happo Kuten*). The old way of learning the no-hands somersault was to first do a somersault with both hands flat on the ground, then with only the five fingers on each hand, gradually reducing them to three fingers to two then one, and finally without using the hands at all. This is then called the 'jumping dragonfly' (*Tonbo-o Kiru*).

Takamatsu Sensei once said, "After the age of forty, it is best to avoid doing the no-hands somersault in regular training. I rarely do it myself now". When I used to train in this, I did it alone. At about midnight I would leave the house while everyone was a sleep and head for the paddy fields. In Japan, a paddy field is about 40 to 50 cm below the normal level of the ground and around the perimeter there is a small pathway at normal ground level. I would scatter hay on the empty field, and then stand on the pathway. From here I would hurl myself into the air and attempt to do a backward somersault and land on my feet without using my hands. Countless times I landed on my head and felt dreadful. Other times I would try to roll off the roof and land on my feet; sometimes I would simply jump

Hicho-Jutsu

Jumping down

Jumping up

PART IV:
NINPO TECHNIQUES

straight down. I would also try running under a horizontal limb of a tree, catching it with one hand and then swinging over it. By learning these things one is able to escape from arm locks that seem impossible to escape from, finally placing the attacker in a counter arm lock. Whenever I teach these techniques, my pupils are usually flabbergasted. Several techniques have my attacker thinking that my arm has broken when actually his has.

Shoten no Jutsu is the way to run up vertical objects. It is very important for a *Ninja* to have this ability. For training, incline a plank of wood about 30 cms by 3 to 6 cms by about 3 meters at an angle. Once you can run up it, jump off it and land on your feet, incline the plank at a steeper angle. The training is then done on trees, walls and even people. The most important things are to concentrate your mind into perceiving the object as horizontal rather than vertical, straighten your back, hold your breath and sprint at full speed. When you reach the top, kick so that you jump off it and do a backward roll to absorb the shock of landing. In olden times, a *Ninja* would run up the wall of house, jump off it and grab hold of one of the roof beams with a pair of claws fitted to the hands (*Shuko*).

Onshin Ho-Ho is a special way of walking in order to pass a guard or guard dog without being noticed. One of the many times I have done this was near my home. When I take my dog for a walk, we usually pass a house with three dogs that bark at us. One night I told my dog we would trick them and pass them without their noticing by using *Sosoku Onshin no Ho-Ho*. The result was just that: they didn't notice us until after we had passed them. This technique involves using the body, breath and above all, mind control. It is impossible to explain this in a book, but I do teach it to the masters in my *Dojo*.

Senko-Jutsu

Walking steaalthily

Backward somersault

Under the earth

Under the water

B.
TAIHEN-JUTSU 「体変術」
(BODY MOVEMENTS TECHNIQUES)

B-1. *MUTO DORI* 「無刀捕り」 (DISARMING TECHNIQUES)

In every type of school (*Ryu-Ha*), disarming techniques or *Muto-Dori* taught as the final and highest-class technique. This is common sense. *Muto-Dori* is a special way of empty-handedly apprehending an attacker who has a weapon. I believe this should be taught both as part of the basics of *Ninpo Tai-Jutsu* and as the final technique, and therefore I teach my pupils these techniques from the very beginning so they can use them properly in real situations.

These are some of the basics taught:

Muto-dori Demonstration in Belgium

B. *TAIHEN-JUTSU* 「体変術」 (BODY MOVEMENTS TECHNIQUES)
B-1. *MUTO DORI* 「無刀捕り」 (DISARMING TECHNIQUES)

B-1-1. *SUKUI-DORI* 「掬い捕り」 (Sweeping catch)

My attacker, carrying both his long *Daito* (sword) and *Shoto* (short sword), only draws his *Daito*. Instinctively, I kick his sword hand upwards with my right foot, and then move forward with the left, catching his *Shoto* with my left hand while punching the bridge of his nose (the *Sancho*). My left hand draws his *Shoto* and thrusts it through him. I then leave in a state of cautiousness (*Zanshin*).

①

②

③

B. *TAIHEN-JUTSU* 「体変術」 (BODY MOVEMENTS TECHNIQUES)
B-1. *MUTO DORI* 「無刀捕り」 (DISARMING TECHNIQUES)

B-1-2. *YUKI-CHIGAI* 「行き違い」 (Passing another)

I am walking towards someone and am about to pass him when he suddenly draws his sword to cut my waist (performs a *Nukiuchi*). I stop him from drawing his blade completely by placing my left hand on his drawing forearm simultaneously punching a nerve point in his upper arm (the *Jakkin*) with my right fist. I then catch his left hand with my left and hold the end of the scabbard (the *Kojiri*) with my right hand, turning it until my attacker is face down on the ground. I restrain him with my knee, and with my right hand I draw his sword, cutting his groin. I finally place his sword to the back of his neck.

①

②

③

B. *TAIHEN-JUTSU* 「体変術」 (BODY MOVEMENTS TECHNIQUES)
B-1. *MUTO DORI* 「無刀捕り」 (DISARMING TECHNIQUES)

B-1-3. *DASHIN* 「拏振」 (Shaking fist)

My attacker thrusts his sword at me (does a *Tsuki*) that I avoid by pivoting on my left leg, catching his right wrist with my left hand. With my right fist I punch the back of his hand making him drop his sword, but he tries to kick me with his left leg. I counter kick his leg and take him down by applying pressure to his wrist. I finally slam my foot down on his body.

①　　　　　　　　　　②

③　　　　　　　　　　④

B. *TAIHEN-JUTSU* 「体変術」 (BODY MOVEMENTS TECHNIQUES)
B-1. *MUTO DORI* 「無刀捕り」 (DISARMING TECHNIQUES)

B-1-4. *MAWASHI-DORI* 「廻し捕り」 (Rolling catch)

From *Daijodan no Kamae* (an overhead sword stance), My attacker cuts downwards to my head. I evade the blade by lunging to the left and hit a nerve point in his lower arm (the Shakkotsu) with a right *Shuto* (knife hand) while kicking his left wrist so that his sword flies from his hand. I push his Adam's apple (the Dokkotsu) with my right hand and sweep his right leg so that he falls face up. I then take his sword and restrain him.

①

②

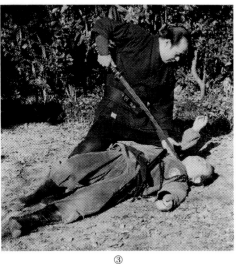

③

B. *TAIHEN-JUTSU* 「体変術」 (BODY MOVEMENTS TECHNIQUES)
B-1. *MUTO DORI* 「無刀捕り」 (DISARMING TECHNIQUES)

B-1-5. *SHIEN* 「獅猿」 (Giant monkey)

My attacker, standing behind me, thrusts his blade towards my back. I avoid his blade by stepping diagonally back with my left leg, catch his right wrist with my right wrist and, as he tries to kick my arm away, counter kick his leg, then lock both his arms, taking him down.

① ② ③ ④

B. *TAIHEN-JUTSU* 「体変術」 **(BODY MOVEMENTS TECHNIQUES)**

B-2. *TAI-GAESHI* 「体返し」 (ESCAPE TECHNIQUES)

Part of the *Ninja*'s *Tai-Jutsu* is ways of escaping from throws and arm locks, etc. by moving the body in a special manner and then taking the opponent to the ground. These techniques are called *Ura-Waza*.

Tai-Gaeshi training

B. *TAIHEN-JUTSU* 「体変術」(BODY MOVEMENTS TECHNIQUES)
B-2. *TAI-GAESHI* 「体返し」(ESCAPE TECHNIQUES)

B-2-1. *KOTE-GAESHI* 「小手返し」(Turning wrist)

As my attacker tries to do a backward wrist throw (Omote-Gyaku), I do not resist, allowing myself to drop first and then roll in front of him as he releases his grip and is thrown. For a forward wrist throw (Ura-Gyaku), again I offer no resistance and do a forward somersault, landing on my feet and immediately delivering a kick.

For *Omote-Gyaku*

①

②

For *Ura-Gyaku*

①

②

B. *TAIHEN-JUTSU* 「体変術」 (BODY MOVEMENTS TECHNIQUES)
B-2. *TAI-GAESHI* 「体返し」 (ESCAPE TECHNIQUES)

B-2-2. *GOJA-GAESHI* 「強者返し」 (Turning elbow)

When my attacker attempts to break my shoulder with a Goja-Dori arm lock, I do a backward somersault, landing on my feet, and then kick him.

①

②

③

B. *TAIHEN-JUTSU* 「体変術」 (BODY MOVEMENTS TECHNIQUES)
B-2. *TAI-GAESHI* 「体返し」 (ESCAPE TECHNIQUES)

B-2-3. *SEOI-GAESHI* 「背負返し」 (Turning back throw)

As my attacker tries to throw me as in *Seoi-Nage*. I roll off his back, landing on my feet, and counter attack. Another way is to allow myself to be thrown and, as I fly through the air, to place my right leg between his, putting him off balance and throwing him.

①

②

B. *TAIHEN-JUTSU* 「体変術」(BODY MOVEMENTS TECHNIQUES)
B-2. *TAI-GAESHI* 「体返し」(ESCAPE TECHNIQUES)

B-2-4. *OSOTO-GAESHI* 「大外返し」 (Turning leg sweep)

This is an escape from *Osoto-Nage*. As the throw is attempted, I twist in front of my attacker and throw him instead, restraining him with my right leg by choking him.

① ② ③

B. *TAIHEN-JUTSU* 「体変術」 (BODY MOVEMENTS TECHNIQUES)
B-2. *TAI-GAESHI* 「体返し」 (ESCAPE TECHNIQUES)

B-2-5. *TAWARA-GAESHI* 「俵返し」 (Turning rice bag)

As my attacker lifts me up in the *Tawara-Nage* throwing style, I use two palm strikes to his ears (Happa-*Ken*), rupturing his eardrums. I then grab his hair and throw him.

Most of these techniques have more than ten variations and, like the character of the *Ninja*, they change constantly being adapted to different situations.

①

②

C.
JU-TAIJUTSU「柔体術」
(GRAPPLING TECHNIQUES)

Ju-*Taijutsu* otherwise known as either *Yawara* or Ju-*Jutsu*, is the ways of defeating an opponent empty handedly. The main techniques are known as *Gyaku-Nage* or Kansetsu Waza (Joint-locking techniques). This *Jutsu* enables one to produce enormous effect with little power. The attacker's power is used against him, enabling him to be thrown or restrained or his bones to be broken.

Ju-Taijutsu with *Kimura Sensei*

C. *JU-TAIJUTSU* 「柔体術」 (GRAPPLING TECHNIQUES)

C-1. *KIMON-DORI* 「鬼門捕り」 (The way to catch the devil)

My attacker takes hold of both my lapels in a threatening manner so I simply take hold of both sides of his ribcage, driving my thumbs in. I step on his right foot, kneel and throw him so that he lands face up. Another way is to lift him on to my hip and suddenly drop him either on his head or back.

①

②

③

C. *JU-TAIJUTSU* 「柔体術」(GRAPPLING TECHNIQUES)

C-2. *KOCHO-DORI* 「胡蝶捕り」(The way to catch a butterfly)

My attacker holds me in *Kumiuchi*. I bring my right arm down and then up under his left arm, catching it against my neck. By sweeping his right leg with my right, he flies into the air before landing on his back.

①

②

③

C. *JU-TAIJUTSU* 「柔体術」 (GRAPPLING TECHNIQUES)

C-3. *ONI-KUDAKI* 「鬼砕き」 (Breaking the devil)

My attacker throws a punch to my face. I block it with my left hand as I lunge backwards with the right leg. I bring my right hand under his elbow, clasp both my hands together and bend his elbow until his shoulder is locked. Turning towards him, I sweep his right leg with my right and take him to the ground.

①

②

③

C. *JU-TAIJUTSU* 「柔体術」 (GRAPPLING TECHNIQUES)

C-4. *HIKI-CHIGAI* 「引き違い」 (Pulling when passing)

My attacker grabs my neck with one arm and is about to throw me to the ground. Holding his right hand with my left, I place my body in front of his then deliver a powerful blow with my left elbow. I then lock his arm and drop to the ground, taking him with me. Finally I restrain him by kicking his chest.

①

②

③

C. *JU-TAIJUTSU* 「柔体術」 (GRAPPLING TECHNIQUES)

C-5. *SHIHO-ZUME* 「四方詰め」 (Stopping in all directions)

Four attackers are restraining me at the same time, two holding an arm each, one holding my collar from behind and the fourth holding my lapels from in front. I begin by kicking the person in front of me in the groin while leaning backwards, hitting the person behind me with my head. I then deal with the other two, who are still holding my arms, by doing a backward somersault and kicking them in the face.

①

②

③

D.
DAKEN-TAIJUTSU「打拳体術」
(STRIKING TECHNIQUES)

Daken-Taijutsu means empty handedly taking an enemy to the point when he thinks he is about to die. It is also considered a mixture of *Ju-Jutsu* and *Kenpo* (拳法; fist techniques).

Daken-Taijutsu Demonstration in U.S.A.

D. *DAKEN-TAIJUTSU* 「打拳体術」 (STRIKING TECHNIQUES)

D-1. *NICHI-GEKI* 「日撃」 (Attacking the sun)

As my attacker attempts to throw me as in *Seoi-Nage*, I step back and slap one of his kidneys with my left palm, suddenly changing it into a thumb strike (*Boshi-ken*), sinking my thumb into a secret point called Shichibatsu. I then strike his face with my right hands fingers, I then thrown the opponent down and stamp on him with my right foot.

①

②

③

D. *DAKEN-TAIJUTSU* 「打拳体術」 (STRIKING TECHNIQUES)

D-2. *UNJYAKU* 「雲雀」 (Skylark)

My attacker throws a right punch to my face. I duck under it and rise up, punching his lower jaw from underneath with my right fist, then take hold of his left ribcage with my right hand I finally bring him to the ground using a *Seoi-Nage* throw.

① ②

③ ④

D. *DAKEN-TAIJUTSU* 「打拳体術」 (STRIKING TECHNIQUES)

D-3. *TENCHI* 「天地」 (Heaven and Earth)

My attacker comes at me with a right punch, left punch, right kick and right punch. I block each one by hitting specific nerve points. I then block the last punch with my left arm, with my right hand outside his left forearm catching his upper arm, and pull his arm towards me. I then deliver a right heel kick to the inside of my attackers right knee, kneel on my left knee, throw him and finally lock his arm.

①

②

③

D. *DAKEN-TAIJUTSU* 「打拳体術」 (STRIKING TECHNIQUES)

D-4. *SETTO* 「雪倒」 (Throwing snow)

My attacker comes at me with a right punch, left punch, right kick, left kick and right punch. After blocking each attack separately, I block the last punch with my right arm, catching his wrist with my left hand. My right hand then reaches over his right shoulder catching a nerve point. I then kick his groin, kneel with the right leg, take him down and restrain him.

①

②

③

④

D. *DAKEN-TAIJUTSU* 「打拳体術」 (STRIKING TECHNIQUES)

D-5. *YAMA-OTOSHI* 「山落とし」 (Dropping a mountain)

After blocking whatever combination of attacks my attacker uses, I block his final right punch with my left arm, grabbing hold of his wrist. I then sink my right thumb into his neck while catching the rest of his face with the other fingers. Finally I twist his hand, place my right leg behind his and throw him.

①

②

E.
KOSSHI-JUTSU 「骨子術」
AND
KOPPO-JUTSU 「骨法術」
(SECRET FINGER AND BONE TECHNIQIES)

Kosshi-Jutsu and *Koppo-Jutsu* are two specialized ways of dealing with an enemy with as little as one finger and with little or no effort.

Koppo-Jutsu is also known as Karate *Koppo-Jutsu*(唐手骨法術). The character for Kara (唐) is the old name for China and, therefore, Karate here means Chinese hand (unlike Kara'空' meaning 'empty' in nowaday's popular Karate). This art was brought to China from India where they called it 'Karani'. *Koppo-Jutsu* was origionally part of *Kosshi-Jutsu* and later developed into a separate branch. From long ago, *Kosshi-Jutsu* and *Koppo-Jutsu* were considered top-secret techniques (almost 'miracle' techniques) and were only taught to those *Ninpo* families above the middle class. On top of this, they were only taught to one member of each family (that is, a father would teach only one of his sons who would then teach only one of his sons.) These techniques were the backbone of the *Ninja*'s martial arts.

Kosshi-Jutsu, the oldest of the *Tai-Jutsu* arts, came to Japan about 1,000 years ago and has developed until the present day. *Koppo-Jutsu*, after becoming independent from *Kosshi-Jutsu*, has also continued to develop.

Kossi-Jutsu and *Koppo-Jutsu* Demonstration in New York

E. *KOSSHI-JUTSU*「骨子術」AND *KOPPO-JUTSU*「骨法術」(SECRET FINGER AND BONE TECHNIQIES)

E-1. *KOKU*「虚空」(Empty sky)

From the *Tenryaku Uchu Gassho* posture, the right hand forms a *Boshi-Ken* and the left arm is straightened. This posture is called *Soko no Kamae* (the posture of an attacking tiger). My attacker punches to my face and I block this with my left arm, doing a *Shuto* to his upper arm and breaking it. He then attacks with a right kick to which I counter kick, punching his ribcage with a *Boshi-Ken*.

① ② ③ ④

E. *KOSSHI-JUTSU* 「骨子術」 AND *KOPPO-JUTSU* 「骨法術」 (SECRET FINGER AND BONE TECHNIQIES)

E-2. *KORAKU* 「虎落」 (Throwing the tiger)

From Futen *Goshin* Gassho (circle of wind) posture, I cross my arms over my chest with the index finger and thumb (*Fu* and *Ku*) fingers again touching each other. This posture is called Kohyo Gassho. My attacker comes at me from the *Daijodan no Kamae* posture with a sword. I move to the left, catching his right wrist and delivering a right *Shuto* to his temple. I then lift his arm, twisting his wrist, and then bring it down again, which throws him to the ground. I finally kick him to end the fight.

① ② ③ ④

E. *KOSSHI-JUTSU*「骨子術」AND *KOPPO-JUTSU*「骨法術」(SECRET FINGER AND BONE TECHNIQIES)

E-3. *KAISOKU*「魁足」(Amazingly fast feet)

From the *Hanno Bon-Itsu Gassho* (circle of water) posture, I place my right hand on my hip with my left hand pointing forward. This posture is known as *Tonryu no Kamae* (the posture of an escaping dragon). My attacker comes at me from the *Daijodan no Kamae* posture and I move to the left, kicking his right hand making him drop his sword. He then tries to draw his short sword (*Shoto*). At this point, I rush in as quickly as possible and deliver a *Shuto* to his right temple. Catching his right elbow with my left hand, I then take him to the ground in a manner resembling *Osoto-Nage*. I end in a state of cautiousness (*Zanshin*).

①

②

③

E. *KOSSHI-JUTSU* 「骨子術」 AND *KOPPO-JUTSU* 「骨法術」 (SECRET FINGER AND BONE TECHNIQIES)

E-4. *HITO* 「飛倒」 (Jumping attack)

My attacker throws a right punch at me. Standing in the *Hoko* no *Kamae* posture, I evade it, hitting his chest with three fingers, and finally kick him in the chest with two simultaneous kicks. I land, do a backward somersault and assume a ready posture.

①

②

③

E. *KOSSHI-JUTSU* 「骨子術」 AND *KOPPO-JUTSU* 「骨法術」 (SECRET FINGER AND BONE TECHNIQIES)

E-5. *SANTO* 「攅倒」 (Finger power)

My attacker attempts to thrust his *Shoto* through my abdomen. Standing in *Seigan no Kamae*, I evade the blade by pivoting on my right leg and catching his hand. With the tips of all the fingers of my right hand, I strike the inside of my attacker's right elbow followed by a right punch to the back of his right hand, making him drop his *Shoto*. I do a wrist throw (Ura-Gyaku) to this hand, heel kick his right thigh and take him down.

① ②

③ ④

02.
BO-JUTSU 「棒術」
(STAFF TECHNIQUES)

A.
HANBO JUTSU 「半棒術」
(HALF STAFF TECHNIQUES)

Hanbo-*Jutsu* is the art of using the Hanbo, a short wooden staff 0.9 m long. There are other similar types of weapons differing only in length. These are the Jo, a staff 1.26 to 1.29 m long, and the *Bo* that is 1.8 to 2.4 m long. In my *Dojo*, I prefer to use a 1.35 m *Jo* and a *Bo* that measure 1.8 m (this is called a *Rokushaku Bo* - Roku means six and a Shaku is 0.3 m). It is from the Hanbo that *Kenpo* (the art of using a sword), *So-Jutsu* (the art of using a spear) and *Naginata-Jutsu* (the art of using a halberd) derived; during battles, a *Samurai* fighting with either a *Yari* or *Naginata* who found his weapon cut in half used the remains of the weapon as either a *Jo* or a Hanbo. They are made from Japanese red oak (*Shogunboku* or Akagashi) and their diameters were between 2.4 and 3 cm.

All *Bo-Jutsu* techniques can only be done properly after one has mastered *Taijutsu*; otherwise the whole exercise will be pointless. Please keep this in mind and continue training. By mastering Hanbo-*Jutsu*, one can develop the highest quality of swordsmanship (*Biken-Jutsu*).

Jinchu-Rei of Hanbo-Jutsu

A. *HANBO JUTSU* 「半棒術」 (HALF STAFF TECHNIQUES)

A-1. *KIRISAGE* 「切り下げ」 (Cut down)

My attacker stands in the *Daijodan no Kamae* posture and attacks with his sword. From the *Hira Ichimonji no Kamae* posture, I step to the left and hit his chest with the right tip of the Hanbo (Migi Bojiri) while holding it in with both hands. Releasing my right hand to hold his sword hand and using the Hanbo to lock his elbow, I then remove sword, cutting his groin in the process. I then stand poised to thrust it through him if necessary.

①

②

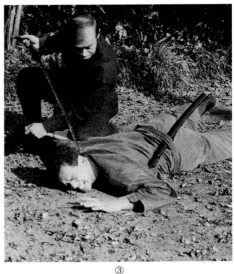

③

A. *HANBO JUTSU* 「半棒術」 (HALF STAFF TECHNIQUES)

A-2. *KOTE-BARAI* 「小手払い」 (Disposing of the hands)

From the *Seigan no Kamae* posture, my attacker thrusts his sword at me. I step to the left from the Otonashi no *Kamae* posture while lifting the right tip of the Hanbo over my right shoulder, using it to deliver a blow to both his hands and then suddenly to his face.

① ②

③ ④

A. *HANBO JUTSU* 「半棒術」 **(HALF STAFF TECHNIQUES)**

A-3. *MAWARI-DORI* 「廻り捕り」 (Encircling catch)

My attacker, bearing a *Yari* (spear), lunges forward, thrusting it at my abdomen. I evade this by moving diagonally to the left and hit the middle of the *Yari* with the right tip of the Hanbo, sending the *Yari* upwards. I then hit a nerve point on my attacker's right wrist with the left tip of the Hanbo (Hidari Bojiri), thrust the Hanbo at his chest and finally restrain both his hands with the Hanbo.

①

②

③

HANBO JUTSU
AND
HENSO JUTSU

Combining the art of disguise with the art of the *Hanbo*.

①

②

B.
JO-JUTSU 「杖術」
(THREE-QUARTER STAFF TECHNIQUES)

The *Jo* (three-quarter staff) and the *Rokushaku-Bo* (full-length staff) were weapons favored by the wandering priest (*Yamabushi*) who used them mainly as walking staffs. The use of special *Jo* such as the *Shikomi-Jo* and the *Shikomi-Gatana* (*Jo* with a concealed weapon) developed from the basics of *Jo-Jutsu*. In training with a *Jo*, one's partner can train in blocking the attacks.

Jo-Jutsu Demonstration - *Katate Jo-Furi Kata*

B. *JO-JUTSU* 「杖術」 (THREE-QUARTER STAFF TECHNIQUES)

B-1. *JUMONJI* 「十文字」 (The cross)

From the Ihen no *Kamae* posture, I begin to twirl the *Jo* in the right hand in a figure of eight. I then hit the left side of my attacker's face, continuing the figure of eight and hitting the right side of his face. Then I use the opposite end of the *Jo* to hit the right side of his face again by holding it in both hands. My left hand releases the *Jo* again to let it hit the left side of my attacker's face again.

① ② ③ ④

B. *JO-JUTSU* 「杖術」 (THREE-QUARTER STAFF TECHNIQUES)

B-2. *ROPPO* 「六法」 (The six directions)

From the *Gedan no Kamae* posture, I swing the *Jo* with my left hand to hit my attacker's legs, and then place it on my shoulders. I then swing out and hit the left side of his face followed by a hit to his head with the left tip of the Jo. Finally I thrust the right tip of the *Jo* at his chest.

B. *JO-JUTSU* 「杖術」 (THREE-QUARTER STAFF TECHNIQUES)

B-3. *HIRYU* 「飛龍」 (Flying dragon)

From the *Tenchi no Kamae* posture, I deliver a blow with the right tip of the *Jo* to my attacker's left shoulder, followed by a hit with the left tip to his head, then a hit with the right tip to his head and then to his left hip. Immediately after this I hit his groin with the left tip followed by a final blow to his left jaw with the right tip.

①

②

③

The following techniques involve the use of disguise (*Henso-Jutsu*) and a *Jo* with a concealed sword (*Shinobi-Jo*):

B. *JO-JUTSU* 「杖術」 (THREE-QUARTER STAFF TECHNIQUES)

B-4. The Priest and the *Shikomi-Gatana* 「仕込刀」

A priest in old Japan wore a Buddhist Rosary and carried a walking staff, a *Ninja* dressed this way carried a sword in his staff. When an enemy attacked from the *Daijodan no Kamae* posture, the *Ninja* would throw the rosary (*Juzu*) at his eyes (this is a *Metsubushi* technique), then draw the sword (*Shikomi-Gatana*) from the staff and cut him down.

①

②

③

B. *JO-JUTSU* 「杖術」 (THREE-QUARTER STAFF TECHNIQUES)

B-5. The Old Man and the *Mezashi* 「目刺」

When disguised as an old man, farmer or hunchback, a *Ninja* normally carried a bamboo *Jo* with an arrow concealed in one end (Mezashi). When an enemy attacked, he flicked his wrists to send the arrow flying into the enemy's eyes. He then used the *Jo* to hit both the enemy's hands, causing him to drop his sword, followed by a blow to the enemy's lower leg to bring him to the ground and a blow to his skull.

①

②

③

C.
ROKUSHAKU BO-JUTSU 「六尺棒術」
(FULL STAFF TECHNIQUES)

There are many different types of *Rokushaku-Bo* (full staffs). Their cross-sections vary between circular, hexagonal and octagonal, some have iron rings attached to each end while others have iron sticks running down the entire length of the *Bo*. The *Nyoibo* (a huge battle club) was covered with armour that was sometimes studded. The *Ninja* sometimes carried other weapons secretly hidden within the *Bo* such as a chain (*Kusari*), weights or an iron sphere (*Fundo*) or even a sword (*Katana*).

Hasso Ihen no Kamae

C-1. *GOHO* 「五法」 (The five ways)

From the *Hira Ichimonji no Kamae* posture, I twirl the *Bo* from left to right, then suddenly attack with the right tip to my attacker's left leg, followed by a swift attack to his face. I then swing the left tip of the *Bo* at his right leg again.

① ② ③ ④

C. *ROKUSHAKU BO-JUTSU* 「六尺棒術」 (FULL STAFF TECHNIQUES)

C-2. *TSURU-NO-ISSOKU* 「鶴之一足」 (Crane's foot)

From the *Tenchi no Kamae* posture, I suddenly slap the entire *Bo* onto the ground so that one tip hits my attacker's foot. I then pick up the *Bo*, swinging the right tip at both his legs, followed by a swing to the right side of his face with the left tip. Again I swing the right tip of the *Bo* downwards, hitting the crown of his head (Tent), continued by yet another swing with the left tip to the right side of his face and another to his left leg.

① ② ③ ④

C. *ROKUSHAKU BO-JUTSU* 「六尺 棒術」 (FULL STAFF TECHNIQUES)

C-3. *TAKI-OTOSHI* 「滝落」 (Drop throw)

From the *Chudan no Kamae* posture, I thrust one tip of the *Bo* at my attacker, then roll it onto my back, holding it with my right hand. From there I swing the *Bo* out to hit the left side of his face, rolling it onto my back again, this time holding it with my left hand. I then swing it at the right side of his face, followed by a hit to the left side with the opposite end of the *Bo*. Of the different *Bo* containing concealed weapons, the *Kusari-Fundo* concealed a weighted chain and is the most famous. The following example shows how it was once used by the *Ninja*.

① ②

③ ④

When dressed as a wandering priest (*Yamabushi*) with an enemy attacking from the *Daijodan no Kamae* posture, a *Ninja* used the left tip of the *Kusari-Fundo* to block the blade so that the enemy had to prepare himself for another attack. He then swings the right tip out, letting loose the chain that snagged the enemy's feet, and pulled him down to the ground. He then used the left tip to hit the enemy's sword hand, disarming him with the chain wrapped around his neck.

Kusari-Fundo Jutsu

03.
KENPO 「剣法」
BIKEN-JUTSU 「秘剣術」
(SWORD TECHNIQUES/SECRETS SWORD TECHNIQUES)

There are many types of swordsmanship or *Kenpo* (*Biken-Jutsu*) such as *Tanto-Jutsu* (using a dagger up to 30 cm long), *Kodachi-Jutsu* (using the *Shoto* - a short sword), *Daito-Jutsu* (using the *Daito* - a long sword), Nito-*Jutsu* (using both the *Shoto* and *Daito*), *Tachi-Jutsu* (using the *Tachi* - an extra-long sword), and *Ninja*to-*Jutsu* (using the *Ninja* sword).

Biken-Jutsu - Ura Gedan no Kamae

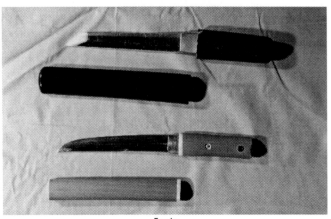

Tanto

A.
TANTO JUTSU 「短刀術」
(DAGGER TECHNIQUES)

A-1. *SHINTEN* 「心転」 (The rolling mind)

My attacker stands in the *Daijodan no Kamae* posture, while I await his first move in the *Migi Seigan no Kamae* posture. As the attack comes, I step to the left with my left foot, placing the blade of the *Tanto* (dagger) onto the back of his neck, twisting my hips and using my left hand to apply pressure to the blade and severing his neck.

①

②

③

A. *TANTO JUTSU* 「短刀術」 (DAGGER TECHNIQUES)

A-2. *KAKUSHI-KEN* 「隠し剣」 (Secret sword)

While I hold the *Tanto* with the blade running down my right forearm (in the Gyakute position) and inside the *Kimono* sleeve so that my attacker is unaware of it, he thrusts his sword at me. At first I avoid attack by moving to the left, but he attacks once more from the *Daijodan no Kamae* posture. I block this with my right forearm (actually with the *Tanto*'s blade resting against my arm), followed by a left punch to a weak point in his chest (the Butsumetsu). I immediately take hold of the handle (*Tsuka*) of his sword and while twisting my body. I remove his sword and force the *Tanto* into his chest.

①

②

③

A. *TANTO JUTSU* 「短刀術」 (DAGGER TECHNIQUES)

A-3. *IKKAN* 「一貫」 (Keep going)

I am attacked from the *Daijodan no Kamae* posture and I escape from the *Hidari Hanmi no Kamae* posture with the *Tanto* held in Gyakute in my right hand by stepping to the left with my right foot and kneeling with my left. I emded the *Tanto* as strongly as possible through his front foot and into the ground, leaving it there so he is unable to move his foot, remove his sword by using a wristlock (*Omote* Gyaku) and finally place his sword to his neck.

① ②

③ ④

The *Tanto-Jutsu* for the female *Ninja* (*Kunoichi*) included ways of concealing the *Tanto* in the sleeve, sash (*Obi*), and hair, under the armpit or in a bunch of flowers.

① ② ③ ④

B.
KODACHI-JUTSU 「小太刀術」
(SHORT SWORD TECHNIQUES)

Since olden times, the most famous schools (*Ryu-Ha*) that taught *Kodachi-Jutsu* (the way of using the *Shoto*) were the *Chujo-Ryu* and *Takeuchi-Ryu*. It was especially important for the *Ninja* to master this art because they often had to go through very narrow areas or had to use jumping and flying techniques (*Hicho Taihen-Jutsu*).

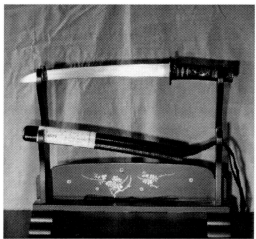

Kodachi / Shoto

Kodachi no Jutsu

B. *KODACHI-JUTSU* 「小太刀術」 **(SHORT SWORD TECHNIQUES)**

B-1. *HICHO-KEN* 「飛鳥剣」 (Flying bird's sword)

My attacker changes his posture from *Daijodan* to *Seigan* to *Hasso* and I stand as if in *Muto no Kamae* (empty-handed posture) with a *Shoto* (short sword) in my right hand. I begin to move to my attacker's right, exposing a little of my back to tempt him into cutting it. At last he attacks with a cut to the right side of my waist but I fly forward like a bird, thrusting the *Shoto* into his ribs.

①

②

B. *KODACHI-JUTSU* 「小太 刀術」 (SHORT SWORD TECHNIQUES)

B-2. *SHISHIGEKI* 「獅子擊」 (The Chinese lion attacks)

My attacker prepares himself in the *Daijodan no Kamae* posture while I stand in *Seigan no Kamae*. I begin to step back and the attacker steps forward, this is repeated two or three times. When he finally decides to attack, I lunge forward thrusting my *Shoto* into a weak point in his upper thigh (the Koe) leaving him unable to stand up.

①

②

B. *KODACHI-JUTSU* 「小太 刀術」 (SHORT SWORD TECHNIQUES)

B-3. *JUJI-KEN* 「十字剣」 (Crossed swords)

While I stand in the *Shizen no Kamae* posture, my attacker comes at me from the *Daijodan no Kamae* posture. I step diagonally back with my right foot and he cuts to my left waist. I then lunge forward with my right foot, catching hold of his sword hand and either thrusting the *Shoto* through his shoulder or simply cutting his shoulder so he is unable to use his arm.

①

②

C.
DAITO-JUTSU 「大刀術」
(SWORD TECHNIQUES)

C-1. *TSUKKAKE* 「突掛け」 (Hooking attack)

My attacker starts from the *Daijodan no Kamae* posture and I lunge forward with the sword (doing a *Tsuki*), kneeling on my left leg. He manages to escape so I cut to the right side of his waist. (A variation of this final part is to cut upwards, severing his arms completely.)

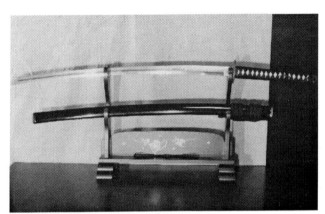

Daito

①

②

③

C. *DAITO-JUTSU* 「大刀術」 (SWORD TECHNIQUES)

C-2. *KOCHO-GIRI* 「胡蝶斬り」 (Cutting a small butterfly)

My attacker lunges forward doing a *Tsuki* from the *Shizen no Kamae* posture while I am in the *Daijodan no Kamae* posture. I step to the right as gently as a 'small butterfly' and cut downwards to his wrists. Other variations of the last part are to cut to his left shoulder or to do a *Tsuki*.

①

②

C. *DAITO-JUTSU* 「大刀術」 (SWORD TECHNIQUES)

C-3. *SHIHO-GIRI* 「四方斬り」 (Cutting the four directions)

My attacker cuts downwards from the *Daijodan no Kamae* posture while I am in the *Tenchi Hasso No Kamae* posture. I step to the right, cutting his left waist, followed by a cut to his right waist and finally a *Tsuki*. Instead of the *Tsuki* I could also cut him vertically in half (*Makko Karatake Wari*) or cut horizontally to both his feet (*Suso Barai*).

①

②

③

D.
NITO-JUTSU「二刀術」
(TWO SWORD TECHNIQUES)

The most famous school of two swords (*Nito-* using the *Daito* and *Shoto*) techniques was the *Miyamoto Musashi Niten Ichi Ryu*. Because a *Samurai* usually carried two swords he therefore had to be proficient in using them both to be considered a true *Samurai*.

Juji-Kiri no Kamae

D. *NITO-JUTSU* 「二刀術」 (TWO SWORD TECHNIQUES)

D-1. *JUMONJI* 「十文字」 (The X-shaped cross)

I stand in the *Hidari Shizen-Tai* posture, holding a *Daito* (long sword) in my left hand and a *Shoto* (short sword) in my right with the two blades crossed and pointing to the ground. From this posture I can defend myself from any type of attack by blocking with the *Daito*, then either thrusting the *Shoto* at my attacker or cutting him down with it.

① ② ③ ④

D. *NITO-JUTSU* 「二刀術」 (TWO SWORD TECHNIQUES)

D-2. *IAI* 「居合」 (Chance cutting)

As my attacker just begins to draw his *Daito* in a horizontal plane (*Nukiuchi*), I draw my *Shoto* throwing it at his chest and leaving it there. I then continue by drawing my own *Daito* and cut him down.

①

②

③

D. *NITO-JUTSU* 「二刀術」 (TWO SWORD TECHNIQUES)

D-3. *HYOHEN* 「豹変」 (Sudden change)

My attacker and I are fighting each other using swords. He disarms me by hitting my sword either towards the ground or in a circular motion. I draw my *Shoto* and cut his wrist with it or throw it at his chest, advancing close to him to remove his *Daito*, and finally cut him down with it.

①

②

③

E.
NINJA TO-JUTSU 「忍者刀術」
(NINJA SWORD TECHNIQUES)

The techniques of the *Ninja* to or *Shinobi-Gatana* are unique since this sword is only about 0.55 m long and is much thinner than a *Samurai* blade. It is therefore very light and can easily be used one-handed to cut an attacker. The main form of fighting used was usually one-handed (slightly resembling European sable fencing), allowing a greater reach. This form of fighting was also very useful in narrow and confined areas.

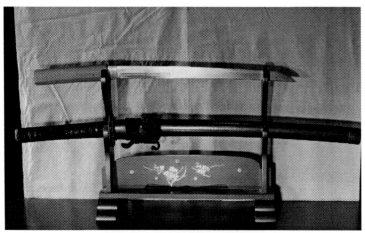

Ninja To / Shinobi-Gatana (Katana)

Ninja-to and *Kamayari*

E. *NINJA TO-JUTSU* 「忍者 刀術」 (NINJA SWORD TECHNIQUES)

E-1. *KAGE-NO-ITTO* 「影の一刀」 (Cutting a shadow)

I am suddenly attacked in such a way that I am unable to draw my sword. In such circumstances, the best thing to do is to roll or jump away and try to hide, for example, behind a tree. At this point, I push my sword back with my left hand, slipping it against my back and turning it so that the handle (*Tsuki*) points to the right. I then lift it over my back with my right hand and draw it over my right shoulder.

① ② ③

④ ⑤

E-2. *ITTO RYUDAN* 「一刀榴弾」(Cutting the Gordian knot)

I stand in front of my attacker in the *Hidari Hanmi no Kamae* posture with my left hand holding the scabbard (*Saya*) horizontally in front of me and my sword poised above my head (this posture is called *Kocho no Kamae*). He then attacks from the *Daijodan no Kamae* posture and I swing the scabbard, releasing a burst of blinding powder (*Metsubushi*) into his eyes, and immediately advance with either a cut or a *Tsuki*. The blinding powder is kept in the base of the scabbard. (If the confrontation occurred after I had emerged from a river, the scabbard would be filled with murky water that I would use as a kind of blinding powder.

①

②

E. *NINJA TO-JUTSU* 「忍者刀術」 (NINJA SWORD TECHNIQUES)

E-3. *HIRYU-KEN* 「飛龍剣」 (Flying dragon sword)

I stand in the *Hasso no Kamae* posture with my sword in its scabbard. As my attacker tries to cut or thrust his sword at me, I escape by moving to the left or right. Just as his sword stops moving, I snap my sword down, releasing its scabbard into his face, then immediately cutting or thrusting my sword at him.

①

②

F.
TACHI-JUTSU 「太刀術」
(LONG SWORD TECHNIQUES)

The length of a *Tachi* (long sword) usually ranges from 0.84 to 1.05 m, although some are more than 1.2 m long. The blade has a very majestic curve and its handle (*Tsuka*) is also long. It is a therefore a very good weapon.

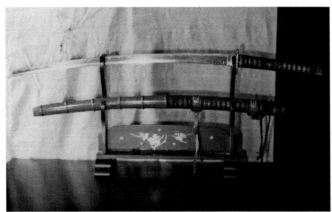

Tachi

Tachi no Jutsu

F. *TACHI-JUTSU*「太刀術」(LONG SWORD TECHNIQUES)

F-1. *ISO-NO-NAMI*「磯の波」(Waves rolling on the beach)

I stand with my legs slightly apart holding the *Tachi* in my right hand with its point directed at my attacker's legs. As he attacks either from the *Daijodan no Kamae* posture or with a *Tsuki*, I simply step to the left and swing the *Tachi* into him like a pendulum.

①

②

③

F. *TACHI-JUTSU* 「太刀術」(LONG SWORD TECHNIQUES)

F-2. *HICHO-GAESHI* 「飛鳥返し」(Flying against)

I stand in the *Seigan no Kamae* posture, as my attacker comes at me from the *Daijodan no Kamae* posture or with a *Tsuki*. I step to the left, digging the tip of the *Tachi* into his temple, then cut off his right leg.

①

②

③

F. *TACHI-JUTSU* 「太刀術」 (LONG SWORD TECHNIQUES)

F-3. *RAIKO* 「雷光」 (Lightning)

I stand in the *Gedan no Kamae* posture with the sword's cutting edge pointing up. As my attacker comes at me from the *Daijodan no Kamae* posture, I raise the blade and cut off his right hand, followed by either a cut to his neck or a sword thrust to his chest.

The *Tachi* was also used on horseback. It is important to learn how to use it on horseback, even though the basics are much the same as for on the ground.

①

②

③

04.
TESSEN-JUTSU AND JUTTE-JUTSU
(IRON FAN AND IRON ROD TECHNIQUES)

A.
TESSEN-JUTSU 「鉄扇術」
(IRON FAN TECHNIQUES)

Tessen-Jutsu (*Sensu Dori*) was a very popular part of the *Samurai*'s martial arts; *Samurai* often carried a *Tessen* (an iron war fan). For the *Ninja* this weapon was very important in the use of disguise (*Henso-Jutsu*), when he had to dress up as a *Samurai*, master less *Samurai* (*Ronin*) or a martial artist (*Bugeisha*).

If one becomes very skilful in these techniques, then even a pencil can be easily used to restrain an attacker. In olden times, when a *Ninja* had to disguise himself as an ordinary citizen (*Chonin*), he would usually only protect himself with a bamboo-smoking pipe with the two ends made of iron (*Kiseru*). A true *Ninja* would rarely fight in the middle of the day with *Shuriken* and a *Ninja* sword (*Ninjato*).

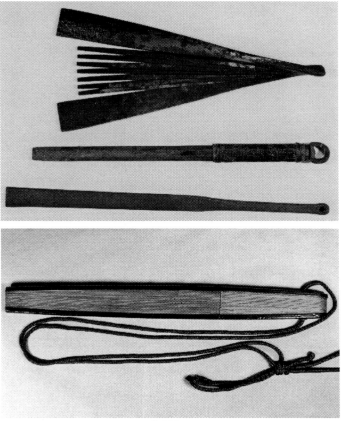

Tessen

A. *TESSEN-JUTSU* 「鉄扇術」 (IRON FAN TECHNIQUES)

A-1. *KOCHO* 「胡蝶」 (Small butterfly)

My attacker attempts to draw his sword to cut my waist. I move to the left while holding his right hand with my left, and hit the back of his hand with the *Tessen*. I then catch a nerve point in his left upper arm (*Jakkin*) and place the tip of the *Tessen* against his chest, bringing him to the ground and restraining him.

①

②

A. *TESSEN-JUTSU* 「鉄扇術」 (IRON FAN TECHNIQUES)

A-2. *SHUKO-KUDAKI* 「手甲砕き」 (Breaking the back of the hand)

My attacker thrusts his sword at my abdomen and I escape by moving to the left, hitting his sword and then his temple before restraining him by applying pressure to his temple with the side of the *Tessen*.

①

②

PART IV:
NINPO
TECHNIQUES

A. *TESSEN-JUTSU*「鉄扇術」 (IRON FAN TECHNIQUES)

A-3. *KASUMI-JIME*「霞締め」 (**Tying up the fog**)

My attacker thrusts his sword (does a *Tsuki*) from the *Seigan no Kamae* posture. I move to the left and hit the side of the blade upwards with my *Tessen* from underneath, then move in close to him. I place the *Tessen* against the side of his head and apply pressure with the aid of the left hand.

①

②

B.
JUTTE-JUTSU 「十手術」
(TRUNCHEON TECHNIQUES)

The *Jutte* (a truncheon with a hook protruding just above the handle) was a very important weapon for the *Ninja*, because during the *Edo* period, they were given the job of being special policemen called (*Yoriki* and *Doshin*): the *Jutte* was their trademark. Short sword techniques (*Kodachi-Jutsu*), truncheon techniques (*Jutte-Jutsu*) and iron fan techniques (*Tessen-Jutsu*) are all used with the same disarming (*Muto-Dori*). A *Ninja*'s highest spiritual levels are: no mind; no thought (*Munen-Muso*) and the natural mind (*Shizen-Shin*). The old name given to *Jutte-Jutsu* means 'the correct way to control evil'.

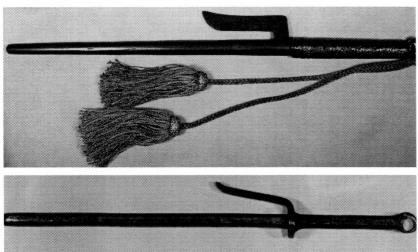

Jutte

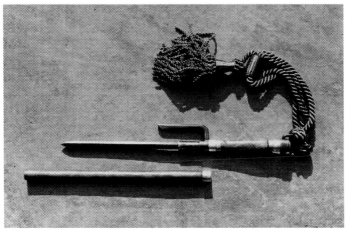

Kakushi Jutte

B. *JUTTE-JUTSU* 「十手術」 (TRUNCHEON TECHNIQUES)

B-1. *KIRI-NO-HITOHA* 「桐之一葉」 (The leaf of a paulownia tree)

My attacker prepares to cut with his sword from the *Daijodan no Kamae* posture, while I stand with the *Jutte* in front of me. As the cut comes, I evade it by moving to the right and hitting the left side of his neck, catching his left wrist with my left. I restrain him by sinking the tip of the *Jutte* into his left armpit.

① ②

③ ④

B. *JUTTE-JUTSU* 「十手術」 (TRUNCHEON TECHNIQUES)

B-2. *RAKKA* 「落花」 (Falling petal)

While I stand in the *Seigan no Kamae* posture, my attacker swings his sword at me from the *Daijodan no Kamae* posture. I block the blade with the *Jutte*, trapping it in the hook on the side of the *Jutte* (*Yokoha*). I then move to the right, placing his sword against his neck, and finally restrain him.

①

②

③

B. *JUTTE-JUTSU* 「十手術」 (TRUNCHEON TECHNIQUES)

B-3. *GORIN-KUDAKI* 「五輪砕き」 (Breaking the five circles)

Again my attacker comes at me from the *Daijodan no Kamae* posture and I wait in the *Seigan no Kamae* posture. As his blade comes down, I escape by moving to the right, hitting his sword hand with the *Jutte*, making him drop it. I follow this with a thrust to his stomach with the tip of the *Jutte*, and then grab hold of his left hand, taking him to the ground and restraining him.

05.
SHUKO-JUTSU「手鈎術」
(HAND CLAW TECHNIQUES)

Within the *Ninpo*'s *Taihen-Jutsu* (body movements techniques) *Muto-Dori* (disarming) styles, there is also a section on iron hand claw techniques (*Shuko-Jutsu*). The *Shuko* (a iron hand claw) are metal tools primarily used for climbing trees, walls, etc. but, when necessary, they could be used as a weapon for defense against an attack. At night they can also be used to surprise an enemy attacking with a sword, who finds it blocked by what seems to be an empty hand. This is a true technique from the ways of catching a sword empty handedly (*Shinken Shiraha-Dori*).

Shuko

1. *KAESHI-DORI* 「返し捕り」 (Returning bird)

As my attacker comes at me with his sword from the *Daijodan no Kamae* posture, I immediately duck, kneeling on one knee, then deliver a crushing blow to his front foot with my right *Shuko*. I then stand up, punch his face with both *Shuko* and deliver two simultaneous kicks to his lower abdomen. As I land, I roll backwards assuming a suitable posture.

①

②

2. *KEN-NAGASHI* 「拳流し」 (Swift punch)

My attacker comes at me from the *Daijodan no Kamae* posture with his sword and I lunge forward with a loud yell (*Kiai*), kneeling on one leg and blocking his blade with my left hand while punching his lower abdomen with my right hand. As I roll away, my left *Shuko* claws his ankle.

① ②

③ ④

3. *ITTO-DORI*「一刀捕り」(Catching the sword)

Once again my attacker comes at me with a sword from the *Daijodan no Kamae* posture while I am in a defensive posture (*Ichimonji no Kamae*). I step forward with the left foot and block the sword with my left *Shuko*. I then drive my right *Shuko* through my attacker's hand as I kick to his groin and pull his sword away from him. I can then use his sword against him.

① ② ③ ④

06.
KUSARIGAMA-JUTSU 「鎖鎌術」
(SICKLE AND CHAIN TECHNIQUES)

The *Kusarigama* was a weapon that came in different styles but was basically made from a sickle (*Kama*) and a length of chain with a weight attached to one end. The *Ninja*, however, had their own special one called a *Kyoketsu-Shoge* (距跋渉毛; meaning moving freely through the mountains and valleys). It was a combination of a *Yari* (spear) blade, a sickle, an iron ring, and a rope made from either women's or horses' hair measuring about 2.4 to 3 m. This style of weapon came to Japan a long time ago from India via China. The normal *Kusarigama* ranged from those with a small sickle with a 2.7 m chain attached to it to those with a very large scythe.

The main ways of using the *Kusarigama* were to either thrust (*Tsuki*) or cut, but it was also used as a climbing aid. When a *Ninja* disguised himself as a farmer, he would cut the grass with the normal sickle and, when necessary, would either untie a rope from his waist or remove a chain from his clothing and clip it on. The tip of the chain would sometimes have a snake or explosive attached to it to produce a more awesome effect. He would hold the sickle in his left hand and twirl the chain in his right, spinning it above the head (*Tenchi-Buri*), spinning it on one side of the body (*Sayu Yoko-Buri*) or twirling it in a figure of eight (*Hachimonji-Buri*). He would attack the enemy's sword, sword hands, head, or neck by wrapping it around the target or hitting it, then suddenly moving close to the enemy, doing a thrust, a cut or if necessary, blocking his sword with the sickle and hitting him with the chain.

The weight (*Fundo*) also varied in size and shape. Some were specialized, such as the iron ones that opened on impact, releasing either poisoned water or powder.

The following techniques are done with the special *Ninja Kusarigama* (*Kyoketsu-Shoge*):

Kaen Kusarigama

1. *KOTE-GAESHI* 「小手返し」 (Hands against)

My attacker stands in the *Seigan no Kamae* posture. I stand spinning the chain (in *Sayu Yoko-Buri*), with the sickle in my left hand. I step to the right, suddenly hitting his hands with the weight, and then begin spinning it above my head (in *Tenchi-Buri*), wrapping it round his legs and pulling him to the ground. I then jump towards him, stepping on his sword hand, and cut his neck.

① ②

③ ④

2. *SHIHO-ZUME* 「四方詰め」 (Blocking up the four directions)

After twirling the chain in a figure eight (in *Hachiji-Buri*), I whip my attacker's left and right sides, but he evades this using *Taihen-Jutsu* (body movements). I then spin the chain above my head and send it towards his neck, which he ducks and blocks with his sword, entangling the chain. We both then begin pulling on the chain and advancing until he attacks me with his sword. I block it with the sickle, drawing my *Shoto* and severing his arm. I finally place the sickle to his neck.

① ② ③ ④

3. *IWA-KUDAKI* 「岩砕き」 (Breaking rocks)

My attacker thrusts his sword at me from the *Seigan no Kamae* posture and I escape by moving to the right, cutting to his wrists and hitting the top of his skull with the weight.

①

②

③

07.
SOJUTSU 「槍術」
(SPEAR TECHNIQUES)

So-Jutsu is the basic ways of fighting with a *Yari* (spear). Whereas a normal *Yari* measured between 2.1 and 2.7m, a short one was normally only 1.8m. There are many different types of *Yari* such as the Te-*Yari* (between 0.9 and 1.2 m, the *Naga-Yari* (a long *Yari*), the *Tetsu-Yari* (an all-steel *Yari*), the *Kama-Yari* (a *Yari* with an additional half-moon blade attached to it) and the *Sanbon-Yari* (a three-bladed *Yari*).

The *Ninja* often used these *Yari* not as weapons but for pole-vaulting over a wall, river, moat or pond. Sometimes, they bound many *Yari* together with pots to make a raft. The half-moon blade of the *Kama-Yari* could be hooked onto a tree branch or wall for climbing.

So-Jutsu (by Yamato Sakura)

Gedan no Kamae

1. *KANPO* 「扞法」 (Keep off and defend)

As my attacker begins to prepare himself, I stand in the *Chudan no Kamae* posture (with the *Yari* pointing at his eyes) and thrust the *Yari* at his chest, then bring it back and thrust again. During his final preparations for an attack from the *Daijodan no Kamae* posture, I swing the iron tip, at the blunt end of the *Yari* (*Ishizuki*), by pivoting on my right leg and hit my attacker's foot with it, disabling him.

①

②

③

2. *HISO*「秘槍」(Secret spear)

From the *Chudan no Kamae* posture, I thrust the *Yari* at my attacker's chest and as I step forward, I swing the blunt end (*Ishizuki*) at his groin, then repeat the thrust to his chest, followed by a swing to his groin. I then use the blade to remove his sword by turning it around his wrists, cutting them, and a final thrust to his chest ends the fight.

① ②

③ ④

3. *TENCHI-KAKU* 「天地推」 (Breaking Heaven and Earth)

From the *Chudan no Kamae* posture, I thrust the *Yari* at my attacker's chest, and then hit both of his hands with the blunt end (*Ishizuki*). I then swing the blade and hit the side of his head, leap backward and throw the *Yari* at him.

①   ②

③   ④

08
NAGINATA-
JUTSU
「薙刀術」
BISENYO-
JUTSU
「眉尖刀術」

08.
NAGINATA-JUTSU
AND
BISENTO-JUTSU

A.
NAGINATA-JUTSU 「薙刀術」
(HALBERD TECHNIQUES)

The *Naginata* (a halberd) was developed from *Bisento-Jutsu* that came from China to Japan during China's *To* period (618 - 898). It was used during the *Heian* period (794 - 1185) by the infantry to cut off the legs of a charging horse. Later it became a *Samurai* weapon, finally ending up as a weapon for women.

The *Ninja's Naginata* was usually light but strong. Sometimes the *Ninja* made one by tying a very short sword (*Tanto*) or *Ninja* sword (*Ninja-To*) to the tip of full staff (*Rokushaku-Bo*) or a piece of bamboo of a similar length. It was used in much the same way as a *Yari* (spear).

Hicho no Kamae

A. *NAGINATA-JUTSU* 「薙刀術」 (HALBERD TECHNIQUES)

A-1. *ASHI-BARAI* 「足拂い」 (Hitting the feet)

As I stand in the *Hira-Ichimonji no Kamae* posture, my attacker comes at me with his sword from the *Daijodan no Kamae* posture. I block his blade with the *Naginata* by lifting my left arm, bringing my right arm back. I then pivot on my right foot, kneeling on my left knee, and cut to his right leg. Circling the *Naginata* above my head, I cut to his left leg and stand up in the *Yoko Ichimonji no Kamae* posture, then in a state of cautiousness (*Zanshin*).

①

②

③

④

08
NAGINATA-
JUTSU
「薙刀術」
BISENYO-
JUTSU
「眉尖刀術」

A. *NAGINATA-JUTSU* 「薙刀術」 (HALBERD TECHNIQUES)

A-2. *KURIDASHI* 「繰り出し」 (Let out)

My attacker again stands in the *Daijodan no Kamae* posture while I stand in the *Naka Seigan no Kamae* posture. I step back and then to the left with the left leg, cutting to the left side of his waist. Immediately I lunge to the right using my right leg, twirling the *Naginata* above my head and attacking the left side of his waist again. I then remain in *Zanshin*.

①

②

③

A. *NAGINATA-JUTSU* 「薙刀術」 (HALBERD TECHNIQUES)

A-3. *SASHI-CHIGAI* 「差し違い」 (Stabbing each other)

My attacker stands in the *Daijodan no Kamae* posture while I stand in the *Hira-Ichimonji no Kamae* posture. I then begin to alternately thrust the blade at his body, with the blade on its side, and then cut to his right foot several times until he drops to the ground.

①

②

③

08
NAGINATA-
JUTSU
「薙刀術」
BISENYO-
JUTSU
「眉尖刀術」

KUNOICHI NAGINATA

Using a *Kimono* as *Metsubushi*

①

②

B.
BISENTO-JUTSU 「眉尖刀術」
(BATTLE FIELD HALBERD TECHNIQUES)

The *Bisento* is a large *Naginata*. It has a broad, hard blade and was mainly used to cut through a warrior's armour or to cut his horse. The techniques for using the *Bisento* came from China during China's *To* period when an accomplished Chinese warrior came and taught them to *Izumo Kaja Yoshiteru* (of the *Minamoto* Family) between 1156 and 1159 A.D..

Bisento

08

NAGINATA-
JUTSU
「薙刀術」
BISENYO-
JUTSU
「眉尖刀術」

B. *BISENTO-JUTSU* 「眉尖刀術」 (BATTLE FIELD HALBERD TECHNIQUES)

B-1. *OSHIN* 「汪振」 (Easy swing)

My attacker stands in the *Daijodan no Kamae* posture while I am in the *Seigan* posture. Stepping to the right, I cut to his left waist but he manages to escape this. I then move to the left and cut to his right rib cage, twirl the *Bisento* above my head and finally bring it down, cutting him diagonally in half from the left shoulder to the right waist. If he blocks during this final cut, his sword will snap in two because the *Bisento* has a strong, heavy (almost 25 kg.) blade.

If it is you who is carrying the sword, the best way to defend yourself is to simply evade the attacks until the attacker tires. It is very important not to allow your sword to touch the *Bisento*'s blade at all.

① ② ③ ④

B. *BISENTO-JUTSU*「眉尖刀術」(BATTLE FIELD HALBERD TECHNIQUES)

B-2. *BATTO*「拔刀」(**Drawing sword**)

My attacker faces me in the *Daijodan no Kamae* posture while I am in the *Hass no Kamae* posture. I step forward with my left leg, swinging the *Bisento*'s blunt end (*Ishizuki*) lightly at his foot, and immediately step forward with my right foot, cutting to the right side of his neck. Again I attack his foot lightly with the *Ishizuki* before cutting to the right side of his neck again.

① ② ③ ④

08

NAGINATA-
JUTSU
「薙刀術」
BISENYO-
JUTSU
「眉尖刀術」

B. *BISENTO-JUTSU* 「眉尖刀術」 (BATTLE FIELD HALBERD TECHNIQUES)

B-3. *SEITO* 「惺刀」 (Clear sword)

    I stand in the *Yoko Ichimonji no Kamae* posture as my attacker comes at me from the *Daijodan no Kamae* posture. I then pivot on my right foot, bringing the blade down onto either his wrists or elbows, severing them.

①

②

09.
KYU-JUTSU AND KISHA-JUTSU

A.
KYU-JUTSU 「弓術」
(ARCHERY TECHNIQUES)

The *Ninja's Yumi* (bow) is called a *Han-Kyu* (half bow). It is very short and light yet very powerful, and so was easy to carry. Some actually folded in half. The arrows (*Ya*) were used in many ways, such as with poison on the tips or with explosives tied to them. They were also used for measuring distances with one end attached to a long, light string. Some had arrowheads made of wood with many small holes in them (*Kaburaya*) that contained explosive devices and blinding powder that exploded on impact, blinding anyone near. They could also be used empty and they would make a loud whistling noise.

The arrow case was made of black cloth and rice-straw padding (*Makiwara*) which the arrowheads were embedded into so they could not fall out. This was useful in training which involved standing, sitting, crouching, lying face up and down, rolling, leaping and even hanging upside down from the limb of a tree. An example of how the *Ninja* used it in real fighting is as follows: The *Ninja* set up the bow and arrow ready to fire in his left hand with his sword in his right, then advanced close to the enemy. Suddenly he shot the arrow at him, then immediately cut with the sword.

There are two main ways of using the bow: on foot (*Busha-Jutsu*) and on horseback (*Kisha-Jutsu*). *Busha-Jutsu* comprises *Ohmato* (large target practice), *Kusajishi* (goat hunting) and *Marumono* (circular target practice), whereas *Kisha-Jutsu* comprises *Yabusame* (target practice), *Inuoumono* (using dogs as targets) and *Kasakake* (hunting). These main divisions are further subdivided as shown in the chart.

The *Yumi* has been around for a long time and used to be made from a cylindrical piece of wood from an *Azusa, Maki, Tsuki, Zumi* or *Haji* tree. Nowadays they are made of a combination of bamboo and wood called *Hase no Ki*. Originally there was no predetermined length for the *Yumi* but during the *Chusei* period (Middle Ages) they were usually 2.25 m long. Later in the *Kinsei* period (from the 16th century to the end of the *Meiji* period in 1913), they were 2.19 m long. The *Ninja's Yumi* was usually about 1.08 m long.

Hankyu-Jutsu

B.
KISHA-JUTSU 「騎射術」
(HORSEBACK ARCHERY TECHNIQUES)

Kisha-Jutsu is the art of using the bow and arrow while on horseback (*Ki* means horseman-ship; *Sha* means using the bow) and so is a union of two arts, *Ba-Jutsu* (horsemanship) and *Kyu-Jutsu*. These techniques were well known to both the *Ninja* and *Samurai*. For *Kisha-Jutsu* it is essential to have mastered *Ba-Jutsu*. The highest point of *Kisha-Jutsu* is called *Meikyo-Shisui* (cleansing mirror; calm water). One's heart must never be over-enthusiastic about shooting arrows; *Kisha-Jutsu* must be done in the purest state the heart can reach.

On the subject of *Ba-Jutsu*, I was taught: "The rider is *Ten* (Heaven) and *Yo* (*Yang*); the horse is *Chi* (Earth) and *In* (*Ying*). Their harmonious union produces the harmonious *Tenchi / In-Yo*. The body must be like a sphere, the mind like a bright light. The human being and the horse are both living creatures; they must both have a pure heart. The rider who attains this spirit and heart will have a horse that moves so smoothly that it flies". I was also taught the ways of using the whip and how to make and use both the harness and secret medicines for the horse amongst other things. The vital thing is to ride and shoot smoothly.

Kisha-Jutsu

10.
SHURIKEN-JUTSU 「手裏剣術」
(HAND-THROWN BLADE TECHNIQUES)

When people think of *Ninja*, often the first image to come to mind is of the *Shuriken* (a hand-thrown blade). In the opinion of these people, a *Ninja* who does not throw the *Shuriken* is not a true *Ninja*. The connection between *Ninja* and *Shuriken* is deeply rooted in these people's minds.

The type of *Shuriken* depended heavily on the *Ryu* (school) or person using it. *Shuriken-Jutsu* began in olden times and was known as *Ishi-Nage* or *Tsubute-Nage* meaning "stone-throwing". The name *Toteki-Jutsu* was given to the ways of throwing anything, and was therefore the old name for *Shuriken-Jutsu*. The *Shuriken* was considered a superior flying weapon (*Tobi-Dogu*) because it was silent, odorless and invisible. In China these weapons were called *Sencheng, Piyau* and *Sanpukosu*.

The Buddhist Chakra was a *Shuriken* from ancient India. From this Chakra all the other *Shuriken* developed: the *Bo-Shuriken, Hiragata-Shuriken, Juppo-Shuriken, Sanpo-Shuriken, Roppo-Shuriken, Happo-Shuriken, Manji-Shuriken*, etc. A special way to stop a *Shuriken* shining was to wrap it in silk and put it in a fire. This made the *Shuriken* black and rustproof.

One-Way to throw the long, thin *Bo-Shuriken* is to point the sharp end in the same direction as the fingers, then throw with the palm downward. This is called the way to a direct hit (*Chokudaho*). *Kaitendaho* is the name for when the tip of the *Bo-Shuriken* rests on the palm and the *Shuriken* is thrown so that it spins.

Shuriken can be thrown while one is standing (*Tachi-Uchi*), kneeling on the leg (*Za-Uchi*), lying (*Ne-Uchi*) or during a roll (*Kaiten-Uchi*) in one of the following directions: forward *Shomen-Uchi*, to the sides (*Sayu Yoko-Uchi*) or backwards (*Gyaku-Uchi*). They can also be thrown using both hands at the same time and repetitively but the most important thing is to be able to throw them freely.

The target areas include the area between the eyebrows, the upper lip, the throat, the heart, the abdomen, the thigh and the foot. It is important to attack with the *Shuriken* when the enemy is off guard; when he has been surprised or scared is the time to escape.

The *Ninja* sometimes laced the tips of *Shuriken* with poison before throwing them, and sometimes attached a small explosive. If a *Ninja* had no *Shuriken*, immediately available, he used a small knife usually kept on the side of the scabbard (*Kozuka*), a *Shoto* (short sword) or even a *Kogai* (a tool used for hairdressing). When necessary, he threw almost anything: hot charcoal, a teacup, an ashtray, a smoking pipe, etc.

The *Shuriken* were not only thrown but were also used as hand-held weapons, climbing tools or even *Makibishi* (sharp objects placed on the ground so an enemy giving chase stepped on them). Other tools used as *Shuriken* included flaming arrows, special candles, hand-thrown explosives (*Horokubi*), blinding powder (*Metsubushi*), fans with blinding powder (*Sensu*), flutes used as blow-guns (*Fukiya*) or even small containers that filled the air with blinding powder (*Sokutoki*).

A *Ninja* who was skilful with the *Shuriken* was equally skillful with the gun. During the reign of *Tokugawa Ieyasu* the *Ninja* were employed as *Teppo-Gumi* that I have already mentioned. *Takamatsu Sensei* often said, "Whenever one uses a pistol, it is the same as using the *Shuriken*".

SHURIKEN NAGE KATA

Zauchi (Senban Nage)

Tachiuchi (Bo-Shuriken Nage)

Tonsochi (Happo-Shuriken Nage)

11.
HOBAKU-JUTSU
AND
NAWANUKE-JUTSU

A.
HOBAKU-JUTSU「捕縛術」
(RESTRAINING TECHNIQUES)

Hobaku-Jutsu is the ways of catching (restraining) and tying someone up. These techniques have many styles such as Tai-*Jutsu*, *Jutte-Jutsu* and *Bo-Jutsu*, and can be done using special tools such as *Sodegarami* (sleeve-catchers) and *Tsukubo*. However, rope is usually used. (But please note that rope techniques are called *Hojo-Jutsu*.)

In the Christian religion the scepter is used for restraining, in Buddhism Buddha used the Chakra and the *Fudomyo-oh* (Protector of the Heavens) holds a rope in his left hand, showing that the idea of restraint has existed since the times of the Gods.

Tying up only using the power of the mind is called *Fudo-Kanashibari no Jutsu*. With spirit power it is called *Toate no Jutsu*. These two are explained in the next section. I will try to explain the usual type of *Hobaku-Jutsu*, especially the *Ninja*'s *Hobaku-Jutsu*. A *Ninja* must be able to untie himself (*Nawanuke*) as well as tie someone up securely. These techniques are used with *Taihen-Jutsu*, *Hicho-Jutsu*, *Kosshi-Jutsu*, *Koppo-Jutsu*, *Shuriken-Jutsu*, etc.

While I was in the *Tokyo* Metropolitan Police Department, I used these techniques to apprehend criminals, drunkards and ruffians, and they were very effective. With this practical experience behind me, I am convinced that the *Ninja*'s *Hobaku-Jutsu* is the best.

The *Ninja* used a tool called the *Kaginawa* (one of the six main *Ninja* tools '*Shinobi-Rikugu*') for tying people up. The true meaning of *Kaginawa* is a tool of someone traveling incognito (a *Shinobi*) for climbing up and down trees, walls and valleys and for carrying other tools. Sometimes it was used for entering an enemy's territory, which was its original purpose. But other times it was used as a martial weapon for battling an enemy or tying someone up. The following examples are ways in which it was actually used.

Hobaku-Jutsu (by 'Sekai no Keibatsu')

The *Ninja* used a hook as the weight with the other end of the rope tied to the hand guard of the sword. He held the sword in his left hand and twirled the hook with his right. This is in fact an adhoc *Kusarigama*.

Another way was to tie the ends of the rope to *Shuriken* and twirl both ends with both hands, like a Chinese rope dart (Piao).

When battling at close quarters, the *Ninja* escaped from the enemy's sword cuts with *Taihen-Jutsu*, suddenly produced the *Kaginawa* concealed in his clothing and hooked it either in the enemy's mouth or hair knot. He then pulled on the rope and used the rope to tie the enemy up. The *Edo* period police used these techniques; however they did not hook the mouth but the shoulder or elbow instead.

An interesting technique used on a forest path at night with the enemy approaching on horse was to tie a rope across the path and dangle from it many strings with hooks just above the level of a horse's head. If he only had one *Kaginawa*, the *Ninja* tied it across the path at the level of the horse's knees as a trip wire, or at the level of the enemy's neck. If the enemy was moving quickly, the effectiveness was increased. Recently someone used this technique to try to deter motorcycle gangs, killing a member in the process. Never do this. Never!

The *Ninja* sometimes used the hand towel or the sash of a sword instead of the *Kaginawa* and chemicals (such as blinding powders *'Metsubushi'* or *'Shibire-Gusuri'*) to help catch the enemy. There are also correct ways of catching someone, as well as specialized tools with their own ways of being used, but it would take too long to explain here.

In conclusion, a *Ninja* must not be preoccupied with the thought of being caught or catching another.

11
HOBAKU-
JUTSU
「捕縛術」
NAWANUKE-
JUTSU
「縄抜け術」

Hobaku-Jutsu (by 'Sekai no Keibatsu')

B.
NAWANUKE-JUTSU 「縄抜け術」
(BOUND ESCAPE TECHNIQUES)

Nawanuke-Jutsu is the ways of untying oneself. When I visited Atlanta's Dekab Police Department in the United States in September 1976, I was introduced to a lieutenant who reminded me of the actor Yule Brunner, because of his shaven head. He said, "You say you are a *Ninja* master, so I shall tie you up with a special nylon cord that has a metal wire inside. If you are able to escape, I will show you all the secret parts of the department". I was a young master then and so I replied, "Okay, I'll try," and watched him tying my wrists as he laughed. Sarcastically he added, "If you can't escape from this, I'll take you around the way you are," to which I told him to watch me carefully to not miss anything. "On the count of three I shall be free. One, two, three," I said and smoothly removed the cord from my wrists. He was amazed but kept his promise and showed me many things in the department, as well as introducing me to the chiefs and making me an honorary policeman.

On another occasion, a military officer attached to the Israeli Embassy in Japan came to the *Dojo*. He was an expert on tying people up in the army and boasted, "Until now I have tied up many people and none have managed to free themselves". I could see very well that he was not lying, that he was a member of the embassy staff and also a person who enjoyed fighting for real. I wanted to avoid his offer of tying me up, but due to certain circumstances, I could not. He began to tie me with my hands behind my back in a criss-cross fashion. Normally I can feel when I can or cannot free myself, and on this occasion I knew I could. In three minutes I freed myself, making him very surprised. He then began shaking my hands and offering his congratulations. However, I am not the type of person who feels pride when I achieve something like this; this is the work of circus men.

The techniques of *Nawanuke-Jutsu* are very good but they do depend largely on the way in which one is tied, the person doing the tying and the type of cord used. In olden times, in Japan, people were sometimes crucified, and in combat there are ways of tying that will cause the captive to die and others that will not allow him to die. Training in how to tie and escape is very important, especially for young women, mothers and children who can easily find themselves in dangerous situations.

During the children's class at my dojo, I have often tried to teach them this and frequently they have burst into tears because they could not free their wrists. But after a while, they become very skillful indeed. Almost all of them never had the feeling of giving up, even when they were suffering from rope burns. One of the most pleasurable incidents that I remember is that of an eight-year-old boy who cried out, "There is no such thing as giving up for the *Ninja*". I also hope you can attain this type of attitude.

Nawanuke-Jutsu not only involves escaping from ropes; there are also times when someone or something has tied up one's heart or spirit and one must get free. Mastering this *Nawanuke-Jutsu* of the heart makes one a true *Ninja* martial artist.

12.
KIAI-JUTSU 「気合術」
(POWER YELLING TECHNIQUES)

In *Ninpo* there are three main types of powerful yelling techniques referred to collectively as '*Sansei Hiden no Ho* 三声秘伝の法'.

① *Shosei no Kiai* (勝声の気合) :

This *Kiai* or powerful yell is for breaking an attacker's spirit to make him feel he has already failed so he is unable to attack again. It is pronounced '*YA*', and for it to work properly it must be well timed; this is done by reading his heart. If an attacker receives this *Kiai*, he will find all his body power drained. It also works well with cats and dogs, making them unable to move.

② *Kosei no Kiai* (攻声の気合) :

This *Kiai*, pronounced '*AA*', means 'now I'll attack you'; the attacker is made to think that his weak point has been found, making him feel insecure and unsafe. His posture then deteriorates.

③ *Chisei no Kiai* (知声の気合) :

When an attacker is about to execute a technique, the use of this *Kiai* will make him think that you already know what his technique will be. His heart as well as his posture will deteriorate at this point you should do a technique of your own. This *Kiai* is pronounced '*TOWA*'.

Once, one of my foreign students asked me to teach him *Kiai-Jutsu* and I did this particular one on him. His face turned blue and his body slumped. When I asked him what was wrong, he replied, "When you did the *Kiai*, I felt my body jump back a meter and my heart seemed to stop. This is a really amazing technique. I now understand this *Kiai* well."

There are ways of using these three forms of *Kiai* together without having to use the voice; with just a *Kiai* of the heart one can paralyze an attacker. This type of *Kiai* is called Kage no *Kiai* (literally 'shadow *Kiai*') or *Toate no Jutsu* (hitting from afar). To be able to use these techniques you need plenty of training and patience.

From *Takamatsu Sensei* comes a very interesting story about this concerning an attacker who was defeated not only with *Kiai*:

"Once two martial artists from the *Sekiguchi-Ryu* (*Jujutsu*) came to *Toda Shinryuken Sensei* (*Takamatsu Sensei*'s Grandmaster) seeking a true fight. Present at that time was a colleague of mine who was 37 years old but, although he had a powerful, well-built body, he was not skillful since he did not train much, however, he did enjoy fighting. One side of his face bore a burn scar. He refused to listen to the advice of *Toda Sensei* or any of the Senpai seniors to stop, and went out and stood in the middle of the *Dojo* facing one of the visitors. After bowing to each other, they both leapt back into a ready stance, staring into each other's eyes. He then opened his eyes as wide as possible, made his scar seem bigger, and yelled '*YAAAH*', stamping his foot on the ground. The *Sekiguchi-Ryu* man, his heart drained, said, 'I give up'. This is a part of *Kosei no Kiai*."

Takamatsu Sensei then added, "To be a true martial artist, one needs '*Banpen-fugyo* 万変不驚', which means that whenever techniques or circumstances are changing, one must never be surprised or scared. One must remain constantly on a single path with an immovable spirit. It is important to have this kind of spirit. This is the truth of the martial arts.

To-Ate no Jutsu

13.
KUJIKIRI:
JUMON 「呪文」, KETSUIN 「結印」
AND GOFU 「護符」

A.
JUMON AND KETSUIN
(INCANTATION AND FINGER ENTWINING)

I have already explained the relationship between *Jumon* and *Ketsuin* mind control techniques. In this chapter I will explain how to do them. Each finger, from the little finger to the thumb, is respectively called *'Chi* 地*'* (Earth), *'Sui* 水*'* (Water), *'Ka* 火*'* (Fire), *'Fu* 風*'* (Wind) and *'Ku* 空*'* (meaning Sky here but at other times Air; it never means Void). The following examples show how to form some in (finger formations).

With the index and middle fingers of your left hand together and pointing upward, clasp the little finger and ring finger to the palm of the hand with the thumb. Hold the two fingers with the right hand (with it's index and middle fingers also straight but pointing to the left). Then place the right thumb on one or both of the two fingers (*Fu* and *Ka*). At this point start to control your mind and channel it. Once this is completed, place your left hand against your hip with the two fingers pointing forwards and place your right hand's fingers into those of the left hand as if putting a sword into its scabbard. The right hand is now called *To-In* (the sword in). Draw it from its 'scabbard' and do a series of cutting motions to either the enemy or to the sky (if there is no enemy). The motions alternate between horizontal cuts (left to right) and vertical cuts (up to down), a total of nine strokes. While doing the motions call out their names: *Rin, Pyo, To, Sha, Kai, Jin, Retsu, Zai* and *Zen*. Do a tenth stroke at the end, like writing a tick (レ), while calling out 'Un'.

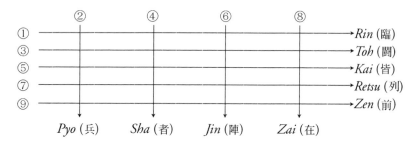

The cutting motions are all done in the same place and it is these that we call *'Kujikiri* 九字切り*'* (*Ku* means nine; *Ji* from the word *'Kanji'* means Chinese character; and *Kiri* means cuts).

The number nine is very significant in the philosophy of most martial arts. It is considered the highest and most complete number. If you do the following arithmetic,

$$1 \times 9 = 09 \rightarrow 0 + 9 = 9$$
$$2 \times 9 = 18 \rightarrow 1 + 8 = 9$$
$$3 \times 9 = 27 \rightarrow 2 + 7 = 9$$
$$\vdots \quad \vdots \quad \vdots \quad \vdots \quad \vdots \quad \vdots$$

the answer is always nine. This holds true for all whole numbers. Our solar system is a sun surrounded by nine planets (Mercury, Venus, Earth, Mars, Jupiter, Saturn, Uranium, Neptune and Pluto), and nine is the highest single-digit number. The mathematicians of ancient Greece thought it an unusual number with magical powers. The old Japanese religions of *Shugendo* and *Mikkyo* as well as *Ninpo* also subscribed to this idea.

13
KUJIKIRI:
JUMON
「呪文」
KETSUIN
「結印」
GOFU
「護符」

After the *Kujikiri* one can do the *Jumon* or an In. For example, it was commonly believed in olden times that saying *'Ga-Ko-Rai-To-Sha-Akuma-Fudo'* would stop an enemy in his tracks. *Un-Ka-Mo-Ta-Ru-Che-Tsu-Pi-Pa* is a *Jumon* that can be used in any situation. In the *Baku-In* there are three secret styles (*Sanpo-Hiden*): *Tenryaku Uchu Gassho, Chiryaku Futen Goshin Gassho* and *Jinryaku Chi-Sui-Ka-Fu Henka Ryoku* (*Hanno-Bon-Itsu Gassho*). For example, *'Tenryaku Uchu Gassho* 天略宇宙合掌*'* is formed by clasping both hands together and using mind control. It means peace and harmony (since all elements of both the right and left hands are united equally), and there is, therefore, no desire to fight.

There is also the *Juji Kiri* (*Ju* means ten). The true *Ninja* had discovered a number much more powerful and far more important than nine. This was ten. Both hands have five fingers; with the hands clasped together, there are a total of ten. If the right hand is considered yang (*Yo*) and the left ying (*In*), then they are together in perfect harmony (ying-yang). Zero is a very powerful number; multiplying it with any other number, no matter how large, always gives zero. Zero is an actual number and not simply nothing. Ten is the union of both one (1) and zero (0). So for this reason I, together with some astronomers, believe that in the near future a tenth planet will be discovered.

Futen Goshin no In

Fudo Kanashibari no In

Suirin Gassho In

Katon Ketsu In

The '*Kunoichi* く ノ 一'(female *Ninja*) also play a part in this philosophy. In Japanese the word '*Onna*' (female) is written using the Chinese character 女 which can be broken down into the following:

女→く (a Japanese *Hiragana* character pronounced '*Ku*', meaning 'nine')

女→ノ (a Japanese *Katakana* character pronounced '*No*', meaning 'of' or 'and')

女→一 (a *Kanji* character pronounced '*Ichi*', meaning one)

Put together as く ノ 一, they are pronounced *Kunoichi*, meaning one of nine. However, its true meaning is 9 + 1 or 10.

The human body has nine holes: two eyes, two nostrils, two ears, one mouth, one anterior and one posterior. However, a woman has an extra tenth one that is very powerful. When used properly it has the same effect as the power of Zero; look at the effect Matahari had.

In *Jumon*, *Kujikiri* may be used but *Juji Kiri* is forbidden because of its immense power. If a person who does not have a superior personality uses it, he will injure himself with it. In Japan there is a proverb that says:

"If you wish a bad thing to happen to someone, not only do you create

a pit for him to fall into, but also one for yourself."

There are ways of making this *Jumon Baku-In* ineffective when it is being used against you, however, this is impossible to teach in a book. This is a *Kuden*, something taught by word of mouth only.

13
KUJIKIRI:
JUMON
「呪文」
KETSUIN
「結印」
GOFU
「護符」

B.
GOFU
(TALISMANS)

I want to say something about good-luck charms, talismans, etc. (*Gofu*). A *Gofu* of the *Shingon Mikkyo* (a Japanese Buddhist religion) is usually a piece of paper with one or more mysterious Chinese characters written on it to be carried on one's person constantly so that God and Buddha can guide one safely through life.

Some people consider these things a total waste of time, others say that believing in them makes the mind stronger and therefore alters situations without one being aware of it, and still others say that they really do work because by wearing them, one is in constant contact with God and Buddha and is therefore guided away from danger, etc. As for me, I cannot say that these beliefs are superstition but I also cannot say I believe all of them. Things such as *Jumon* and *Gofu* are sometimes poisonous, sometimes like a medicine, depending on how they are used. It also depends on the state the person's heart, and the quality of and objectives in life.

People who sell these *Gofu* give a variety of promises, depending on what is written on the paper. The following are a few examples:

If you wear this *Gofu* you will be able to escape from any unnatural danger:

覧 戟 喼 急 如 律 令

躬 鬼 喼 急 如 律 令

If it is written in the following manner:

尻 朋朋朋 國 樂 有 疋 念

date
name (your own)
name (another person)

with the date, the name of another person and your own, it has a different effect depending on how it is used. If you fold it, then place it on your body, it signifies a deeper relationship with the other person. If it is left unfolded, it signifies a deteriorating relationship with the named person. The choice is entirely up to you.

This one helps keep peace within a family or a friendship:

又 鬼 喼 急 如 律 令

This one is especially for a woman who wants to get married or fall in love:

叕 尻 皿 喼 急 如 律 令

This *Gofu* protects you from all accidents and injuries. It is made by mixing your blood with red ink, writing the following on a sheet of red silk, then placing it near the heart:

畢 鍏 品 軍 喼 急如律令 卌 ☆

畢 鍏 品 軍 喼 急 如 律 令 卌

舍 譜 甲 㕔 喼 急 如 律 令 卌

Finally, this one is a protection against sexually transmitted diseases:

屍 腳 腳 腳 唵 急 如 律 令
萌 䀹 胆 胆 唵 急 如 律 令

Kujikiri and *Jumon* from a *Ninjutsu* Scroll

14.
AIZU AND ANGO JUTSU 「合図・暗号術」
(SIGNALLING TECHNIQUES)

Aizu are ways of making secret signals, such as by using smoke, a mirror or another shiny metal object, flags, colored rice, or noise such as from a shell horn, hand held-drum, large drum, or bell. There are actually many ways but here I will concentrate on the written aspects.

The written Japanese language consists of *Kanji* characters that originally came from China as well as two other sets of characters collectively called *Kana*. A *Kanji* may be made up of just a single character or two or more. These components are called radicals.

I will now explain the written code (*Ango*) called *Shinobi Iroha* from the *Iga* region. The following *Kanji* are used as left radicals:

木 (tree); 火 (fire); 土 (earth); 金 (gold); 水 (water); 人 (person); 身 (body)

Another group of *Kanji* are used as right radicals:

色 (color); 青 (blue); 黄 (yellow); 赤 (red); 白 (white); 黒 (black); and 紫 (purple).

These are then combined to make new *Kanji* that are not used in Japanese (or Chinese) and put into rows and columns as follows. The rows are for the 'material' *Kanji* and the columns are for the colors. The corresponding *Kana* and its equivalent in the Roman alphabet are given under each set of radicals.

栬 い(i)	精 ち(chi)	横 よ(yo)	栭 ら(ra)	柏 や(ya)	標 あ(a)	襟 ゑ(we)
炮 ろ(ro)	熿 り(ri)	壙 た(ta)	焭 む(mu)	焰 ま(ma)	爅 さ(sa)	燦 ひ(hi)
土色 は(ha)	堵 ぬ(nu)	壊 れ(re)	坾 う(u)	坧 け(ke)	壂 き(ki)	壖 も(mo)
鉋 に(ni)	錆 る(ru)	鑛 そ(so)	鈳 ゐ(wi)	鉑 ふ(fu)	鏍 ゆ(yu)	鑗 せ(se)
氵色 ほ(ho)	清 を(wo)	潢 つ(tsu)	泋 の(no)	泊 こ(ko)	氵黒 め(me)	潫 す(su)
亻色 へ(he)	倩 わ(wa)	横 ね(ne)	侊 お(o)	伯 え(e)	偶 み(mi)	襟 ん(n)
身色 と(to)	鯖 か(ka)	黌 な(na)	跡 く(ku)	䶍 て(te)	䮾 し(shi)	紫

(a pronounciation modifier)

PART IV:
NINPO TECHNIQUES

This chart should be read from top to bottom and from left to right. So for example, if someone writes: '僙洂泊躰標潢焔墴', it would not normally be understood. But a *Ninja* who knows the code can decipher it as *'Nenokoku Atsumare'* which translated into English means, 'we will meet at midnight'.

Another example is *Shichiji no Kana* from the *Kenshin-Ryu*. There are two types of Japanese *Kana*, *Hiragana* and *Katakana*, each comprising a total of 48 characters. *Hiragana* is used in this example. They are divided into seven groups as follows with the y-axis reading, *'Mikataso Tsuyoki'* (meaning 'we are very strong') and the x-axis reading *'Tekiwa Horofuru'* (meaning 'the enemy will lose').

y-axis / x-axis	て (te)	き (ki)	は (wa)	ほ (ho)	ろ (ro)	ふ (fu)	る (ru)
み (mi)	い (i)	ち (chi)	よ (yo)	ら (ra)	や (ya)	あ (a)	ゑ (we)
か (ka)	ろ (ro)	り (ri)	た (ta)	む (mu)	ま (ma)	さ (sa)	ひ (hi)
た (ta)	は (ha)	ぬ (nu)	れ (re)	う (u)	け (ke)	き (ki)	も (mo)
そ (so)	に (ni)	る (ru)	そ (so)	ゐ (wi)	ふ (fu)	ゆ (yu)	せ (se)
つ (tsu)	ほ (ho)	を (wo)	つ (tsu)	の (no)	こ (ko)	め (me)	す (su)
よ (yo)	へ (he)	わ (wa)	ね (ne)	お (o)	え (e)	み (mi)	ん (n)
き (ki)	と (to)	か (ka)	な (na)	く (ku)	て (te)	し (shi)	

And so if someone writes 'そてたろ゛ みは' again no one would understand it except someone who was familiar with the code. Decoded, it means *'Nigero'* or 'let's get away'.

These are but examples and there are many other ways of doing this, for example:

	1	2	3	4	5
1	あ (a)	い (i)	う (u)	え (e)	お (o)
2	か (ka)	き (ki)	く (ku)	け (ke)	こ (ko)
3	さ (sa)	し (shi)	す (su)	せ (se)	そ (so)
4	た (ta)	ち (chi)	つ (tsu)	て (te)	と (to)
5	な (na)	に (ni)	ぬ (nu)	ね (ne)	の (no)
6	は (ha)	ひ (hi)	ふ (fu)	へ (he)	ほ (ho)
7	ま (ma)	み (mi)	む (mu)	め (me)	も (mo)
8	や (ya)		ゆ (yu)		よ (yo)
9	ら (ra)	り (ri)	る (ru)	れ (re)	ろ (ro)
10	わ (wa)	ゐ (wi)	ゑ (we)	を (wo)	ん (n)

With this, the coded message 16 29 44 11 51 31 can be decoded as 'Pari de Aou' or 'see you in Paris'. These ways are very good now for letters such as love letters, making them very good for couples.

15.
HO-JUTSU 「法術」
(ILLUSION TECHNIQUES)

It is sometimes thought that *Ho-Jutsu* only consists of techniques of hermits and aesthetics, that it is magical, or that it involves some mysterious power. In olden times it was even considered to be *Ninpo*. However, *Ho-Jutsu* is but one part of *Ninpo*. And *Ho-Jutsu* has never actually been mysterious; it is academic knowledge. A few examples follow which I hope you are not tempted to use just to be a showman.

To make a frog fall a sleep, turn it upside down with one hand and stroke it with the other. It will then stay motionless with its legs apart. This also applies to dogs and cats when they are massaged. However, if you massage the frog too much, its stomach will inflate and consequently burst so do not do this. You must be kind to the frog.

With a common snake, hold it by the back of the head, and stroke the entire length of its body with the other hand. The control point of an elephant is its ear. If you can demonstrate your understanding of the habits and weak point of animals, then to the average bystander it will seem that you have performed a miracle.

The demonstrations shown on television and in theatres involving chickens and small birds are explained later in the section on *Kinton no Jutsu*. A person making a 'human bridge' between two chairs and then having a colleague sit on him or smash a concrete slab on his stomach with a sledgehammer is also not performing a miracle. Anyone can do this. The important thing is to arch your spine so that it can support a large weight. And the person hitting with the sledgehammer must hit the concrete dead on.

Breaking rocks with a *Shuto* is done by merely holding the rock in one hand above a hard surface and then doing the chop. The rock breaks by being smashed onto the surface. Sometimes a person strokes a red-hot iron rod, making a scorching sound, yet his hand is unharmed. This too is *Ho-Jutsu* and there is a theory behind it. The human skin is usually humid; tiny droplets of water protect the hand when it passes down the rod in a uniform motion. Coating the hand with salt produces an impressive noise, making the demonstration even more dramatic, as well as helping to insulate the hand further. Ceremonies in Japan in which priests walk over red-hot charcoal are also based on the same theory, since they always throw salt before walking. The ways of emerging the hand in boiling water or oil, thrashing a priest with leaves that have just been removed from boiling water, and placing a lit candle in the mouth also rely on the same basic theory.

Kaen Kugatachi Jutsu

Passing needles through the body is done by passing them through the parts of the skin where there is little or no pain as well as between the bloodroots. They must be driven right through the skin to minimize the pain. Once *Takamatsu Sensei* pushed a sewing needle into a vein in his wrist and moved it vigorously, smiling at the people around him. We were all very surprised, but I understood very clearly that at that time he was trying to convey to me a simple message: one must not only concentrate on martial art theories, but one must also be very bold. *Ho-Jutsu* techniques such as these have their secret points and theories, but if one has no knowledge of them, one cannot understand them let alone do them. However, it is important to train a lot and to be very bold.

There are people who can walk on the cutting edge of a Japanese sword (*Katana*), or tie it firmly to their face or hand, then pull the blade out without cutting themselves. This is possible simply because the *Katana* has a unique construction. If you try this with a Western razor, you will surely cut yourself. If you wish to try these techniques, by all means feel free to ask me. They are not merely techniques of hermits and ascetics.

There are also ways of cutting a banana or orange with only a yell (*Kiai*); however a needle and thread are used beforehand to cut it. As well as the tricks and theories in *Ho-Jutsu*, there is also the high risk of danger to take into consideration. Courage is the essence. There are many other things like the examples given in *Ho-Jutsu*, but they are impossible to explain in a book.

Hikui Jutsu

16.
SHINOBI-SHOZOKU 「忍び装束」
(NINJA EQUIPMENT)

A.
SHINOBI-GI 「忍び着」
(NINJA UNIFORM)

When a *Ninja* had a mission to perform, such as infiltrating an enemy camp, he usually wore the *Ninja* uniform (*Shinobi-Gi*). This became the trademark of the *Ninja*.

The underwear was commonly called *Ecchu-Fundoshi*. It was a rectangular piece of white cotton of about 30 to 45cm wide and about 150 to 165cm long with cords attached to each corner. One end was tied round the neck so that the material hung loose in front and the other end was then passed between the legs before being tied round the waist. For going to the toilet, it was first loosened at the neck.

The next thing put on was the jacket (*Dogi* or *Uwagi*), a *Kimono*-style jacket coming to the waist. The sleeves were wide so that things could be carried in them but when this was not necessary, they could be wrapped around the arms and fastened with buttons. Inside were many pockets (mainly one on each breast and one on the side of each waist) for carrying variety of utensils such as an iron or copper mirror (in the left breast pocket), a hand towel (in the right breast pocket), *Shuriken* (in the left waist pocket) and paper (in the right waist pocket). The trousers were called *Iga-bakama*, these were exactly the same as those worn by the farmers in the *Iga* and *Koga* regions. The legs were narrow and the waist very large so that one size fit all. The excess on the sides was wrapped around the front before being tied. At the back was a small pocket for either *Shuriken* or a small shovel (*Shikoro*).

Shinobi Shozoku

The sash (*Obi*) was worn around the waist for carrying the sword. Sometimes the sash contained concealed chain mail. The forearm guards (*Tekko*) had clasps that were fastened around the forearm. This too had a small pocket for *Shuriken*.

The one-peace hood (*Fukumen*) was a rectangular piece of cloth about 2.1 m long and 24 cm wide. The center part was put on the head and the sides were wrapped round the neck, then the back of the head, over the mouth and nose and finally fastened at the back of the head. There was also a two-piece hood, each piece being about 90 cm long and 45 cm long. One piece was use to cover the head and was fastened under the chin, the second piece was used to cover the mouth and nose. The two pieces had a variety of uses, for example as a bandage, a rope for climbing down or tying up a captured enemy, or even as a utility bag for carrying several weapons at a time. The two-piece is my favorite because it is very practical.

The split-toed socks (*Tabi*) had silk padding under the soles to protect the feet from dangerous objects on the ground. In winter, they helped keep the feet warm and also aided a silent entry into an enemy's fortifications. The sandals (*Waraji*) were made of cotton or leather with three or four little spikes protruding from them to prevent slipping. The leg wraps (*Kyahan*) for the lower legs were constructed in a similar way to the forearm guards and also had pockets for *Shuriken*.

A *Ninja* also carried a coat called a *Haori*. It was a reversible coat with the outside the same color as the rest of the suit and the inside another color such as red or white. Sometimes he wore two so that if the enemy gave chase, he could place one of the coats on a rock or tree. If the enemy attacked it, the *Ninja* had enough time to run away. Sometimes it was thrown at the eyes of an enemy and at other times, according to legend, it was used as a kind of parachute.

The best color for the *Ninja* uniform was red/black, made by a special process called Suhozome. In olden times, the *Ninja* believed that by drinking water from a towel of this color, they would be protected from poisoned water. The uniform was not only worn, but was also used for a variety of purposes, for example as a weapon, tool, or water filter.

Shinobi Shozoku

B.
SHINOBI-KATANA 「忍び刀」
(THE NINJA SWORD)

The *Ninja* usually felt uncomfortable without their swords (*Shinobi-Katana* or *Ninja-To*). They used two types, one with a straight blade and the other with a curved blade. The former was very good for thrusts while the latter was excellent for cutting. The straight blade was very popular during the *Nara* period (710 - 760 A.D.) when most swords carried by the nobility were also straight. After that, when sword makers began producing the curved type, the *Ninja* also began adopting it until there were very few straight blades. The *Ninja* never used straight swords during battle; they considered curved ones better weapons to fight with. I too think the curved bladed is better because if a *Ninja* walked down a street wearing a straight one, it was the same as advertising himself.

The blade itself was made of steel and, whether straight of curved, it was usually about 54 cm long. The hand guard (*Tsuba*) was normally the same as any other, so as not to attract attention, but was slightly bigger and thicker than the conventional ones. The tip of the scabbard (*Kojiri*) was made of strong steel and the sash (*Sageo*) was longer than usual, so that when the sword was used as an aid in climbing walls, the *Sageo* could be clenched in the teeth. The tip also could sometimes be removed by twisting it, allowing the scabbard (*Saya*) be used as a snorkel or, with a special accessory as a poison-water gun. The reason the blade was so short was that it was practical for fighting in narrow, confined areas such as in lofts or under the floor. The tip of the scabbard could conceal blinding powder (*Metsubushi*).

There were seven ways of using the *Sageo*, commonly known as *Sageo Nana Jutsu*. For example, for climbing a wall it was held in the teeth and for fighting it served to bind the sleeves of the *Kimono* to give more freedom. The *Shinobi-Katana* is the last piece of the *Ninja* costume to be put on. I do not understand why people think it should have a special design or construction; any sword a *Ninja* used was called a *Ninja-To* or *Shinobi-Katana* (*Ninja* sword) even if it was a *Shoto* or a *Daito*.

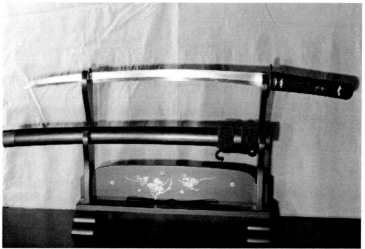

Ninja-To

C.
SHINOBI-RIKUGU 「忍び六具」
(SIX BASIC NINJA TOOLS)

When a *Ninja* was on a mission, he usually carried six basic tools collectively called *Shinobi-Rikugu*;

a. *Amigasa* 「編笠」:

A straw hat which was very good for concealing the face but giving the wearer an unobstructed view. It was a very common hat that attracted little or no attention. It was used to transport secret letters, to catch food and, when folded in half, to carry small weapons and explosives. Sometimes it was used as a *Shuriken*.

b. *Kaginawa* 「鉤縄」:

This was a rope about 8.4 m long made of women's hair with a two-pointed grappling hook called an *Uchi-Kagi* attached to one end. The *Uchi-Kagi* was made of steel and had a hole at the base through which the rope was threaded. It was used for climbing, tying up an enemy or even as a trip-wire.

c. *Sekihitsu* 「石筆」:

This was a chalkstone used for writing something on a tree, wall, etc. which was erased by the *Ninja*'s colleagues after they had read it. It was also used as a stone *Shuriken* (*Tsubute*). Another type commonly used was a brush and an inkpot kept in a small carrying case (*Yatate*).

d. *Kusuri* 「薬」:

A *Ninja* usually carried a small case with a large variety of medicines such as a restorative (*Kitsuke-Gusuri*), ointments for wounds (*So-Yaku*), ointments for insect bites (*Chu-Yaku*), suicide capsule which were sometimes used on the enemy (*Doku-Yaku*), explosive powder (*Baku-Yaku*), a poison antidote (*Gedoku-Yaku*), indigestion medicines (*Icho-Yaku*), compact pellets of food rations (*Hyorogan*) and thirst quencher (*Kikatsugan*). All were carried in only one small box with many compartments (*Inro*) or a small leather pouch tied to the body.

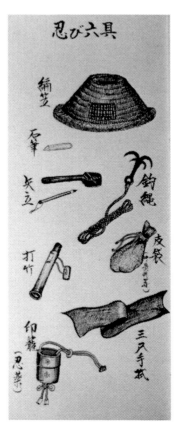

Shinobi Rikugu

e. *Sanjaku Tenugui* 「三尺手拭い」:

A small three-foot towel usually carried in a pocket or in the sash (*Obi*). It was used for many things, for example as a mask (*Fukumen*), water filter, sweatband, *Kusari-Fundo* (a chain about three feet long for fighting), a bandage or climbing aid when slapped wet over a small wall. The *Ninja* were very practical and saw a large number of applications from a single thing: any weapon can be used in combination with *Ninpo Taijutsu*.

f. *Uchi-Take* 「打ち竹」:

Also called a *Donohi* or *Tsuketake*, this was a small, portable, bamboo hand warmer which was also used to ignite explosives, light fires, etc. It was normally strapped to the outside of the sash but in winter, it was carried inside the sash. In summer, the insides of the *Uchi-Take* were removed and used either as a water bottle or to transport insects. To scare people off, the *Ninja* wore 'devil masks' and made it appear as if they were spitting fire.

The reason why this collection is called *'Rikugu'* originates from the Buddhist ideology called *Rikudo Shiso*. This says that man must go through six different worlds:

① *Jigoku-Kai* 「地獄界」: The world with no mutual trust
② *Gaki-Kai* 「餓鬼界」: The world of the eternally hungry and thirsty
③ *Chikusho-Kai* 「畜生界」: The world of the half-man/half animal
④ *Shura-Kai* 「修羅界」: The devil's world where everyone is eternally angry
⑤ *Ningen-Kai* 「人間界」: The human world
⑥ *Tenjo-Kai* 「天上界」: Heaven

The *Ninja* thought that by having these six tools they could go anywhere, no matter how dangerous. However, *Takamatsu Sensei* taught that one had to carry an extra item a bamboo walking staff containing a concealed weapon (*Yonshaku Shikomi Chikujo*), connecting it with men's seven reincarnations (*Shichisho*) or "lucky seven".

17.
NINKI AND NINGU 「忍器・忍具」
(NINJA TOOLS AND WEAPONS)

A.
TOKI 「登器」
(CLIMBING TOOLS)

Toki are tools for climbing up and down trees and walls. They include the *Kaginawa*, *Kasugai*, *Kunai*, *Shuko*, *Nekode*, *Kakushi*, *Shinobi-Zue*, *Shinobi Kumade*, *Ipponsugi*, *Shinobi-Gatana*, *Rikuzen* and *Hashigo*.

a. *Kaginawa* 「鉤縄」:

The *Kaginawa* is simply a length of rope with a hook at one end.

b. *Kasugai* 「鎹」:

The *Kasugai* is an implement used by both the *Samurai* and *Ninja* which stopped two sliding screens from opening. It's secondary use for the *Ninja* was either as a climbing tool or weapon.

c. *Kunai* 「苦無」:

The *Kunai* was originally for breaking objects but the *Ninja* also used it as a shovel, and when tied to one end of a rope, for climbing (when used this way it is called a *'Tobi-Kunai'*). When covered with straw, ignited and thrown onto a roof, it was called a *Tobi-Taimatsu*. Of course, it was also used as a weapon.

d. *Shinobi-Zue* 「忍び杖」:

The *Shinobi-Zue* is a length of bamboo (about 1.5 m long) with an iron hook attached to one end. It has five or six holes drilled through it, through which a piece of rope is tied.

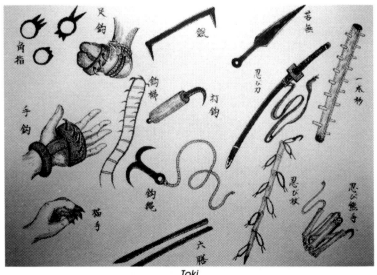

Toki

e. *Shinobi Kumade* 「忍び熊手」:

The *Shinobi Kumade* is another climbing tool made of five or six pieces of bamboo, each about 30 cm long. A rope with a grappling hook is threaded through them and a knot tied. When the rope is pulled tight, the climbing tool becomes a staff.

f. *Ipponsugi* 「一本杉」:

The *Ipponsugi* is a tube between 21 and 24 cm long with three rows of spikes. A rope with a hook on both ends is threaded through the tube.

g. *Shinobi-Gatana* 「忍び刀」:

The *Ninja* sword (*Shinobi-Gatana*) can be used in many ways. One example is resting the sword against a wall, holding the tip of its sash (*Sageo*) in the teeth and stepping onto the hand guard (*Tsuba*) to climb over a wall. Another way is threading the *Sageo* through the little hole in the *Tsuba*, throwing the sword over a wall or tree and then climbing using the *Sageo*.

h. *Rikuzen* 「六膳」:

The *Rikuzen* is a set of 12 long metal spikes like chopsticks with a hole at one end through which a rope is threaded. They can be hammered into a tree or stonewall and used as steps for climbing. Tugging the rope from the top of the tree or wall removes the spikes.

i. *Hashigo* 「梯子」:

The *Hashigo* is basically a ladder. There are many types such as the *Musubi-Bashigo*, *Tobi-Bashigo*, *Kumo-Bashigo*, *Nawa-Bashigo*, *Tatami-Bashigo* and *Taka-Bashigo*. Rope ladders were usually made of rope and bamboo. Also included under this heading is the *Kassha* (flying fox).

Tree climbing with *Shuko*

B.
KAIKI 「開器」
(BREAKING AND ENTERING TOOLS)

Kaiki is the collective name for tools used for breaking and entering. These include the *Shikoro, Kunai, Nata, Kama, Nomi, Kiri, Kagi* and *Kuginuki*.

a. *Shikoro* 「錣」:

The *Shikoro* is a steel hand-saw with a very sharp tip. They came in three sizes, small, medium and large, with the small one usually being worn in the clothing. Because of its jagged edge, if it was used to cut an enemy, the wound was very difficult to treat.

b. *Nata* 「鉈」:

The *Nata*, also called the *Yamagatana*, was used for cutting through bamboo, etc. much like a machete.

c. *Kagi* 「鈎」:

The *Kagi* is simply a hook. There were many types such as *Toikaki, Hamagari, Nobekagi, Irikokagi* and *Kakegane-Nuki*. Chisels also come under this heading but are called *Nomi*. *Kuginuki* was a way of using nearly square blades (Senban *Shuriken*) to remove nails and the like.

d. *Kama* 「鎌」:

The *Kama* (sickle or scythe) was also called the *Shinobi-Gama* and was basically the same as a normal sickle or scythe, except that it had two cutting edges. They were either very large or very small and were used for climbing, cutting trip wires and even cutting through the supporting beams of a house.

e. *Kiri* 「錐」:

The *Kiri* has an iron, needle-like tip and a wooden handle for boring holes to allow eavesdropping.

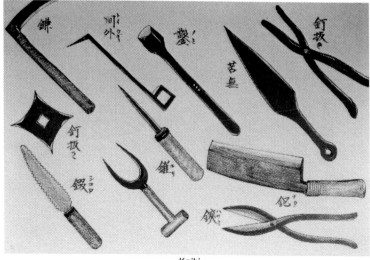

Kaiki

C.
SUIKI 「水器」
(WATER TOOLS)

There are two types of *Suiki* (water-crossing tools), ones used on water and the ones used in water. An example of the former is a raft made of bamboo, wood, *Shino* (similar to but smaller than bamboo), reeds (*Ashi*), pampas grass (*Susuki*), buckets or poles (*Oke*), barrels (*Tsuru*), large ceramic jars (*Kama*), large wooden pounders (*Kine*) or large wooden mortars normally used as a *'Kine'* (*Usu*). The *Mizugumo* (water spider) is an inflatable harness made of either cowhide or rabbit skin used for walking on water. This became a very famous *Ninja* tool because people believed that one could walk on water with it like a water spider. This is actually very difficult to do. The *Ninja* normally sat on it and rowed across the water. For moving many things across a stretch of water, three were lashed together to make a raft.

The *Ukibashi* are types of instant bridges. There are two main types: one has two poles covered with pampas grass, and the other is two lengths of rope held at both sides of the bank by hooks which the *Ninja* used to wade across a body of water by holding onto the ropes to stop him from being washed downstream. Another way was to put pampas grass across the ropes and walk on it.

Tools used in the water include the Mizukaki (a wooden sandal with a large piece of wood hinged on the sole so that when the foot was pushed backwards, the piece of wood acted as a fin. This was used together with the *Mizugumo*.

A variation of the *Mizugumo* is the Hyotan, a lifejacket made with gourds sewn into a coat. The *Shinobi-Bune*, also known as the *Hasami Hakobune*, was a portable boat.

Other things such as a snorkel made of bamboo with a hole drilled through it or a scabbard (*Saya*) were also used. However, it was vital to block the nose to prevent the entry of water. These tools were sometimes used as water guns or flutes for signaling.

Swimming techniques included the breast-stroke (*Hira Oyogi*), treading water (*Tachi Oyogi*), and swimming on the river bed (*Moguri*). In these techniques it is important to move silently. An average *Ninja* was able to remain under-water for two or three minutes.

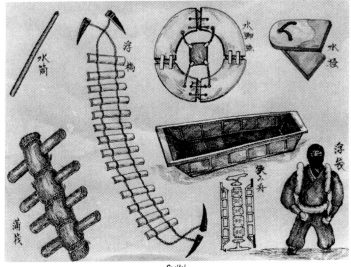

Suiki

D.
KAKI 「火器」
(FIRE TOOLS)

Kaki (fire tools) and their techniques increased the *Ninja*'s power, mostly because in olden times everyone was afraid of fire.

Noroshi is a technique of using smoke for signaling. It used to be called *Tobuhi* or *Ho* and was done using a mixture of branches, straw, rice stalks, mugwort, and either reeds or wolf faeces. Wolf faeces were very important because, as with mouse faeces, the smoke they emit rises straight up, not staying close to the ground. Later camphor, sulphur, etc. were used instead of faeces.

During the night, signaling was done using torches (*Taimatsu*) made from pine tree roots and straw. The *Mizu-Taimatsu* was a special torch used on rainy nights. It was prepared with a mixture of camphor, sulphur, and gunpowder and mixed with *Sake* (*Shochu*).

The *Ryusei* was a special signaling torch that worked as a flare. It was a piece of bamboo filled with saltpeter and sulphur.

The *Kemuri-Dama* (smoke ball), also known as a *Torinoko* (special bond), was made from a sphere of special strong paper filled with gunpowder. It was used for both fighting and signaling.

The *Hiya* (fire arrows) included the *Yabiya*, *Uchibiya*, *Tebiya*, *Horokubiya*, *Ishibiya*, *Ohkunibiya* and *Teppobiya*. A *Hiya* was simply an arrow with an explosive charge attached to it (before explosives were known about, oil was used).

The *Horokubiya* was made of two ceramic tea cups sealed together and filled with iron balls and gunpowder. It was used in much the same way as a hand grenade.

The *Ohkunibiya* was a weapon imported from China. It was a type of arrow cannon that had a range of some 500 to 1000 meters. The cannon was made of wood and had an explosive charge inside. A massive arrow with an explosive charge was then placed inside.

The *Higurumaken* was a *Shuriken* with a small explosive charge with a long fuse on it. It was used for attacking, signaling or arson.

The *Uzumebi* was a land mine consisting of a wooden box filled with gunpowder and iron balls laced with poison. It also had a fuse of variable length attached to a lighting mechanism that acted as a time delay.

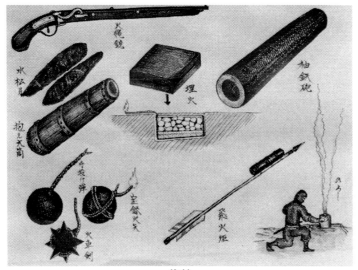

Kaki

The gun was first brought to the Japanese island of *Tanegashima* by the Portuguese on August 25th, 1543. It's Portuguese name was the 'espingarda' but the two types that entered Japan were given the name *Tanegashima-Ju* which spread all over Japan. It was this introduction of the gun that was responsible for ending the warring period. The *Ninja* were very skilful in using the gun and they diligently studied the ways of making gunpowder. During the *Tokugawa* period, many *Ninja* worked in special army gun groups (*Teppo-Gumi*). The *Taiho* (cannon) was also introduced by the Portuguese at about the same time and was known by several names such as *Kunikuzushi, Furoki, Shimoho* and *Harakanzutsu*. The Portuguese called it a 'cahnao'. The normal cannon was made of iron, but a wooden cannon called the *Kakae-Ozutsu* was used.

The *Ninja* also used a small hand held cannon called *Sodezutsu* or *Sode-Teppo* that was 33 cm long and made of either wood or bamboo. Another was the *Shinobi-Bi* that was 75 cm long. This one was buried underground and it's fuse was lit to frighten the enemy when they came close to it.

Later the *Moppan* was used, a chemical substance kept in a glass container that was smashed either on the floor or better still in the enemy's face. It had a powerful smell that produced a variety of effects such as an inability to breathe, sleepiness, or a stream of tears.

Most techniques involving gunpowder came from China, where in the seventh century the Chinese discovered how to mix saltpeter, sulphur and soot. In the 11th century, it was developed as a fire weapon and then in the 13th century it was brought to Europe by Marco Polo. There guns and cannons were invented and used by the English, French, Dutch, Spanish, Portuguese, etc., In the 16th century, the gun and cannon came to Japan.

The Japanese already knew how to make gunpowder long before guns came to Japan, and so too did the *Ninja*; therefore they became very skilful in the gun techniques very soon after guns were introduced.

E.
KAKUSHI BUKI 「隠し武器」
(CONCEALED WEAPONS)

The weapons of people traveling incognito (*Shinobi*) have the collective name of *Ninki* or *Kakushi Buki* (concealed weapons), whereas the tools are given the collective name of *Ningu*.

Ningu are further subdivided into several parts such as *Toki* (climbing tools), *Kaiki* (tools for breaking and entering), *Kaki* (tools for making fire) and *Suiki* (tools for water). *Ningu* were also sometimes used as weapons.

I will give a few examples of *Kakushi Buki*.

a. *Kakushi* 「角指」 (Hidden fingers):

This is a finger ring made of either iron or steel with two to four spikes protruding from it. The ring was worn so that when the hand was closed the spikes could not be seen. It was then used for gouging or catching an enemy's hand, foot, face, etc. It is useless however if one is not skilful in *Taijutsu Muto-Dori*. The *Kakushi* was also used as a climbing tool.

b. *Shuko* 「手鈎」 (Hand claw):

Also called a *Tekko* or *Tekagi*, this is a steel band that fits over the hand with three or four spikes protruding from the palm. It was sometimes used for blocking a sword blow, for attacking an enemy's face or hands, or as a climbing tool (*Toki*). *Shuko Taijutsu* has already been explained in a previous section.

c. *Nekode* 「猫手」 (Cat's nails):

The *Nekode* resembles the tool used by Japanese harp (*Koto*) players, but was made with sharp pieces of iron. They were put on all five fingers and were then used for blocking and attacking. When they were used together with special *Ninja Taijutsu* (*Koppo-Jutsu* or *Kosshi-Jutsu*), the effect was even more devastating. Both the *Kakushi* and the *Nekode* are well suited to the female *Ninja* (*Kunoichi*).

d. *Sokutoki* 「息討器」 (Blowing tools):

This is a small wooden box into which a mixture of poisonous powder was placed. On one side was a mouthpiece through which one blew into and on the opposite side was a small hole which the powder would come out of.

When using this tool, one must be very aware of the weather and ground conditions as well as a master of *Taihen-Jutsu*. A bamboo or paper tube instead of the box is equally effective.

e. *Tekken* 「鉄拳」 (Iron fist):

This is simply a brass knuckles. It encloses by all five fingers and has a guard protecting the hand. The guard had small spheres or spikes sticking out of it. It was mainly used to deliver blows.

After the Second World War, they were commonly known as *Meriken-Sakku* and were often used in street fights.

f. *Kakushi-Bo* 「隠し棒」 (Concealed short staff):

Also known as *Tenouchi*, this is a small cylindrical piece of steel or wood slightly longer than the width of a hand. Some foreigners call them *Yawara*, but this is totally incorrect; the meaning of *Yawara* is '*Jujutsu*'.

Some *Kakushi-Bo* had a small iron ring in the center, which the middle finger was placed through. Sometimes they could be spun. It was used to block a sword blow, attack the enemy or catch his hand or foot.

As a variation, it was sometimes tied to the end of a hand-towel (*Tenugui*) and used as a *Kusari-Fundo*. It could also be placed at the end of a *Kusari-Fundo* itself.

g. *Kusari-Fundo* 「鎖分銅」 (Weighted Chain):

Any combination of a chain (*Kusari*) and a weight (*Fundo*) is a *Kusari-Fundo*. If it also includes a sickle or scythe (*Kama*), it is called a *Kusari-Gama*. A *Shikomi-Bo* or a *Shikomi-Jo* is a pole with a *Kusari-Fundo* hidden inside it; with no *Kusari-Fundo* inside, it is called a *Chigiriki*.

A chain 90 cm long with a weight of about 90 to 100 g and an iron finger ring is called a *Konpi*.

A chain 90 cm long with a 100 g weight at one end, a *Kakushi Buki* at the other end and a two-spiked hook that can be moved along the entire length of the chain is called a *Konpei*. Both the *Konpi* and *Konpei* were very much *Ninja* weapons.

A finger ring to which three chains each 21 cm long are attached, with each one having a weight of 100 g is called a *Mijin* (meaning 'to completely smash').

A *Manriki-Gusari* (commonly known as a *Kusari-Fundo*) has a chain between 60 and 90 cm long with a weight attached to both ends. This was used by the police in the *Edo* period.

h. *Makibishi* 「撒菱」 and *Fukiya* 「吹き矢」 (Throwing water-chestnuts and Blowgun):

The *Makibishi* (literally 'throwing a water chestnut') was used for slowing down or stopping perusing enemy. They were sometimes laced with poison. Although natural, dried water chestnuts were used, others were made from wood, bamboo or iron. The water chestnut plant is found in ponds and fully grows in only one year. It's leaves are triangular, and the nuts resemble small pyramids, which are dried in the sun to turn them into weapons. They were not only thrown or scattered around, but were sometimes used as hand-held weapons or even eaten, since the inside is edible. Sometimes, when a *Ninja* was being chased, he attached a long rope to his body with many chestnuts threaded onto it, trailing it behind him and preventing those giving chase from getting too close without injuring themselves.

The *Fukiya* (blowgun) was considered a mysterious weapon that was mainly used for scaring people. They were sometimes very long, 1.2 to 1.5 m, but were usually only 30 cm. They were made of bamboo, wood or brass. The *Shakuhachi* (a bamboo flute) was also used as a *Fukiya*. The darts normally had tips coated with poison or sulphur.

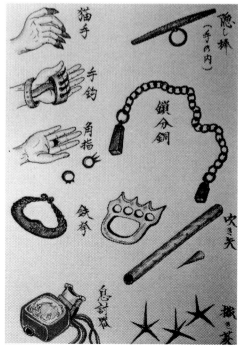

Kakushi Buki (隠し武器)

KUNOICHI KAKUSHI（角指）JUTSU

①

②

③

18.
NINJA-SHOKU AND NIN-YAKU
(NINJA FOODS AND MEDICINES)

A.
NINJA-SHOKU 「忍者食」
(NINJA FOODS)

Ninja foods (*Ninja-Shoku*) were studied a lot and developed over a long period of time because the *Ninja* often had to be in places where there was no food. This food is compact, yet very nourishing. Some of the more common ones are *Hyorogan, Kikatsugan, Enmeigan, Suikatsgan* and *Ninjutsu*gan.

The recipes for the first four are given below.

a. *Hyorogan* 「兵糧丸」:

Powdered wheat:100g; powdered rice cake (*Mochi*): 100g; and garlic:33g are all simmered with *Sake* and honey until the mixture can be made into little spheres. These are then dried. A total of 20 should be sufficient for one day.

b. *Kikatsugan* 「飢渇丸」:

Powdered carrot: 150g; buckwheat: 300g; wheat flour: 300g; yam: 300g; stellaria negrecta (*Mimikusa*): 15g; pearl barley: 150g; glutinous rice: 300g are all mixed together with 5.4 liters of *Sake*, then stored for three years so that all the alcohol evaporates. They are then made into small spheres about the size of a peach pit. Three per day is enough.

c. *Enmeigan* 「延命丸」:

Powdered carrot: 3.75g; white rice: 0.9 liters; and powdered pine bark: 3.75g are all mixed together with *Sake* and stored for three days, then made into spheres. This is enough for three days.

d. *Suikatsugan* 「水渇丸」:

Powdered plum: 15g; hard sugar: 30g; ophiopogon Japonicus (*Bakumonto*): 15g are mixed and simmered, then made into small spheres.

These are all old-fashioned ways of preparing food; with the present-day canned and instant foods, you would be well advised to mix new and old techniques to create new forms of *Ninja* food.

I have often heard of people who have been able to survive for many days with nothing but chocolate, and therefore this is also a good form of nourishment for the modern *Ninja*. These are things one must study to learn more.

Ninja Shoku

B.
NIN-YAKU 「忍薬」
(NINJA MEDICINES)

Nin-Yaku is the collective name for both *Ninja* medicines and secret medicines. They are classified into four main parts:

These remedies are from ancient time and some have present usages while others do not.

a. *Doku-Yaku* 「毒薬」:

Doku-Yaku is the background use of poisons. If you use these techniques they can be very dangerous and they are, especially nowadays, very anti-social. There are some recent books on the subject of *Ninpo* poisons and this fact makes me very sad. The ways of making and using these poisons were and still are meant for those masters with pure hearts. If a master does not have such a spirit, it would never be taught to him and that, in turn, would bring about the end of a *Ryu*. Many *Ryu* have ended this way.

Nowadays, some writers think it necessary to introduce these techniques and the readers tend to believe it to be their right to know these things.

These writers try to evade responsibility by saying, "This was already written in such and such an old book" or, "Some old man taught me these things". I believe that in *Ninpo*, if a secret is necessary, it must be kept.

If not and the knowledge is used badly, severe problems arise. I will therefore only give the following list of poisons so that people can be aware they exist: aconite, *Konpeto*, *Manjushage*, buttercup, *Yatsude*, *Shikimi*, Korean morning glory, toadstool, mercury, lead, *Gyokuro-Cha*, toad, swell-fish (*Fugu*), verdigris, arsenic, *Doku-Hebi* (poison snake), *Doku-Gumo* (poison spider), *Okuguro Tessa*, *Kongosa*, *Machin*, *Hanmyo* and *Irakusa*. And nowadays there are even more such as hydro cyanic acid, potassium, agricultural chemicals and weed killers with worse things collectively called *Baidoku* that includes syphilis and other sexually transmitted diseases.

b. *Gedoku-Yaku* 「解毒薬」:

Gedoku-Yaku is means of removing poisonous substances from the body.

In cases such as when having taken a poisonous fungus, the best and most logical place to go is the nearest hospital. However I have included certain other old-fashioned remedies for you to study.

If you have taken a simple poison, first drink between ten and 20 egg whites, immediately put your fingers to the back of your throat and vomit everything out. Then make up and drink one or two small cups of indigo juice.

If the poison has made you totally disorientated, the best thing to do is to drink as much water as possible, vomit everything out, and then again drink as much water as possible. This can save your life if you have been poisoned. In Japan, there was a very famous murder case involving the *Teigin* Bank. Everyone there had been poisoned and only one person survived after going to the bathroom and doing the above.

If you have been poisoned by either a lead-based poison or silver dust, again you must drink egg-whites, vomit, then drink the juice of the white part of the welsh onion.

If you get a stomach problem after eating young bamboo shoots, fish or meat, after drinking and vomiting egg-whites, drink ginger juice or the juice made from the swollen areas of orchid roots. This is also very good for stomach ulcers.

If you get a stomach problem after eating buckwheat noodles, wheat-flour noodles, fish or fowl, eat, then vomit egg whites, then drink fresh horseradish or orchid juice.

If you get a stomach problem after eating crabmeat, boil black soya beans and add ginger to it before drinking it. Aloe, if only a little is drunk, is a good remedy but if too much is eaten it is very dangerous since it is a laxative. If you vomit a long time after having taken the poison, it is best to drink either aloe juice or carbonic acid. Laxatives also bring down the body temperature. Parsley juice is also good for curing stomach problems while pickled plums are very good for preventing these problems. It is very important to eat plenty of vegetables such as lettuce, carrots, parsley and radish when eating fish or meat.

Another important thing is to be careful of being poisoned in the first place. For centuries there have been ways of finding out whether food or drink has been laced. One common way was to use teacups and other dishes with a gold rim so that if the contents contained poison, the gold changed color. Fans usually had a small coral bead that crumbled if placed near any poison. The gold decorations on the handle of a sword can also be used to test for poison. Even using the tip of the tongue is enough. If you feel a burning sensation or swelling, then do not consume the food or drink. Be aware also of the actions and reactions of those who may be trying to use poison. The way a poisoner's eyes, hands and facial muscles move will not be normal.

When syphilis has been transmitted, one usually knows about it by the appearance of an inflammation on the sides of the groin. Place egg whites on the inflammation several times. This will make the inflammation disappear, but it does not mean the syphilis has been destroyed, it has only gone deeper into the body. Next place a mixture of smashed *Konpeto* (round lumpfish) and salt on either the buttocks or the spine and after about 15 minutes a new inflammation filled with puss will have formed. Puncture it with a needle (preferably an acupuncture needle). Finally apply the leaf of a *Ju-Yaku Dokudami* (houttuynia cordate), which has been baked inside the leaves of a paulonia plant until it is very soft, to the puncture hole. This will remove the syphilis. This was the way it was done in olden times, but since we are now in far more modern times it is best to go to a doctor.

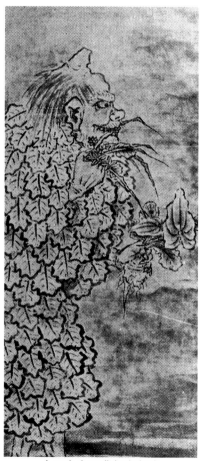

A god of medicinal plants

c. *Gan-Yaku*「癌薬」:

Gan-Yaku is medicines that are good for fighting cancers. The following are very good to eat for this: *Kawaratake*, pearl barley, buck-wheat noodles, *Dokudami*, garlic, leeks, ginger, white nandin, peppermint, shepherd's purse, *Obako*, goosefoot, dandelion, *Yomena*, mandarin oranges, eel, liver of; sardine, salmon, as well as carrots, eggplant, tomato, persimmon, loquat, mandarin, apricot and plum juice.

d. *So-Yaku*「創薬」:

So-Yaku is the use of medicines for wounds, etc. If you get cut, first wash the wound with mixture of 60 % *Shochu* (a strong alcoholic drink made from sweet potatoes) and 40 % juice from the leaves of a Japanese cedar. The *Shochu* works as a disinfectant while the juice works as an anesthetic.

If the wound is very infected, apply a mixture of smashed peppermint and *Shochu* directly to the wound. If you are cut by a sword, thoroughly mix baked black cowpea and chenopodium then apply this to the wound.

To stop the loss of blood, place the ashes of rice stalks directly on the wound. Chewed paulownia or tea leaves are also good for this. If you are bitten by a dog, apply charred garlic and oil of Toshibi or even concentrated nitric acid to the wound. If you are bitten by a mouse, it is best to apply a mixture of smashed, dried persimmon and ginger.

If you get hit in the groin, mix the juices of ginger and Japanese cedar leaves together and place this on the area with gauze. It is also good to drink some of this. Bruises left by a kick or a punch are best dealt with by applying either egg white or a mixture of viper, deer antler and crab that has been baked until black and pulverized.

If you have a swelling, ferment some Japanese cedar and pine leaves. Heat the mixture and then apply it. If after a fall a joint is either broken or very painful, boil some willow tree to make a soup and apply it. For neuralgia, apply smashed radish directly to the affected area or use it as a moxa. If you have a high temperature, boil bark from the cherry tree and a chamomile flower to make a soup, then drink it.

If you have a fishbone lodged in your throat drink the juice of either mugwort or a leaf of a banana tree.

Another way is to bake a mixture of pine needles and balsam and drink a little of it.

If you have been burnt, you can apply the juice of a cucumber, boiled roots of lily-turf or boiled leaf of aucuba japonica. But the best thing to do is to place the burn under cold running water, and then apply aloe. This method is very good; both my family and I have used it.

If your energy is lacking, boil a vine of the houttuynia cordate (*Tsuru Dokudami*) and grandiflorum (*Ikariso*) and drink it. If you have a mental disease, limit your daily food intake, and wash your hair at least three times a day, placing radish juice on your head with gauze after each wash.

19.
NINJA YASHIKI 「忍者屋敷」
(NINJA HOUSES)

If one can say, "Ah, this is a *Ninja Yashiki* (*Ninja* house)", then it is no longer a *Ninja* house. The true *Ninja* house looks like a normal everyday house from both the outside and inside. But it can be transformed suddenly into a small fortress filled with secret passages. The following houses have been considered to be *Ninja* houses.

The *Koga Ninja* house in *Shiga* Prefecture is said to have been the home of the *Mochizuki Ninja* Family. It is now owned by a pharmaceutical company called *Ohmi Seizai* Co., Ltd. The way it is constructed makes it seem to be a single-storied building, but inside there are several entrances to a secret basement, as well as trapdoors for catching an enemy. A squeaky corridor seems to have only one wall, but in fact it hides a secret passage. A paper sliding door is opened by being pushed. An alcove on a wall in the main room reserved for paintings has a rope attached to an alarm system. Another rope opens up a secret staircase. Secret rooms are stockpiled with weapons, explosives and food supplies and from here one can go up to another floor with three rooms: one with three *Tatami* (a mat about 1.8 m by 0.9 m), one with four-and-a half *Tatami* and one with a wooden floor and many weapons hanging on the wall. Yet another floor can be found after a climb up a rope ladder. This one has only a large wooden floor that leads to the garden.

Another *Ninja* house is in *Koka* (*Koga*) in *Shiga* Prefecture and belongs to Mr. *Koyama Tadahiko*. He calls it *Shinonome-Sha* and again from the outside it seems to be a single-storied house. Inside there are five rooms with three, four, four-and-a-half, eight, and ten *Tatami*. At the entrance there is a small shoe cupboard that conceals a secret passage leading straight to the ten *Tatami* room located deep within the house.

At the end of a corridor, what appears to be a wall can be opened, revealing a four-and-a-half *Tatami* room with a ladder leading to another floor with two large rooms of eight and ten *Tatami*. At one end there is a large circular window about 50 cms in diameter that leads to the roof. From there, there is a rope ladder for climbing down.

Other places called *Ninja* houses (but not true ones) are purely tourist attractions. One is the *Nijo-Jinya* in *Kyoto*; the *Myoryuji* Temple in *Kanazawa* is another.

Ninja Yashiki

20.
HENSO-JUTSU 「変装術」
(THE ART OF DISGUISE)

One part of the *Ninja*'s art of disguise (*Henso-Jutsu*) is known as *Shichihode* (七方出) (the seven ways of going). They are:

① *The Komuso* 「虚無僧」:
A priest of the *Fukeshu* religion who, as part of his religious training, wandered throughout Japan wearing a large straw hat and playing the *Shakuhachi* (a bamboo flute).

② *The Shukke* 「出家」:
A person who left his home to learn the Buddhist religion. If he studied outside a temple, he was a *Shukke*, whereas if he was admitted into a temple, he was a *Soryo* (or *Shukke*).

③ *The Yamabushi* 「山伏」:
A student of the *Shugendo* religion who usually trained in a special mountain district. He normally carried a *Jo* (a four foot staff) and a shell horn.

④ *The Shonin* 「商人」:
A traveling salesman or merchant, also called a *Gyoshonin*.

⑤ *The Hokashi* 「放歌師」:
A traveling entertainer who while playing a musical instrument, entertained the public with a monkey, magic tricks, etc. He usually wore a cap called a *Zukin*.

⑥ *The Sarugakushi* 「猿楽師」:
Another type of traveling entertainer who was essentially a dancer.

⑦ *The Tsune no Kata* 「常の形」:
An ordinary citizen, sometimes a *Samurai*, sometimes a master less *Samurai* (*Ronin*), at other times a mere farmer, etc.

When the *Ninja* disguised themselves as one of the above characters, they attracted very little, if any, attention, since these disguises were designed to blend into the background easily.

Shichihode Sanpo Kata

Sanpo-Gata (三法型) is the collective name given to another set of *Ninja* disguise techniques. It consists of:

① Techniques for changing the appearance of the face
② Techniques for changing the appearance of the body
③ Techniques for looking like the opposite sex

Shichihode and *Sanpo-Gata* have a total of ten methods, making *Henso-Jutsu* one of the most effective set of *Ninja* techniques.

The old *Ninpo* book *Shoninki* refers to five styles of *Henso*:

① The beautiful woman and the handsome gentleman
② The nobleman
③ A refined person, expert in etiquette, flower arranging, and the tea ceremony, who lived in a secluded mountain house
④ Entertainers, including dancers
⑤ An artist who specialized in calligraphy and painting

According to *Shoninki*, with these five techniques one could easily fool the enemy. The following are examples of *Henso-Jutsu* techniques: Changing the appearance of the face by removing the eyebrows and painting them back on in a different way; using a fine iron powder to blacken the teeth (as was the custom for married women in the *Edo* period); using soot or a similar material to make the face look like that of a poor person, and undoing the hair knot and putting the hair in the mouth to imitate the behavior of a mad man. These acts changed the appearance of the face dramatically. Methods of producing make-up for *Henso-Jutsu* were also taught; for example, mixing a black and a red powder stick to produce a color that simulated a healing sword cut on the face. Another technique was to use a yellow substance made from any white powder mixed with finely ground bark, or a bluish liquid made from finely crushed grass and ink for simulating bruises.

To appear ill, a *Ninja* went without sleep for several days and then acted ill, using a lot of moxa, or he fasted for several days.

Not shaving or cutting his finger nails for several months gave him the appearance of someone with long-term illness. To make an iris seem cloudy, making it look as if he were blind, he made a contact lens from the scale of a sea bream and inserted this in his eye.

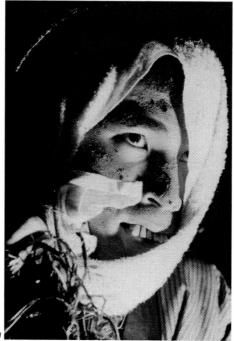

Henso-Jutsu

The normal hairstyle of both male and female *Ninja* was called *Shihohatsu* and resembled a ponytail. The sideburns were kept long so that at short notice any hairstyle could be effected. To change one's appearance it is very important to change one's costume, face and posture.

Henso-Jutsu was not just a technique one could pick up easily; it was also necessary to put one's heart into it. When pretending to be a *Komuso*, one needed to be a skilful flute player; when pretending to be a priest, one needed to be able to chant prayers properly; when pretending to be a dancer, one needed to be an expert dancer; when pretending to be a woman one needed to be able to show the feelings of a woman.

Since the words and accents used in different areas and different professions differed, the mastering of various dialects was crucial. Habits were also important. During the Second World War, a Japanese spy who had infiltrated a Chinese city was executed by the Chinese Secret Police. They had discovered he was not really Chinese because he used the toilet totally different from the way a Chinese would. Very small details of everyday behavior such as the way of washing the face and the example above vary from one place to another.

Henso-Jutsu

21.
ONGYO-JUTSU 「隠形術」
(DISAPPEARING TECHNIQUES)

A.
GOTON SANTON NO HO 「五遁三遁の法」
(THE 30 METHODS)

The highest set of techniques in *Ninpo* are the ways of concealing and disappearance called *Onshin Tongyo no Jutsu* 「隠身遁形の術」or *Ongyo-Jutsu*. If you can do these techniques, you can make the impossible possible. Their essence is *Goton no Ho* which has elements of wood, fire, earth, metal and water. These five escape techniques are called *Omote Goton no Ho* and *Ura Goton no Ho*, and were once absolute secrets, being taught only by word of mouth. *Ura Goton no Ho* is the following: using a person, bird, animal, insect and fish. Together *Omote Goton* and *Ura Goton* are called *Jutton*.

A more comprehensive name for *Ongyo-Jutsu* is *Ten-Chi-Jin Santon no Ho* 「天地人三遁の法」(*Ten* means heaven, *Chi* means earth, and *Jin* means person). *Tenton* is the collective name given to the following ten ways of disappearing: using the sun, moon, a star, a cloud, fog, thunder, lightning, wind, rain and snow.

Chiton is the collective name given to the following ten ways of disappearing: using wood, grass, fire, smoke, earth, house, metal, stone, water and boiling water. (These are very much like the *Ura Goton*.)

Finally *Jinton* is the collective name given to the following ten ways of disappearing: using males, females, old people, infants, the nobility, the poor, birds, animals, insects and fish. All in all, there are 30 ways.

In olden times, if one specialized in only one of these thirty, one could open one's own *Ryu* and, as *Takamatsu Sensei* used to say, this is why there were over seventy different *Ryu*.

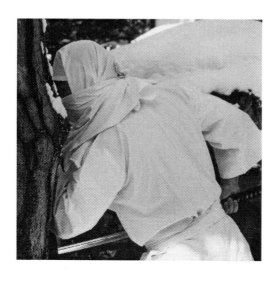

Ongyo-Jutsu

B.
OMOTE GOTON NO HO 「表五遁の法」
(THE TEN EARTH METHODS OF DISAPPEARING)

Onshin Tongyo no Jutsu is a very logical and academic art. By using it together with the body, the spirit and strategies, one can develop very powerful, almost magical abilities. The following are examples of *Omote Goton no Ho*:

a. *Mokuton* 「木遁」:

Mokuton is the way of disappearing using wood and/or grass, with the specialists among the various *Ninja* clans being the *Togakure-ryu*.

The techniques included ways of using the shadows of trees or grass during both the day and night. A distraction such as the use of a piece of string to move a bush so that the enemy turned his back or the placing of one's clothing on a tree to distract the enemy, allowed one to leave the scene unobserved.

Of course, these techniques were not only used for disappearing, but were also used for attacking. Climbing a tree with *Shuko* (hand claws) and *Sokko* (foot claws) is one example of *Mokuton*. Other ways of climbing trees included using such tools as the *Ipponsugi*, *Kyoketsu Shoge* and *Kaginawa*. Throwing water-chestnut caltrops and waxing the wooden floor of a corridor are all part of *Mokuton*.

In China, there was once a hero called *Tsuang Hoi* who used to distract people by toppling long wooden poles; while everyone was inspecting the area, he would disappear by climbing a tree with his *Shuko*. 'Kusa' means 'grass' and is therefore used to refer to a *Ninja* who is expert at *Mokuton*. Using a mixture of *Mokuton*, *Juton* and *Katon* increases the effectiveness several times.

b. *Katon* 「火遁」:

Katon is the way of using fire to disappear, for example, by gathering dry leaves and setting them on fire to distract the enemy and escape. Another way is to light a small explosive with a portable lighter, throw it, then escape. A small explosive device can be thrown into a fireplace or a small portable fireplace with the escape being made while everyone is recovering from the shock.

Mokuton

Katon

The *Uchitake, Onibi, Hiya, Higurumaken, Hifukidake, Ohzutsu, Kakaezutsu, Sodezutsu, Nageteppo, Uzumebi* and *Kaengusari* are all tools of *Katon*. In the past, fire was both respected and feared by everyone as if it were a god and therefore the use of *Katon* was the most effective form of escape. Before one can use *Katon*, it is vital to learn about climatic conditions and ground conditions, especially when it comes to using the wind, otherwise it can be very dangerous.

These are the physical applications of *Katon*, but there are also psychological aspects to it. For example, making an enemy so furious that his face becomes red makes him unable to judge things correctly. His body also becomes tense and rigid, leaving him unable to use *Taijutsu* properly. Sometimes his anger may become so great that he runs the risk of having a cerebral hemorrhage or an ulcer, which could eventually kill him. Another example is fabricating a scandal about the enemy so that his honor is tarnished, putting him in a very unpleasant position. This is also a part of *Katon*; the following shows why:

If the enemy is imagined to be a pillow and a small piece of red-hot coal is placed in the center (the fabrication of the scandal), the pillow begins to smoke (the scandal). This smoke is then seen and smelt by everyone around and slowly the whole pillow catches fire, destroying it (the enemy) completely. The *Ninja* also used natural fires to their own advantage. Once, a *Ninja*'s home often had many calabashes filled with water, mainly for extinguishing fires. However, some of these were filled with inflammable liquid or poisoned water so that if an enemy entered while the house was on fire, it could be used against him.

c. *Doton* 「土遁」:

Doton is the way of using the earth to disappear. This includes throwing stones or sand at the enemy, digging a hole with a trowel (*Kunai*), hiding in a man-made 'rock', setting up a trap so that the unsuspecting enemy falls into it and using dirt to change the appearance of the face.

The soil is the parent of everything that is born on it. We too are born upon the soil and die upon the soil. The seasons change depending on the angle between the earth and the sun. Between heaven and humanity is the earth. And so earth is the most vital part of everything. For instance, if there were no earth, there would be no plants and so no wood (*Mokuton*) and consequently no fire (*Katon*).

The Japanese expression 'Doron-Doron', when referring to a *Ninja*, is used to indicate an actual appearance or disappearance of the *Ninja*. It comes from theatrical dramas such as *Kabuki*. The appearance or disappearance of a ghost is indicated by the sound of drums, which is imitated verbally by 'Doron-Doron'. This is the popular idea but from the *Ninja*'s point of view, the words 'Doron' and 'Doron' are the same. *Doton* in *Ninpo* means 'the way to disappear'. Doron in *Kabuki* means 'the time of a disappearance'. And so from *Doton* comes all other techniques.

Doton

Even the *Ninja*'s costume has a close relationship with *Doton*; its red-black colour makes it easy to disappear into the darkness and the earth. Before the Second World War, the Japanese Imperial Army wore dark-brown uniforms and now the armed forces of Europe and the United States use a mixture of dark-brown and green for almost everything including tanks. These are the colors of earth and wood. The octopus and the squid are also very skilful at using black ink to perform a vanishing act. Even the skunk uses smell to its advantage.

The phrase "As silent as a forest, as steadfast as a mountain" is also about *Doton*.

d. *Kinton* 「金遁」:

Kinton is the way of using metal tools to produce reflections or noise. These are good diversionary actions. Using a blade or mirror to reflect the sun into the enemy's eyes as a form of *Metsubushi* (blinding powder) or for signaling, suddenly throwing a small flame from a portable hand heater to startle the enemy, reflecting moonlight into his eyes with a sword, banging on a gong, bell or drum or shouting to startle an enemy are all part of *Kinton*.

Even throwing a stone into a pond making the enemy's mind focus in that direction so that you can enter from a different direction is part of this. The following is a famous *Haiku* written by *Matsuo Basho*: 'An old temple pond, a frog jumping, the noise of the water'. From this I can understand perfectly well that *Basho* was a secret *Ninja*.

The psychological aspects are as follows: If an enemy wants money, giving it to him can open many doors. The Japanese word for money and gold is *Kin*, hence *Kinton*. So when large quantities of money are involved, everything is possible. If a person wants money, status, and honor, the *Ninja* can already control him. Money has a direct influence on status, honor and also women. So if one wishes to be a true *Ninja*, one must be very careful not to be blinded by gold.

I am not saying, however, that one should not think about it. We are presently in a period in which we need to have the following five powers well balanced: spiritual power, physical power, technical power, wisdom power and momentary or economic power. A true *Ninja* never drowns in the sea of gold, yet he knows how to produce it well.

A *Ninja* is also very skilful at using the 'Golden Spheres'. 'Bed techniques' are used by the *Ninja* as a background technique, while the *Kunoichi* uses them as foreground techniques. In *Gyokko-Ryu Ninpo*, using a pair of iron balls to make the fingers strong and agile was a basic everyday technique. Sometimes they were used as a weapon. If a person is skilful with these balls, he is also skilful at manipulating the enemy as if he were a ball. Matahari was therefore very skilful at using *Kinton*.

e. *Suiton* 「水遁」:

Suiton is the way of disappearing using water. Floating on it; swimming over or under it, using special boats, rafts, or water spider (*Mizugumo*) or water pistols (*Mizuteppo*) or even cutting through the banks of a river to flood a village are all part of *Suiton*.

If a person likes alcohol, giving him an excessive amount is also part of this. If a person has a great weakness for women, drowning him with them is also a part. This also holds for material things, a *Ninja* must be very skilful in using money, alcohol, women and any material thing. He must be able to determine whether the drinks offered to him have been poisoned.

Using the five senses as well as the sixth sense is the only way of doing these things, but certain tools may also be used. For example, gold placed in a drink laced with poison changes colour. And a coral bead put near poison breaks up. A *Ninja* never allows himself to drown in anything, whether it be alcohol or women, he must swim freely and easily.

In the last five sections I have explained *Omote Goton*; this is about half of *Chiton Juppo*. I will not elaborate further on this, but will next explain a little about *Ura Goton*.

Kinton

Suiton

C.
URA GOTON NO HO 「裏五遁の法」
(THE TEN PEOPLE METHODS OF DISAPPEARING)

a. *Jinton* 「人遁」:

Jinton is the way of using one or more people to disappear, for example, using one's family or friends. Even the enemy himself or total strangers can be used. This can be done either directly or indirectly. The art of disguise (*Henso-Jutsu*) is also part of this.

Jinton includes the use of males, females, old people, infants, people from the noble class and people from the poor class. *Shichihode* is also a part of this, for example, using *Komuso, Shukke, Yamabushi, Shonin, Hokashi, Sarugakushi, Tsune no Kata* and all other aspects of *Henso-Jutsu*.

Jinton requires that all types, classes and manners of people be studied. One needs to learn things from make-up to acting, and so it is very important to learn how to do demonstrations.

b. *Kinton* 「禽遁」:

This is the way of using birds to disappear and it includes using birdcalls as well as imitating them. For example, startling a flock of birds making them take to the air and can be used to surprise the enemy, making surprise attacks on the enemy's chickens and ducks, using eagles and falcons to attack, using homing pigeons for communication, and using hypnosis (*Saimin-Jutsu*) to paralyze chickens and other domesticated birds on the enemy's property.

Two examples of how to use hypnosis to paralyze birds are as follows. Close the eyes of a chicken with one hand and stroke its back with the other to paralyze the bird completely. To awaken it, clap your hands next to its head. To do the same to a lovebird, remove it from its cage and close its eyes with one hand, then shake it vigorously. The bird appears to be dead. If it is thrown into the air with a yell (*Kiai*), it will not fly but will fall to the ground as it tries frantically to flap its wings. (Note that *Kinton* in this section is not the same as the *Kinton* in the previous section.)

c. *Juton* 「獣遁」:

This is the way of disappearing using animals. For example, there are two ways of dealing with dogs. The first is knowing how to use them, which is well known all over the world since there are police dogs trained for specific tasks such as detecting drugs or explosives

Jinton

Kinton

and also dogs for the blind. The second knows how to control dogs. When entering an enemy's home, you must know how to control his guard dogs. Many of these techniques remain secrets within the *Ninpo* scrolls.

There are basic ways such as befriending a dog by giving it food or, if a more drastic measure is necessary, poisoning it. Placing a dog of the opposite sex near the guard dog or putting a cat in front of it is another way. There are also ways of making one's body odor 'disappear'. A special way of using a secret poison called *Machin* is to mix it with baked rice and offer it to the animal. This will make the dog collapse and if it is not resuscitated in time it will die. If the mixture includes iron filings, the dog will die instantly.

Carrying a mouse in one's pocket and letting it loose in a room in the enemy's house where people are sleeping can cause great panic. Or if an even greater diversion is necessary, one can attach fireworks to its tail.

Recently in South Asia, someone used this technique. Perhaps this person had studied a little about *Ninpo*. However, this is a very bad example of a modern *Ninja*. For those involved in crime detection, such a person will have traces of explosive powder on him and he will stand out in a crowd by the way his eyes shine and move.

In olden times, a herd of cows or sheep with candles on their horns were sometimes stampeded towards the enemy. This is a mixture of both *Juton* and *Katon*. The most important thing to know is an animal's weak point and how to control it. For example, a cow's and horses weak point is the nose; a cat's is at the back of the neck. And most animals have one weakness in common, a fear of fire.

d. *Chuton* 「虫遁」:

Chuton is the way of disappearing using snakes, toads, etc. These are disliked by most people, they are easy to transport in the hand or pocket.

The Japanese theatre contains the stories *Orochi Maru*, about a man who is very skillful at using snakes, and Jiraiya, about a man who rides an enormous toad and commands it to release a poisonous gas that either kills everyone around or simply puts them to sleep. This is *Chuton*.

Other creatures used instead of a snake include the newt, gecko, lizard, centipede, and a frog can be used instead of a toad. Sometimes even large, poisonous spiders are usually placed in the most unexpected places.

e. *Gyoton* 「魚遁」:

This is the way of disappearing using fish. For example, when disguised as a fishmonger, one could transport either a dagger (*Tanto*) or a secret message inside the fish. *Gyoton* is very similar to *Suiton* especially in areas such as diving into and moving through water.

Juton

Chuton

Gyoton

D.
TENTON JUPO 「天遁十法」
(THE TEN HEAVEN METHODS OF DISAPPEARING)

I have already explained two of the three parts of *Ten-Chi-Jin Santon no Ho* (*Chiton Juppo* and *Jinton Juppo*). The remaining part is *Tenton Juppo*. *Tenton Juppo* is a very important part of the strategies of *Tenmon* (see the next section).

a. *Nitton* 「日遁」:

Nitton (*Ni* means sun) is the way of positioning oneself and directing one's movement when facing an enemy. Standing with one's back to the sun so that it shines in the enemy's eyes is important. This has been an important element in fighting for over 2,000 years. Even the use of the sun's reflection is part of *Nitton*. Also included under this title are ways of hiding in the shadows and observing the enemy.

b. *Getton* 「月遁」:

Getton (*Ge* means moon) is the way of using both the moonlight and the shadows it causes. The poem 'The Moon on a cloud, to the flower the wind' contains many hidden teachings. One-way of looking at it is as follows: When the moon is shining, the *Ninja* does not move. At the moment a single cloud moves in front of the moon, he moves like the wind, swaying the flowers. One must therefore be aware of the slightest change before moving. When clouds come, many things, such as the temperature, change or it may even rain.

From these techniques of using the moon and clouds, a 'new' style of *Ninpo* called *Kumogakure-Ryu* emerged (*Kumo* means cloud; *Gakure* means to hide behind).

c. *Seiton* 「星遁」:

Seiton (*Sei* means star) is the way of appearing or disappearing on starry nights. When there are only stars in the sky it is slightly brighter than a pitch-black night, yet not as bright as on a clear moonlit night. *Seiton no Jutsu* involves using the constellations with which time, direction and life waves can be predicted.

d. *Unton* 「雲遁」:

Unton (*Un* means cloud) is the way of appearing and disappearing using clouds during the day and night. It is on cloudy days and nights that the *Ninja* feels most comfortable.

It is very important to train in the ways of seeing at night, whether it is moonlit, cloudy,

Nitton

Getton

rainy or snowy. In olden times the *Ninja* trained in how to see distant objects at night. One way was to observe things from as close to the ground as possible. From this position one could recognize figures very easily. One must, however, be very careful of white objects at night. There are also ways of using In (energy channeling) to see at night, called *Meikyo no In* or *Ankoku Toshi Jutsu*.

e. *Muton* 「霧遁」:

Also called *Kirigakure no Jutsu*, *Muton* (*Mu* means fog) involves moving an army or disappearing in fog. There are two main ways, the first is to determining when the fog will come down and the second is using it at the moment it arrives. For example, fog usually arrives after a lot of rain has fallen when there is warm, still air or when rain comes from the sea to the land in the morning, followed by a warm southerly air current in the afternoon, then a cool northerly wind in the evening.

f. *Raiton* 「雷遁」:

Raiton (*Rai* means thunder) is the way of using thunder together with heavy rain. There are again two ways: the first is determining their arrival and the second is using them once they have arrived.

g. *Denton* 「電遁」:

Denton (*Den* means electricity) is very like to *Raiton* and is the way of using lightning with heavy rain, both when they appear suddenly and when they have been forecast.

h. *Futon* 「風遁」:

Futon (*Fu* means wind) is mainly used with strong winds. Using fire when a strong wind is blowing, disappearing with the howling of the wind, or even positioning oneself so that the wind blows into the enemy's face are examples. Sometimes typhoons or hurricanes are used.

i. *Uton* 「雨遁」:

Uton (*U* means rain) is the ways of using rain. When these techniques are used, it is of the utmost importance to know when the rain will begin and when it will stop. This is often used in conjunction with *Futon*.

j. *Setton* 「雪遁」:

Setton (*Se* means snow) is the way of using snow. This is extremely difficult since when walking in it, one leaves tracks and one's silhouette can be seen easily. However, there is the advantage that the enemy will be relaxed on such days; this is the chance a *Ninja* needs.

The *Setton Ninja Isho* is a reversible cloak with one side reddish-black and the other white. After entering the enemy's property using the white side, the *Ninja* can then use the black side.

There are several ways of camouflaging footprints left behind. One is to wear the footwear the wrong way round so that it seems as if you are walking in the opposite direction. Another way is to attach five pieces of bamboo to the soles, leaving tracks similar to those of an animal.

Setton

22.
TENMON AND CHIMON

A.
TENMON 「天門」
(ASTRONOMY)

The subject of astronomy (*Tenmon*) has already been mentioned as part of *Tenton Juppo*. The important thing about *Tenmon* is meteorology, which I will introduce in this section. Although the study of modern meteorology is necessary, the old type, which was also studied for a long time, is very accurate. If one masters *Chimon* (see the following subsection), *Tenmon* and *Jinmon* in addition to *Tenmon*, then one will never fail. This is the best *Ninpo* strategy. The theories for each area, province and country are sometimes totally different. You must learn them for the relevant areas. The theories below are for areas in Japan.

a. Rain:
★ If it starts raining at about midnight or 4 p.m., it will rain for a long time.
☆ If it is raining about 10 a.m. or 6 a.m., the rain will stop soon and the rest of the day will be fine.
★ If it starts raining about 8 p.m., 4 a.m. or midday, the rain will stop shortly.
☆ If it starts raining at about 2 p.m., 6 p.m. or 10 p.m.. The rain will last for about 12 hours.

b. Wind:
★ If the wind blows from the east, it will rain. And if this happens at the beginning of the rainy season or the hottest period of the year, the rain will continue for a long time.
☆ If the east wind is strong during the day, the night will be fine.
★ If the wind blows from the north-west in either the spring or summer, it will probably rain.
☆ If a westerly wind blows in the autumn, it will definitely rain.
★ If a southerly wind blows in the winter, within three days there will be a frost.
☆ If the wind blows from either the west or north-west, it will be fine.
★ If the wind blows from either the east or the south, it will be rainy as well as windy.
☆ If the wind blows from either the north in the spring or the south in winter, the area to the east will have rain.
★ If an easterly wind blows, the following area will have rain: the north in autumn, the south in spring and the west in summer.
☆ In the *Kanto* area (around *Tokyo*), if the wind blows from the west, the days will be fine, but in the *Kansai* area (around *Osaka* and *Kyoto*), it will be rain.

c. Sun:
☆ If the sky is either red or blue when the sun is setting, the wind will blow.
★ If there are scaled clouds when the sun is setting, it will rain.
☆ If the clouds are red when the sun is setting, the following day will be fine.
★ If the sun has a ring around it, it will rain.

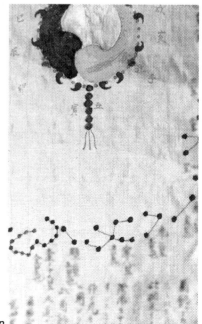

Babsenshukai's Tenmon

d. Clouds:
☆ If the clouds are moving fast, strong winds will blow.
★ If the clouds are still but there is wind at ground level, the wind will soon stop.
☆ If the clouds are red and white, there will be strong winds at ground level.
★ If fog descends at night, the following day will have very strong winds.
☆ When the clouds seem to have 'heads' and 'tails' with the tails pointing to north east, it will rain later. If the tails are pointing to the south, there will be rain, but the day may become fine.
★ If fog falls, later on the day will be fine.
☆ If the fog seems bright, the day will be fine.
★ If the fog seems to be rising, it will rain later.

e. Stars:
☆ If a falling star falls to the east, later the wind will blow.
★ If one falls to the south, the day will be fine.
☆ If one falls to the west, the following day will be rainy.
★ If the stars flicker a lot, it will rain.

f. Moon:
☆ If the moon seems very white while it is rising, it will rain.
★ If there is a ring with stars in it, around the moon's perimeter it will rain.
☆ If there are two rings around the moon, there will be strong winds.
★ If the moon shines very strongly while it is setting, there will be a lot of rain.
☆ If the moon is weak while it is setting, the wind will blow.

g. Rainbows:
★ If there is a rainbow in the west in the morning, three days later it will rain.
☆ If there is a rainbow in the east, the following day will be fine.

h. Mountains:
★ If the mountains can be seen clearly, warm winds will blow.
☆ If the mountains cannot be seen clearly, cold winds will blow.
★ If the mountains seem to be very close on a windless day, it will rain.

i. Birds:
☆ If a crow or raven takes a bath, it will definitely rain.
★ If a pigeon coos and another one replies, it will be a fine day.
☆ If a pigeon coos and there is no reply, it will rain.
★ If a black kite cries in the morning, it will rain.
☆ If a black kite flies upwards in a circle, it will be a fine day.
★ If a black kite flies downwards in a circle, it will rain.

j. Miscellaneous:
☆ If thunder is heard everywhere, there will be strong winds and rain.
★ If a rock is damp, it will soon rain.
☆ If smoke from a campfire stays down, it will rain. However if the smoke rises straight up, it will be a fine day.

Tenmon is also very closely related to the divination (*Kimon Tonko*) and to strategies, but these are very difficult to explain; I only teach them by word of mouth.

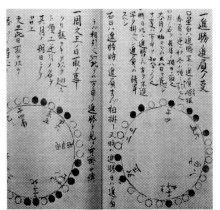 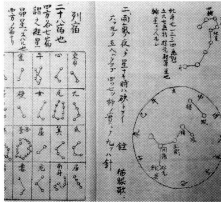

The secret scroll of *Tenmon*

B.
CHIMON 「地門」
(THE GATE OF EARTH)

Chimon not only includes *Chiton Juppo* (the ten earth methods of disappearing) but also includes Geography, ways of recognizing mountains and surrounding areas and their flora and fauna, ways of choosing a good day from a bad day, ways of judging tracks and determining the exact time and how something died. *Jinmon*, the ways of judging people's faces and minds and moving their heart is also necessary, however, this subject is only taught by word of mouth.

★ If a spider's web has water droplets on it, it will be a fine day.
☆ If a sparrow or chicken does not eat any food and goes straight back to its nest, the day will be rainy.
★ If a sparrow or chicken eats well until late or wants to be in the sunlight, it will be fine.
☆ In the summer, if a lot of fireflies and other insects come into the room or a carp jumps in the pond, it will rain.
★ Usually insects live high up in the trees, but if they come down, if a lark flies low and cries or if the reeds (or pampas grass or turf grass) are bent over, strong winds will blow.
☆ If the earth tastes salty, many people use this track; if however it tastes sweet or spicy, it is rarely used.
★ With the ear placed to the ground, it is possible to determine where a person or a horse is and the direction of travel.
☆ For researching how many houses are occupied or the population of a village, keep a known quantity of red beans in one sleeve and soya beans in the other. Dropping one of one type for each empty house and one of the other types for every ten occupied houses found allows an accurate record to be kept. Another way is to use rice painted five different colors; this can also be used for food.
★ When staying at an inn, one must know the types of locks used and location of such things as toilets, fire exits and the inn itself.
☆ Being in a full town is better than being in an empty one. Living in a brothel is also very good.
★ When a *Ninja* builds a secret house, there are only two styles: those without any tricks and those full of tricks. (There are a few houses like these left such as the *Koga Mochizuki* and *Kyoto Nijo-Jinya*, and even my parents' house has several secret rooms from which one can go onto the roof and from there to other parts of the house. Around the house there are also boards that can be removed to escape).
☆ When going around the side of a mountain after a long rainy period, one must be very careful of landslides. One must not live in an inn that is either at the foot of a mountain or next to a river.

Geography and topography must also be learned together with possible points of attack and escape. The *Ninja* also used *Kimon Tonko* (divination) for fortune telling, even though the styles of the *Iga* and *Koga* regions differed somewhat. They also used Chinese and *Yoshitsune-Ryu* ways of forecasting the type of day. However this does differ from season to season and month to month.

★ From a person's face, palm lines and body structure, forms of attack and defense can be determined. These things have been used throughout history and are very accurate, but not 100%.
☆ *Sanmyaku no Ho* are the three places where the pulse can be taken. If all three are balanced, everything is fine, if not, something is wrong. Sometimes martial artists check them while traveling. This is a good thing, but it is far better to clean and purify the heart so that happenings can be foreseen.
★ If you want to know where you are at night, the best thing to do is to use the constellations. To determine direction the *Ninja* used a small iron 'boat' with a magnet at one end placed on water (*Kishaku*). Another good way is to study the rings of a tree.
☆ For fighting at sea, the important things to know are the currents and tides. In *Ninpo*, using the lunar calendar which was previously used in Japan, we say that the highest tides

occur between the 14th and 18th days and between the 29th and 3rd days; the medium tides occur between the 4th and 8th days and between the 25th and 28th days; the lowest tides occur between the 9th and the 13th days and between the 19th and 24th days.

★ One must learn the customs, habits and dialects of each area.

☆ If the water in a moat is blue-black, the moat is very deep. If the colour is light, waves form very easily in a soft breeze and there is grass, the moat is not very deep.

★ If there are sagittaria trifolia (*Omodaka*), irises, reeds, etc. in the mountains, the mountains contain an underground river.

☆ Do not fall into the traps of the five desires: material things, sex, honor, eating and drinking too much good food and habits. Their use is, however, very good for strategies.

★ Do not allow your mind to wonder; the *Ninja* needs a steady heart and always keeps the same heart because there are times when the enemy will use pleasurable things, anger or even an appeal to the heart. For these a *Ninja* needs an immovable heart (*Fudoshin*) and an unchanging heart (*Heijoshin*).

☆ Before entering a dark area from a bright area, close the right eye and once inside, close the left and open the right. After a while, the left can also be opened.

★ On a dark night, if you cannot find your direction, lie on the ground and look up to the sky to find out where things are. For example, ponds and rivers look bright, whereas fields are black.

☆ At night on a road, if you see a strange shadow, kneel down and look at the object over a fan, sword or something similar. If it does not move, it is most probably a fence or tree. If it moves, it is probably either a person or an animal. If a lamp seems to be rising above the fan, the person carrying it is approaching. If it seems to be getting lower, the person is moving away.

★ When entering a place secretly, move downwind. Advance from a point the enemy cannot see.

☆ If you must pass through a wall of fire, drench the body with water, wrap a wet towel around the head, then move keeping as low as possible.

★ In an earthquake, the best place to be is where bamboo is growing.

☆ The best times for entering at night are 9 p.m. - 1 a.m., 4 - 9 p.m. and when clouds are covering the mountain peaks.

★ When advancing on a moonlit night, do not move towards the moon.

☆ Telling the time from the eyes of a cat was done in olden times; however this is not as reliable as the 'stomach clock'.

★ To enter noiselessly, do it on a rainy, windy or thunder night.

☆ When walking on tiles, tread on the point where they overlap. On *Tatami* (Japanese mats), walk along their edges. On a wooden floor, lay your sash on the floor and walk on it.

★ If a person seems to be sleeping, use the following to confirm it: If he moves a lot, he is not in a deep sleep; if the intervals between snores are not regular, it is very doubtful that he is asleep and the best way to check this is by letting loose a mouse or some ants. Another way is to use hollow bamboo with a piece of paper over one end as a stethoscope to listen from outside.

☆ Sleep during spring is deep and long. In the summer it is very shallow, but from 9 - 11 p.m. one can get a good sleep. In autumn it is very good but very short, and in winter it is very long but shallow. These things however do depend on the person's age and health.

The changes within *Tenmon* and *Chimon* must be studied carefully and researched deeply.

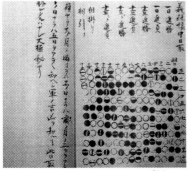 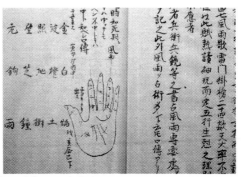

Chimon Section of Bansenshukai

23.
GUNRYAKU HEIHO 「軍略兵法」
(STRATEGICS)

Gunryaku Heiho is the use of strategies. This I have already explained in several sections of this book, such as those on *Tonpo* and *Tenmon/Chimon*, but I will try to explain more about *Ninja* strategies. This has already been done in a book called *Bansenshukai*, which is divided into two sections called *In no Jutsu* (ying techniques) and *Yo no Jutsu* (yang techniques). *Yo no Jutsu* is the way of entering an enemy's territory while being physically visible but with the ability to change the personality when confronted by different people. *In no Jutsu* is the way of entering an enemy's territory by disappearing out of the direct line of vision.

Yo Nin no Jutsu is the way of entering enemy's territory secretly with the ability to adapt to any changes in circumstances and to use the correct opportunity, such as when the enemy is off-guard. *In Nin no Jutsu* are the ways of secretly entering an enemy's territory using tools and *Ongyo no Jutsu* (see section 21). Using these *In/Yo* (ying/yang) techniques under any circumstances results in the highest quality technique.

Yo Nin no Jutsu is further subdivided into three sections:
a. *Jo* (Upper) : *To-Iri no Hen* (Being close, yet far)
b. *Chu* (Middle) : *Chika-Iri no Hen* (Being near)
c. *Ge* (Lower) : *Kenbun no Hen / Kanken no Hen* (Surveillance / eavesdropping)

In Nin no Jutsu has five sections:
a. *Joeinin - Jo* (Sneaking into castles - Higher techniques)
b. *Joeinin - Ge* (Sneaking into castles - Basic techniques)
c. *Ieshinobi* (Sneaking into houses)
d. *Kaiko* (Opening doors)
e. *Shinobi Youchi* (Attacking at night)

If you want to know more, you can consult *Bansenshukai* as well as *Taiheiki* (the story of the *Genji* and *Heike*), *Koyo-Gunkan* (*Yoshitsune-Ryu* strategies), *Chikujo* (The Construction of a Castle) and other history books of which there are many good publications.

The most important thing I want to emphasize is that if one can do *Taijutsu* and master the spiritual part of *Ninpo*, the use of strategies will come naturally. If you read this book over and over again you will surely become a true martial artist and a true *Shinobi* person. I also strongly hope that you use this book in your daily life and pass through life with good fortune.

A scene from *Gunryaku Heiho* (by *Yamato Sakura*)

The scroll of *Heiho*

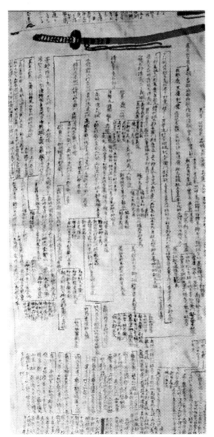

The secret scroll of *Gunryaku*

PART V
OTHERS

ACKNOWLEDGEMENTS

I have been planning this book for 15 years ago and have finally finished it after seven years of work. It is being published in English. I am very glad to be able to speak to the world as an authority in the *Ninpo* martial arts through this book. My motto is, "My gates are open to all who wish to enter, and they remain open to all who wish to leave."

I shall always try to teach with pleasure those who are very honest and earnest and will try to make a union with those who study and walk together with me along my path.

My reasons for writing this book are that I intend it to be a guidance text for martial artist about the true meanings of *Ninpo*, *Ninjutsu* and *Ninja*. It is also a meaningful volume containing the philosophy, history and techniques of the *Ninpo* martial art. It must be realized that this book contains only about 10% of what I really want to write, the reason is for lack of space. So I plan to write more books following this.

This English book was transcribed from my unskilled English into more comprehensible English by Robert Hughes, and was edited by Michael Collins. I have also been helped by Ross & Jane Edwards, James Wright, Scott Stamps, Nicola D'Onofrio, Tomoko Hirakata, Roy Ron, Ricci & Teresa Vidal, David Parmer, David Pinsker and Kirpa Nakamura. Yoshikazu Morisawa is responsible for some of the illustrations and Mr. Seiji Yokoyama took the excellent photographs. I thank these people, as well as the many others, from the depths of my heart. Thank you very much. Domo Arigato!

GLOSSARY

Aizu and *Ango Jutsu* : Techniques for signaling and writing.
Aruki Kata : The name given to the methods of walking.
Ashinami Jukka Jo : The ten ways of walking according to the *Ninpo* book *Shoninki*.
Asuka Period : 592 until 710.
Ba-Jutsu : Horsemanship.
Bakufu : The Shogunate 's system.
Banpenfugyo : The spirit of never is surprised or afraid. See Part II-01-B.
Bansenshukai : Translated as "All Rivers flow to the sea" is a book on *Ninpo*.
Biken-Jutsu : Specialized Sword techniques.
Bisento : A long-handled battlefield halberd.
Bisento-Jutsu : Techniques for using a *Bisento*.
Bishamonten : A guardian of the Heavens of the Buddhist religion.
Bo : The collective name for all types of staff; a staff usually between six and eight *Shaku* in length.
Bo-Jutsu : Staff techniques.
Boshiken : Thumb strike.
Bu : A measurement of length. 1 *Bu* = 0.33 cm. (10 *Bu* = 1 *Sun*)
Bufu : A code of conduct. See Part II-01-B.
Bufu Ikkan : Keep going code of conduct. See Part II-01-B.
Bugei Juhappan : 18 basic categories of martial art techniques.
Bugeisha : A martial artist.
Bukkyo : The Buddhist religion.
Bumon : The Martial Art component consisting of the *Ninpo Sanjurokkei*.
Bunmon : The learning and understanding of culture.
Buppo : The theory of the Buddhist religion.
Busha-Jutsu : Normal archery.
Butoku Iko : The Shining virtue of the martial arts,
Butsumetsu : A secret weak point in the chest.
Chimon : Geography, etc.
Chonin : An ordinary citizen.
Chudan no Kamae : Standing with one tip of the *Bo* pointing towards the opponent's midsection.
Chusei Period : The middle ages. (14th Century until the 16th Century).
Daijodan no Kamae : A posture where the sword is above the head. The cut is done in a vertical manner.
Daimyo : Feudal lord.
Daito : A long sword.
Daken-Taijutsu : Striking techniques.
Do : Way, path.
Dokkotsu : The Adam's apple.
Dokyo : Teachings from China.
Doshi : The title of Master origionally from the Chinese *Dokyo*, later adopted by the *Ninja* until the *Kamakura* Period.
Doshin : Name given to the police of the *Edo* Period.
Edo Period : 1603 until 1868.
Fudo Kanashibari no Jutsu : Immobilizing any living thing with the power of the mind.
Fudochi : The immovable wise heart.
Fudomyo-oh : Guardian of the Heavens.
Fudo Shichi Baku In : Techniques used to immobilize an enemy.
Fudoshin : An immovable heart.
Fundo : An iron weight.
Furin-Kazan : A motto used by *Takeda Shingen* meaning 'Wind/forest/fire/mountain'.
Gedan no Kamae : Standing, one point of a *Jo* resting on the floor behind one.
Genbukan Ninpo Bugei Dojo : The *Dojo* /organization name of *Genbukan Ninpo* Martial Arts *Dojo*.
Genji : *Minamoto* Family.
Genjutsu : Magical techniques.
Genzen Okusezu : An air of dignity.
Geta : Wooden thronged sandals.
Gofu : Talisman, good-luck charms, etc.
Goku : See 'Koku'.
Goshin : Defense of the body, spirit and soul.
Goton Santon no Ho : The 30 methods for disappearing.
Gunryaku Heiho : Strategies.
Gyaku Nage : Joint-locking techniques.
Gyakute : A way of holding a sword or blade so that the blade runs down the forearm.
Gyoja : A mountain priest.
Hachimon Tonko no Ekisen : Techniques for fortune telling from China.
Han-Bo : A half-staff, 3 *Shaku* long.
Hanbo Jutsu : Techniques for using the *Hanbo*.
Happa : Ear breaker.

Happa-Ken : A strike done with both palms.

Happo Kuten : Somersaulting without the use of hands in eight directions.

Happo Tenkai : Somersaulting with the use of the hands in eight directions.

Hashiri Kata : The name given to the methods of running.

Hasshodo : The eight ways for the correct mental state Buddhism. See Part II-01-E.

Heian Period : 794 until 1192.

Heike : *Taira* Family.

Heishi : *Heike* Family.

Henso-Jutsu : The art of impersonation and disguise.

Hicho-Jutsu : Leaping and flying techniques.

Hidari Bo-Jiri : The left tip of a *Bo*.

Hira Ichimonji no Kamae : Standing upright with the *Bo* in front of one and keeping it horizontal.

Ho : See Part I-01.

Hobaku-Jutsu : Techniques for restraining an opponent.

Hojo-Jutsu : Techniques for using ropes.

Ho-Jutsu : Techniques for making illusions.

Hoko no Kamae : Standing upright with both hands in the air slightly in front of one's head.

Ichimonji no Kamae : A defensive posture.

Iga : *Mie* Prefecture.

Ihen no Kamae : Standing upright with a *Bo* behind one and in a horizontal position.

In-Jutsu : See *In/Yo*.

In : A form of concentration adopted from the *Mikkyo* Religion.

In/Yo : The Japanese pronunciation on *Ying/Yang*.

Ishizuki : An iron tip located at the non-blade end of a *Yari* or *Naginata*.

Jakkin : A secret nerve point in the upper arm.

Jiai : Affection and benevolence.

Jiai Ni Tomi : See *Jiai*.

Jingai-Jutsu : Signaling techniques.

Jo-Jutsu : Techniques of a three-quarter staff.

Joruri : A Japanese-style puppet play.

Juji-Kiri : See Part IV-13-A.

Jujutsu : See *Ju-Taijutsu*.

Jukyo : The theory of moral and governmental ruling from China.

Jumon : A secret chant.

Junanajo no Kenpo : The Seventeen-Article Constitution made by *Shotoku Taishi*.

Jun Shihan : A title rank of Assistant Master (7th *Dan*) in the *Genbukan Dojo*.

Ju-Taijutsu : Grappling techniques.

Jutsu : See Part I-1.

Jutte : A short iron truncheon with a hook protruding just above the handle.

Jutte-Jutsu : Techniques for using the *Jutte*.

Kabuki : A Japanese-style play.

Kago : A palanquin.

Kagura : Sacred music and dance about the Gods performed at shrines.

Kaiki : The collective name given to tools used for breaking and entering.

Kajo Chikusei : Bearing and respecting the qualities of the flower and the spirit of the bamboo.

Kajo Waraku : Having a heart as peaceful, joyful and lovely as that of a flower. (From the poem *Ninniku Seishin*)

Kaki : Fire tools.

Kakushi Buki : Hidden weapons.

Kama : A sickle.

Kamae : A posture (offensive or defensive).

Kamakura : period : 1192 until 1334.

Kamari : Name once given to a group of *Ninja*, meaning is 'scout'.

Kama Yari : A *Yari* with a half-moon blade attached to it.

Kan : Japanese pronunciation of the Chinese word '*Chen*' by which the *Ninja* were once known.

Kancho : The President/Headmaster of the *Genbukan* organization.

Kan-i Junikai : A law passed by *Shotoku Taishi* that changed the social structure of Japan into twelve classes of people.

Kanji : Chinese characters.

Kankoku Juhakkei : The 18 fundamental Chinese-style Martial Arts.

Kansetsu Waza : Joint-locking techniques, see *Ju-Taijutsu*.

Katana : A sword.

Katon no Jutsu : Fire techniques.

Keisotsu : Thoughtlessness.

Kenpo 「拳法」: Fist techniques.

Kenpo 「剣法」: Sword techniques.

Ketsu-In : The forming of special knots with the fingers.

Ki : Spirit power.

Kiai (*Kiai-Jutsu*) : Power yelling (techniques).

Kinsei Period : The Modern Ages (from the 16th Century to the early 20th Century).

Kinton no Jutsu 「禽遁の術」: Techniques for using birds.

Kinton no Jutsu 「金遁の術」: Reflection techniques with mirrors.

Kiseru : A smoking pipe made of a bamboo shaft with two iron ends.
Kisha-Jutsu : Archery from horseback.
Kito : Prayers for general good.
Kocho no Kamae : Standing in upright holding a sword in front of one's forehead and keeping it horizontal.
Kodachi-Jutsu : Techniques for using the *Shoto*.
Koe : A secret nerve point in the thigh.
Koga (Koka) : *Shiga* Prefecture.
Kojiri : The end (or tip) of a scabbard.
Koku : A measurement of rice with a volume of 180.39 cm^3.
Koppo-Jutsu : Techniques developed from *Kosshi-Jutsu*.
Kosei no Kamae : Standing upright with one hand at head level and the other at groin level.
Kosshi-Jutsu : The oldest form of *Taijutsu* using the fingers for striking.
Kuden : A teaching only passed by word of mouth.
Kuji Kiri : A form of cutting the air nine times with a 'Sword' In.
Kunoichi : The name given to female *Ninja*.
Kusa : Grass; A name once given to *Ninja*.
Kusari : A chain.
Kusarigama : A weapon usually consisting of a sickle and a weighted chain.
Kyojutsu Tenkan : Diversionary tactics.(From the poem *Ninniku Seishin*)
Kyoketsu Shoge : A specialized *Ninja Kusarigama*.
Kyoshi : A title rank of Teacher in the *Genbukan Dojo*.
Kyu-Jutsu : Archery.
Makibishi : Small pointed objects usually scattered on the ground in order to stop or slow down an enemy.
Makiwara : Rice-straw padding.
Makko Karatake Wari : A way to cut an opponent vertically in half.
Meiji Period : 1868 until 1912.
Metsubushi : Eye-blinders.
Mezashi : A bamboo Jo with an arrow concealed in one end.
Migi Bo-Jiri : The right tips of a *Bo*.
Mikkyo : An esoteric Buddhist religion.
Muromachi Period : 1394 until 1603
Muto-Dori (-Jutsu) : Techniques for defending against an armed opponent without resorting to weapons.
Muto no Kamae : A weaponless posture.
Naga Bishaku : A farmer's implement consisting of a pole about six feet long with a cup attached at one end which was used tospread human faeces around the fields as fertilizer.
Naginata : A halberd.
Naginata-Jutsu : Techniques for using a *Naginata*.
Nanboku-Cho Period : 1334 until 1394.
Nara Period : 794 until 1192.
Nawanuke no Jutsu : Techniques for escaping from bindings.
Nigite : Shrine papers cut and folded in a zigzag manner.
Nin : An entire or patience.
Ninja : A master of *Ninpo*.
Ninja Juhakkei : The 18 parts of the *Ninja*'s training.
Ninpo Sanjurokkei : The 36 parts of the *Ninja*'s training.
Ninja-Shoku : *Ninja* food.
Ninja-To : A *Ninja* sword.
Ninjato-Jutsu : Techniques for using the *Ninja*to.
Ninja Yashiki : A *Ninja* house.
Ninpiden : Translated as "Secret Teachings Of *Ninjutsu*", a book on *Ninpo*.
Ninpo Bugei : The Martial Art of *Ninpo*.
Nintai Seishin : The ability to pocket insults and humiliation and later throw it away together with all traces of resentment. (From the poem *Ninniku Seishin*)
Nin-Yaku : *Ninja* medicine.
Nito-Jutsu : Techniques for using both the *Daito* and *Shoto*.
Nukiuchi : A way of drawing a sword to cut an opponent's waist.
Nyoibo : A huge battle club.
Obi : A sash.
Ofuro : A Japanese bath.
Ongyo no Jutsu : Leaping and concealing techniques.
Oniwaban : Name given to *Ninja* whose undercover job was as castle guards.
Onshin no Ho : Techniques for attaining invisibility.
Onshin Tongyo no Jutsu : Techniques for concealment and escaping.
Otonashi no Kamae : Standing upright with a *Bo* behind one, keeping it horizontal.
Ranbo-Rozeki : Ranbo means 'violence and rudeness'; *Rozeki* means 'rioting'.
Rappa : Name once given to a group of *Ninja*, meaning 'guide'.
Reishi-Sen : A 'lifeline' between God and all living things.
Ri : A measurement of distance. 1 *Ri* = 4 km.
Rokushaku-Bo : A staff six *Shaku* in length.
Ronin : A master less *Samurai*.
Ryu (or *Ryu-Ha*) : Type of school or tradition.
Sageo : A cord usually fitted on swords.

Sageo Nana Jutsu : Techniques for using the *Sageo*.
Sakki : Killing intention.
Salary-man : An office worker.
Sanbon Yari : A three bladed *Yari*.
Sanbyo no Imashime : The law of the three illnesses.
Sancho : The bridge of the nose.
Sanpo-Gata : The collective name given to certain techniques of *Henso-Jutsu*.
Sansei Hiden no Ho : The collective name given to three main forms of *Kiai*.
Sanzui : A radical (or part) of a *Kanji* meaning 'Water'.
Saru : A radical (or part) of a *Kanji* meaning 'Going forth'.
Satori : Comprehension.
Saya : A scabbard.
Sayu Yoko-Buri : Spinning the chain/rope of a *Kusarigama* on one side of the body.
Seishinteki Kyoyo : Spiritual Culture.
Sekko-Jutsu : Techniques on surveillance and on how to employ an army.
Sendo : See *Senjutsu*.
Sengoku Period : Japan *Samurai* War time (1467 - 1573).
Senjutsu : Techniques for becoming super-human.
Sennin : A practitioner of *Senjutsu*.
Senpai : A senior practitioner.
Seppuku : Ritual suicide.
Sessho : Regent of the empire.
Shakkotsu : A secret nerve point in the lower arm.
Shaku : A measurement of length. 1 *Shaku* = 33 cm.
Shibire-Gusuri : Poisons that produce a numbing or paralyzing effect.
Shichibatsu : A secret nerve point in the back.
Shichihode : The collective name given to seven forms of disguise of *Henso-Jutsu*.
Shichiju no Kana : A secret form of writing.
Shichisho : The collective name given to a set of seven books on strategy.
Shihan : A title rank of Master in the *Genbukan Dojo*.
Shihan-Cho : A title of Chief Master in the *Genbukan Dojo*.
Shiko : Japanese pronunciation of the Su Chang Province in China.
Shikomi-Gatana : A Jo with a concealed sword.
Shikomi-Jo : A Jo with a concealed weapon.
Shinai : A bamboo sword.
Shinken Shiraha-Dori : The way of empty-handedly catching the blade of a real sword.
Shinobi : A *Ninja*.
Shinobi-Bi : A small *Ninja* cannon, 2 *Shaku* 5 *Sun* long.
Shinobi-Katana : See *Ninjato*.
Shinobi-Gi : A *Ninja*'s uniform.
Shinobi Iroha : A secret form of writing.
Shinobi no Mono : Emphasizes a person involved in stealth and disguise.
Shinobi Rikugu : The six essential *Ninja* tools.
Shinobi Shozoku : A *Ninja*'s equipment.
Shinto : Japanese *Shinto*ism religion.
Shinzen Rei : A ceremonial bow to the *Dojo* shrine.
Shizen no Kamae : A posture where one is standing upright as normal.
Shoji : A paper sliding door.
Shoninki : Translated as "Correct *Ninjutsu* Memories", a book on *Ninpo*.
Shoten no Jutsu : Techniques for running up vertical objects.
Shoto「小刀」: A short sword.
Shoto「匠刀」: The name of Grandmaster *Tanemura*.
Showa Period : 1926 until 1989.
Shugendo : Combination of Buddhism and *Shinto*.
Shuko : An iron claw fitted to the hands.
Shuko-Jutsu : Techniques for using the *Shuko*.
Shumon : The religious and spiritual aspect.
Shunkan Saimin jutsu : Hypnosis and mind control techniques.
Shuriken : Hand-thrown blades.
Shuriken-Jutsu : Techniques for using *Shuriken*.
Shuto : A strike done with the side of an open hand. Hand sword.
So「宋」: Japanese pronunciation of the Song Province in China.
So「槍」: The *Yari*.
Sodegarami : A sleeve-catcher.
Sode-Deppo : See Sodezutsu.
Sodezutsu. A small hand-held cannon, 1 *Shaku* 1 *Sun* long.
So-Jutsu : Techniques for using a *Yari*.
Soko no Kamae : A posture where one hand is in *Boshiken* and the other extended.
Sokotsu-Biro : Carelessness, indelicacy, impoliteness.
Sokuho : Ways of using the feet.
Sokutoki : A small container that fills the air with *Metsubushi*.

Sonbu : Japanese pronunciation of *Sun Tsu,* author of the book '*Sonshi*'.
Sonshi : The Chinese book of strategies '*Sueng Tsu*'.
Soshi : Grandmaster of the *Genbukan Ninpo Bugei*.
Sosoku-Jutsu : Techniques for rapid walking and running.
Suiki : Water-crossing tools.
Sun : A measurement of length. 1 *Sun* = 3.3 cm. (10 *Sun* = 1 *Shaku*).
Suso Barai : A way of cutting horizontally to an opponent's feet.
Suzu : Striking point of groin.
Tachi : An extra-long sword.
Tachi-Jutsu : Techniques for using a *Tachi*.
Tai : Physical, Body.
Taiho : A cannon.
Tai-Jutsu : Unarmed self-defence techniques.
Taisho Period : 1912 until 1926.
Tamakazari : A gigantic string with 500 colorful stones.
Tanto : A dagger up to one *Shaku* in length.
Tanto-Jutsu : Techniques for using a *Tanto*.
Tatami : A mat made of rice-straw measuring 1.8 meters x 0.9 meters x 6 cms, which is used as the floor in most Japanese rooms.
Tenchi-Buri : Spinning the chain/rope of a *Kusarigama* above the head.
Tenchi Hasso no Kamae : Standing upright with the *Bo* or sword next to the ear, keeping it vertical.
Tenchi no Kamae : See *Tenchi Hasso no Kamae*.
Tengu. Demon.
Tenmon : Astronomy.
Tento : The crown of the head.
Tenugui : A towel.
Teppo : Gun, musket.
Tessen : An iron fan.
Tessen-Jutsu : Techniques for using an iron fan.
Te-Yari : A very short *Yari* between 3 and 4 *Shaku* in length.
Tetsu Yari : An all-steel *Yari*.
Tobi Kaiten : Jumping-rolls.
Tobi-Kata : The name given to the methods of jumping.
Tobi Roppo : The collective name given to the six main ways of *Tobi-Kata*.
Toda-Jutsu : Chinese Karate.
To-Gakure : The feeling given to an opponent of one being far away when in fact one is very near.
Togakure-Ryu : The *Ninpo* style of *Togakure*.
To-Jutsu : Techniques for using a *Daito*.
Toki : Climbing tools.
Tokonoma : An alcove on a wall of a main room reserved for paintings.
Toki : The highest position of a member of the government according to the *Kan-i Junikai*.
Tsuba : The hand guard of a sword.
Tsuka : The handle of a sword.
Tsukubo : A long staff with one end having another piece of wood perpendicular to it and full of spikes. Used for restraining.
Tsuki : A thrust with a weapon including a fist.
Tsutsushimi Bukaku : Modesty, discretion and carefulness.
Ukimi no Jutsu : Techniques for walking on ice especially with *Geta*.
Yakuza : Japanese Mafia.
Yamabushi : Mountain *Samurai* / warrior.
Yamabushi Hyoho : Strategies of the *Yamabushi*.
Ya : Arrow(s).
Yari : A spear.
Yata no Karasu : A three-legged raven.
Yojo Shiketsu : The form main points to preserve health. See Part II-01-E.
Yo-Jutsu : See *In/Yo*.
Yokoha : The hook of a *Jutte*.
Yoriki : Name given to the Police of the *Edo* Period.
Yuga : Graceful elegance.
Yumi : A bow.
Yuyo Semarazu : A sincere, calm and well-composed attitude.
Zanki : The perception of a cutting intention.
Zanshin : A state of cautiousness.
Zui : The old Japanese name for China.

BIBLIOGRAPHY

Anata mo Ninja ni Nareru : *Nawa Yumio - Keibunsha*
Araki-ryu Torite Gokui no Maki : Scroll
Bansenshukai : *Ishida Yoshito - Seishudo*
Doron Ron Saigo no Ninja : *Fujita Seiko - Nihon Shuhosha*
Gendaigoyaku Bansenshukai : *Ishida Yoshito - Seishudo*
Hiroku Sengoku Ninja Den : *Miyazaki Jun - Toen Shobo*
Hichibuku Goshinjutsu : *Densho* by *Takamatsu Toshitsugu*
Hyoho Sonshi : *Ohashi Takeo - Management-Sha*
Itto-Ryu Gokui : *Sasamori Junzo - Itto-Ryu Gokui Kankokai*
Iga-ryu Ninjutsu no Maki : Scroll
Jinbutsu Tanbo Nihon no Rekishi : *Akatsuki Kyoiku Tosho*
Korega Ninjutsu-da : *Koyama Ryutaro - Kubo Shoten*
Kukishinden Zensho : *Ago Kiyohiko - Shin Kokuminsha*
Kuki Bunsho no Kenkyu : *Miura Ichiro - Hachiman Shoten*
Kyu-Jutsu Gokui Kyoju Zukai : *Dai Nihon Koryukai*
Maho Zensho : *Daigakurin Koshubu*
Nakatomi Shinden Hiho no Maki : Scrolls and *Densho*
Ninpiden : *Okimori Naosaburo - Okimori Shoten*
Ninpo Chojin no Sekai : *Ohira Yosuke - Ikeda Shoten*
Ninjutsu no Gokui : *Ito Gingetsu - Bukyo-Sekaisha*
Ninjutsu sono Rekishi to Ninja : *Okuse Heishichiro - Jinbutsu Oraisha*
Ninjutsu no Kenkyu : *Nawa Yumio - Nichibo Shuppansha*
Ninjutsu Tejina no Himitsu : *Nawa Yumio - Gakuken*
Ninjutsu Hyoho Tora no Maki : Scroll
Nito-Ryu o Kataru : *Yoshida Seiken - Kyoiku Sha*
Ninja : *Tobe Shinjuro - Tairiku Shobo*
Ninja no Seikatsu : *Yamaguchi Masayuki - Yuzankaku*
Ninja Ninpo Dai Hyakka : *Nagakata Kaneaki - Keibunsha*
Ninja Ninpo Gaho : *Shonen Champion - Akita Shoten*
Ninja no Himitsu : *Kitagawa Sachihiko - Kodansha Bunko*
Ohtsubo Ryu Bajutsu : *Densho*
Ranger Ninpo : *Miyazaki Jun - Koseido*
Rekishi Dokuhon : *Shin Jinbutsu Oraisha*
Shinsetsu Nihon Ninja Retsuden : *Koyama Ryutaro - Arachi Shuppansha*
Shinobi no Sato no Kiroku : *Ishikawa* Masatomo - *Suiyosha*
Shinden Ryuko no Maki : Scroll
Shinden Reikan Ho : *Densho* by *Takamatsu Toshitsugu*
Shoninki : *Mori Senzo - Nissin Shoin*
Shuriken : *Naruse Kanji - Shin Taishusha*
Tenmon Chimon Kubikazari Magatama Den : Scroll by *Takamatsu Toshitsugu*
Zukai Kakushi Buki Hyakka : *Nawa Yumio - Shin Jinbutsu Oraisha*

THE DISTRICTS, PROVINCES AND PREFECTURES OF JAPAN

PART V:
OTHERS

DISTRICT	No.	PROVINCE		PREFECTURE	
HOKKAIDO 北海道	1	EZO	蝦夷	HOKKAIDO	北海道
TOHOKU 東北	2	MUTSU	陸奥	AOMORI	青森
	3	RIKUCHU	陸中	IWATE	岩手
	4	RIKUZEN	陸前	MIYAGI	宮城
	5	IWAKI	磐城	FUKUSHIMA	福島
	6	IWASHIRO	岩代		
	7	UGO	羽後	AKITA	秋田
	8	UZEN	羽前	YAMAGATA	山形
KANTO 関東	9	AWA	安房	CHIBA	千葉
	10	KAZUSA	上総		
	11	SHIMOUSA	下総		
	12	HITACHI	常陸	IBARAKI	茨城
	13	SHIMOTSUKE	下野	TOCHIGI	栃木
	14	KOZUKE	上野	GUNMA	群馬
	15	MUSASHI	武蔵	SAITAMA	埼玉
	16	EDO	江戸	TOKYO	東京
	17	SAGAMI	相模	KANAGAWA	神奈川
CHUBU 中部	18	IZU	伊豆	SHIZUOKA	静岡
	19	SURUGA	駿河		
	20	TOTOMI	遠江		
	21	MIKAWA	三河	AICHI	愛知
	22	OWARI	尾張		
	23	MINO	美濃	GIFU	岐阜
	24	HIDA	飛騨		
	25	SHINANO	信濃	NAGANO	長野
	26	KAI	甲斐	YAMANASHI	山梨
	27	SADO	佐渡	NIIGATA	新潟
	28	ECHIGO	越後		
	29	ECCHU	越中	TOYAMA	富山
	30	NOTO	能登	ISHIKAWA	石川
	31	KAGA	加賀		
	32	WAKASA	若狭	FUKUI	福井
	33	ECHIZEN	越前		

Note: In the TOHOKU district, provinces 2–6 (MUTSU, RIKUCHU, RIKUZEN, IWAKI, IWASHIRO) correspond to MUTSU 陸奥, and provinces 7–8 (UGO, UZEN) correspond to DEWA 出羽.

KINKI 近畿	34	OHMI	近江	SHIGA	滋賀
	35	KOGA (KOKA)	甲賀		
	36	YAMASHIRO	山城	KYOTO	京都
	37	TANGO	丹後		
	38	TANBA	丹波		
	39	TAJIMA	但馬	HYOGO	兵庫
	40	HARIMA	播磨		
	41	AWAJI	淡路		
	42	SETTU	摂津		
	43	IZUMI	和泉	OSAKA	大阪
	44	KAWACHI	河内		
	45	YAMATO	大和	NARA	奈良
	46	IGA	伊賀	MIE	三重
	47	ISE	伊勢		
	48	SHIMA	志摩		
	49	KI-I	紀伊	WAKAYAMA	和歌山
CHUGOKU 中国	50	MIMASAKA	美作	OKAYAMA	岡山
	51	BIZEN	備前		
	52	BICCHU	備中		
	53	BINGO	備後	HIROSHIMA	広島
	54	AKI	安芸		
	55	SUOH	周防	YAMAGUCHI	山口
	56	NAGATO	長門		
	57	OKI	隠岐	SHIMANE	島根
	58	IZUMO	出雲		
	59	IWAMI	石見		
	60	HOKI	伯耆	TOTORI	鳥取
	61	INABA	因幡		
SHIKOKU 四国	62	AWA	阿波	TOKUSHIMA	徳島
	63	TOSA	土佐	KOCHI	高知
	64	IYO	伊予	EHIME	愛媛
	65	SANUKI	讃岐	KAGAWA	香川
KYUSHU 九州	66	CHIKUZEN	筑前	FUKUOKA	福岡
	67	CHIKUGO	筑後		
	68	BUZEN	豊前		
	69	BUNGO	豊後	OHITA	大分
	70	HYUGA	日向	MIYAZAKI	宮崎
	71	OHSUMI	大隅	KAGOSHIMA	鹿児島
	72	SATSUMA	薩摩		
	73	HIGO	肥後	KUMAMOTO	熊本
	74	HIZEN	肥前	SAGA	佐賀
	75	IKI	壱岐	NAGASAKI	長崎
	76	TSUSHIMA	対馬		
	77	RYUKYU	琉球	OKINAWA	沖縄

THE GENEALOGY
NINPO MARTIAL ARTS

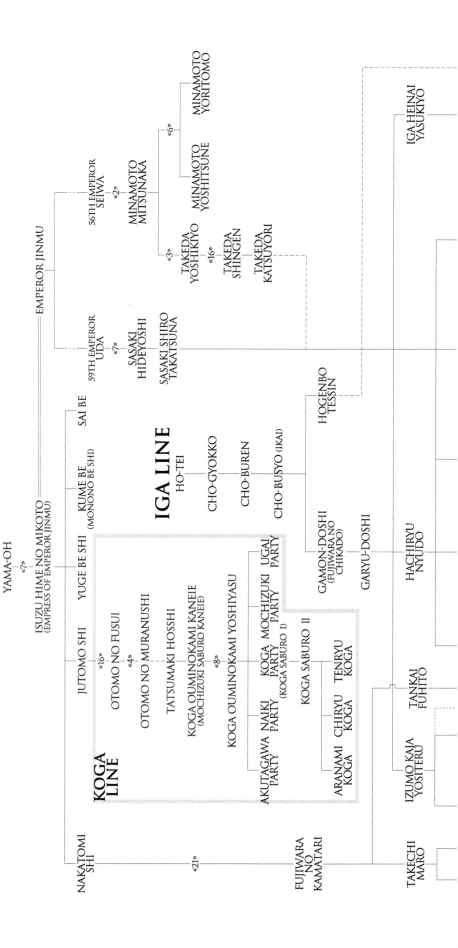

AMATSU LINE
YAMA-OH

ISUZU HIME NO MIKOTO
(EMPRESS OF EMPEROR JINMU)

«7»

EMPEROR JINMU

56TH EMPEROR
SEIWA

59TH EMPEROR
UDA

«2»

MINAMOTO
MITSUNAKA

«6»

MINAMOTO
YOSHITSUNE

MINAMOTO
YORITOMO

«3»

TAKEDA
YOSHIKIYO

«16»

TAKEDA
SHINGEN

TAKEDA
KATSUYORI

«7»

SASAKI
HIDEYOSHI

SASAKI SHIRO
TAKATSUNA

SAI BE

KUME BE
(MONONO BE SHI)

YUGE BE SHI

JUTOMO SHI

«16»

OTOMO NO FUSUI

«4»

OTOMO NO MURANUSHI

TATSUMAKI HOSSHI

KOGA OUMINOKAMI KANEIE
(MOCHIZUKI SABURO KANEIE)

«8»

KOGA OUMINOKAMI YOSHIYASU

**KOGA
LINE**

AKUTAGAWA
PARTY

NAIKI
PARTY

KOGA
PARTY
(KOGA SABURO 1)

MOCHIZUKI
PARTY

UGAI
PARTY

KOGA SABURO II

ARANAMI
KOGA

CHIRYU
KOGA

TENRYU
KOGA

IGA LINE
HO-TEI

CHO-GYOKKO

CHO-BUREN

CHO-BUSYO (IKAI)

HOGENBO
TESSIN

GAMON-DOSHI
(FUJIWARA NO
CHIKADO)

GARYU-DOSHI

HACHIRYU
NYUDO

IGA HEINAI
YASUKIYO

TANKAI
FUHITO

IZUMO KAJA
YOSITERU

NAKATOMI
SHI

«21»

FUJIWARA
NO
KAMATARI

TAKECHI
MARO

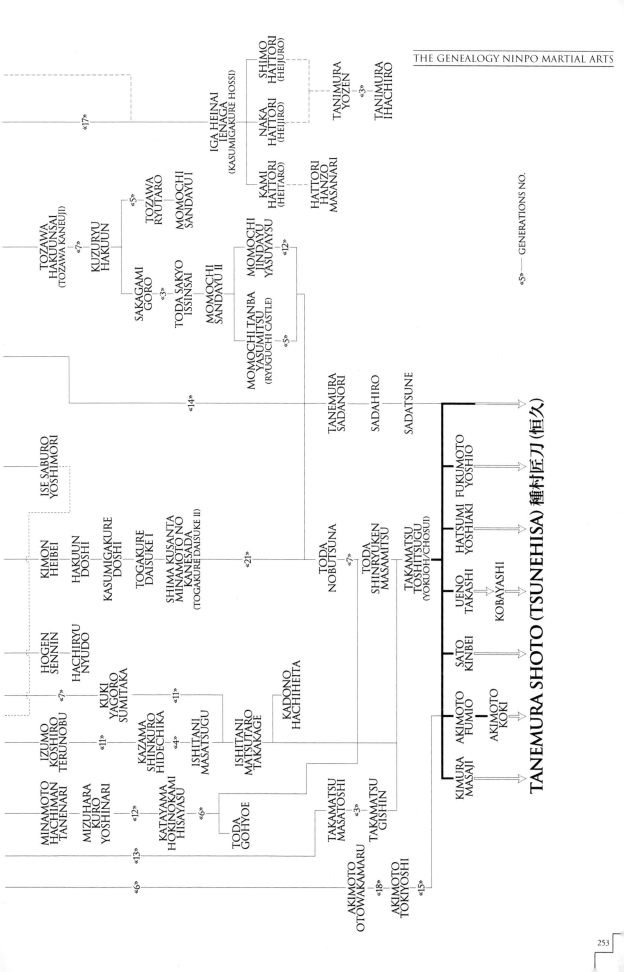

TANEMURA SHOTO (TSUNEHISA) 種村匠刀 (恒久)

«5» —— GENERATIONS NO.

IGA HEINAI TENAGA (KASUMIGAKURE HOSSI)

SHIMO HATTORI (HEIJURO)

NAKA HATTORI (HEIJIRO)

KAMI HATTORI (HEITARO)

HATTORI HANZO MASANARI

TANIMURA YOZEN

TANIMURA IHACHIRO

«3»

«17»

TOZAWA HAKUUNSAI (TOZAWA KANEUJI)

KUZURYU HAKUUN

«7»

TOZAWA RYUTARO

MOMOCHI SANDAYU I

«5»

SAKAGAMI GORO

TODA SAKYO ISSINSAI

«3»

MOMOCHI SANDAYU II

MOMOCHI TANBA YASUMITSU (RYUGUCHI CASTLE)

MOMOCHI IINDAYU YASUYAYSU

«12»

«5»

«14»

TANEMURA SADANORI

SADAHIRO

SADATSUNE

ISE SABURO YOSHIMORI

KIMON HEIBEI

HAKUUN DOSHI

KASUMIGAKURE DOSHI

TOGAKURE DAISUKE I

SHIMA KUSANTA MINAMOTO NO KANESADA (TOGAKURE DAISUKE II)

«21»

TODA NOBUTSUNA

TODA SHINRYUKEN MASAMITSU

«7»

TAKAMATSU TOSHITSUGU (YOKUOH/CHOSUI)

HOGEN SENNIN

HACHIRYU NYUDO

IZUMO KOSHIRO TERUNOBU

KUKI YAGORO SUMITAKA

«7»

KAZAMA SHINKURO HIDECHIKA

«11»

«1»

«4»

ISHITANI MASATSUGU

ISHITANI MATSUTARO TAKAKAGE

KADONO HACHIHEITA

MINAMOTO HACHIMAN TANENARI

MIZUHARA KURO YOSHINARI

«12»

«13»

KATAYAMA HOKINOKAMI HISAYASU

«6»

TODA GOHYOE

TAKAMATSU MASATOSHI

TAKAMATSU GISHIN

«3»

AKIMOTO OTOWAKAMARU

«6»

AKIMOTO TOKIYOSHI

«18»

«15»

KIMURA MASAJI

AKIMOTO FUMIO

AKIMOTO KOKI

SATO KINBEI

UENO TAKASHI

KOBAYASHI

HATSUMI YOSHIAKI

FUKUMOTO YOSHIO

253

PART V:
OTHERS

ABOUT THE AUTHER

Shoto Tanemura, whose martial arts names are *'Bikokuryu* 秘黒龍*'* (secret black dragon) and *'Kogyoku* 光玉*'* (shining ball), was born on 1947 in the town of *Matsubushi* in *Saitama* Prefecture, Japan. He majored in law at *Hosei* University after which he became a police officer, later an instructor, at *Tokyo*'s Metropolitan Police Academy. He has been trained in *Ninpo* and other martial arts since the age of nine and is now the *'Soshi' 'Soke'* (Grandmaster) of, not only *Genbukan Ninpo*, but also of various *'Ryu-Ha'* (Martial Traditions). Currently, he is teaching *Ninpo* as the 'Art of the martial arts'. His organization, the *Genbukan* World *Ninpo Bugei* Federation has it's headquarters at his home where he also maintains his position of *Kancho* (Head of the Federation). The *Genbukan* is international in scope with branches existing in the American, European and Asian continents.

NINPO SECRETS
NINPO PHILOSOPHY, HISTORY AND TECHNIQUES

By Shoto Tanemura

3rd Edition : 29th, May 2003

Published by Genbukan World Ninpo Bugei Federation
P.O. Box 1, Matsubushi-Machi, Saitama-Ken, 343-0105, Japan
Tel. 048-991-2103
Fax. 048-992-3221
www.genbukan.com
www.genbukan.org